# ZOO 2000

# ZOO 2000
## A LOOK BEYOND THE BARS

### JEREMY CHERFAS

BRITISH BROADCASTING CORPORATION

For my parents

So many people have been involved in *ZOO 2000* since its inception that it is impossible to thank every one of them individually. The people in the institutions we visited gave freely of their time and both this book and the television series it accompanies are much improved as a result of their assistance. I am grateful to them all.

Some people I must single out. Damien McGreevy in Queensland and Billy Dhillon in Kenya made things happen. Everyone on board the Executive allowed us to disrupt their lives. Nancy Heneson, Colin Tudge and especially Ruth West were critical and encouraging as needed.

Finally, I cannot thank the BBC enough. Susan Kennedy edited this book with great care. Linda Blakemore was responsible for the excellent design, and Jennifer Fry for picture research. George Inger and Moira Mann turned scraps of ideas into television programmes, aided and abetted by Nicola Davies, Mark Jacobs, Liz Nicol and countless others. I hope they all agree that it was worth it.

*Jeremy Cherfas*

Published by the British Broadcasting Corporation
35 Marylebone High Street, London W1M 4AA

ISBN 0 563 20281 5

First published 1984   © Jeremy Cherfas 1984

Set in 11pt Monophoto Times Roman
and printed in England by Jolly & Barber Limited, Rugby

# CONTENTS

# THE PANTHER
Jardin des Plantes, Paris

His gaze has traced the limits of his prison
So often that it sees no more than this:
A picture of a thousand bars. A vision
Of a thousand bars, behind them nothingness.

Softly he moves with strong and supple strides
And makes a circle, endless, fine and small.
A dance of strength that round a centre glides
In which a mighty will is held in thrall.

But when the curtains of his pupils part
In silence, one image rushes in to fill
The tense and quiet limbs, and then the heart,
Where finally it ceases and is still.

*Rainer Maria Rilke* (translated by Nancy Heneson)

Chapter One

# CAPTIVATION

The mountains of the Pyrenees throw a high wall between France and Spain. Just below the tiny principality of Andorra, on the French side, the river Ariège begins the journey that will take it through Toulouse to join the Garonne, and then to the sea. The limestone peaks it rises among, bubbling from many streams in the ground, are riddled with caves that were shaped during the last Ice Age, some 50,000 years ago, when powerful streams melted at the edges of the glaciers that filled the valleys to carve their way through the rock. With them the meltwaters brought sand and boulders, and this cargo, which now lies in great heaps on the cave floors, polished the walls smooth.

Visit the vast cave complex at Niaux and you can take a guided tour into the heart of one set of caves. There, following the flickering torch of the guide ahead, you tread silently down unlit corridors. As your guide waves his torch you can make out the unremarkable walls and roof of the tunnel. Smooth cool stone, but nothing more. Then, after half an hour or so, and as you are beginning to feel perhaps the slightest bit apprehensive, the roof has vanished. The tunnel opens out, and rather than being in a corridor, you are now clambering up the side of what seems to be a steep sand dune. There is a feeling of space all around, but you can see nothing because all the guides keep their torches aimed at the floor. Expectancy runs high, and even whispers echo in the darkness.

Suddenly, and with no warning, a guide raises his torch and lights up a panel of rock in the great cavern. There, beautifully drawn and as fresh as yesterday, is a magnificent black ibex. On another panel is a bison, suffused with an enormous vitality. Each panel is illuminated in turn, and on each is a magnificent beast. The guide tells you that you are almost a full kilometre from daylight, in the famous Salon Noir of Niaux. He points out the animals, tells you about the Ice-Age people who painted them some 15,000 years ago, and leaves your imagination to run riot.

It is very easy to come away feeling that you have just visited a temple, a cathedral, that was sacred to the people who decorated it and was used by them for ritual purposes. But what purposes? Look again at the bison, and you see

7

that in its flank are four crudely drawn arrows, two red and two black. So this is hunting magic. Kill the painting, and you will surely kill your quarry. But the arrows are so crudely drawn, the animals so artistic. Perhaps the hunt was re-enacted here many times, unaesthetic hunters adding their talismans to the efforts of the true artists. Then, too, the arrows do not seem to have the slightest effect on the animals, who stand there taut and full of life.

Other painted caves, here in the Pyrenees, elsewhere in France, and throughout Europe, make any simple interpretation difficult. There are some like the Salon Noir, great chambers filled with lively paintings, chambers that could easily have accommodated all the members of the tribe. But there are tiny caves, too, into which a person can barely squeeze. Were these even more magical, hidden away from prying eyes? Some of the paintings include weapons and even hunters, but many of them do not. In many the animals are very realistic and lifelike. In others they look as if they have been drawn from dead models. The variety of cave art makes it almost impossible to come up with any single satisfactory explanation. Some paintings undoubtedly represent art for art's sake, the product of leisure, involving very good hand and eye co-ordination, and a sense of the purely aesthetic. Others are examples of hunting magic, drawn to ensure a good hunt or propitiate the prey. Still others of these caves must have been places of ritual where many people could gather not just to practise such magic but to engage in all manner of ceremonies. Each cave, and its art, must be interpreted in context, and each is different.

Bison from the Salon Noir at Niaux in France, a crude arrow in its flank

There is, however, one overwhelming property that unites all the painted caves: the animals. The artists of the Ice Ages were intimately involved with animals. As hunters, of course, they would need to be, but the art of the caves seems to go beyond the fieldcraft and knowledge of the hunter. It indicates, if not reverence, then a very special relationship between men and the animals around. We can never know what the Stone-Age artist thought about his animals, though I believe that we are not so far from him, 20,000 years or so along the evolutionary road, that our own feelings are useless in helping us form an idea of how he felt. And we can ask other hunters today.

Among such people everywhere there is a peculiar reverence for the animal world, and an ambivalence towards it too. The hunter respects his prey, and he is glad to kill it. There need be no problem here, for it is entirely consistent to feel deeply for the life on which your own life depends. The Eskimos of the far Arctic make no bones about the intimacy of their relationship with their prey. For them, every animal has an *inua* or spirit, and the *inua* enjoys being hunted with a beautiful implement. The *inua* of a dead animal returns to enter the body of one as yet unborn and remembers how it was treated. So the prey must be treated with respect, for an offended *inua* will lead its fellows away from the hunters. The Eskimo's relationship goes further, for animal spirits can be used and harnessed. The float for a seal net is shaped like a seal's head, not expressly as a decoy, but to ensure that the 'sealness' of the net is enhanced. A hunter from Cape Nome keeps his lance points inside a little box shaped like a seal, not simply because seals are a part of his life to be celebrated in art, but for sound practical reasons. 'Thus,' he explains, 'the points would grow accustomed to being inside a seal, making them more likely to find their marks and the quarry more likely to accept them.' To drag a dead seal home over the ice needs some kind of thong with a handle. The thong is of leather, the handle of ivory, carved as a wolf's head. Again this is not empty art. The wolf's predatory qualities are gathered into the implement, making it a better hunting tool.

Western Eskimo seal-shaped box, a container for harpoon points

9

It is the same all around the world. Animals inhabit the same spiritual world as people, and may be seen as true brethren. Totem animals, sacred to a particular clan, are very special. The word itself is derived from an Algonkian Indian word *ototeman* that means brother-sister kin. In other words, the members of a clan are related to their totem animal as brother and sister. This prevents members of a clan marrying one another, but that is just one consequence of having a totem. Identifying with an animal also lends the clan some of its properties. It is impossible to generalise about people and their totems, and academic anthropologists continue still their learned debates about what exactly constitutes totemism and, indeed, whether it even exists. But, as with the cave artists, some unifying threads do emerge.

Animals in general, and the totem in particular, are often regarded as humans with superhuman qualities. The strength of the bear, the cunning of the fox, the swiftness of the deer, are qualities that the clan members may share in. The totem is a companion, a relative, a protector and often a progenitor; the first member of the clan may have been a totem animal, or the clan may have sprung from a union between man and animal. The clan reveres the totem, and has taboos against killing, eating, and even touching it. Where sacrifices of the totem must be made, they are usually conducted for one clan by another that has no such special feeling for the animal in question, for different clans or subgroups of the tribe have different totems. For this reason, totemism is not, in most experts' eyes, a religion. It is more restrictive than that; a religion would involve an entire ethnic group, worshipping the same animal – as, for example, the ancient Egyptians, all of whom worshipped baboons and cats.

Animals feature strongly in true religion and in myth and legend, often helping to explain aspects of life that people find puzzling, or frightening, or simply wonderful. Eclipses are just such a phenomenon. The moon vanishes, only to reappear a minute or two later. More frightening still, the sun itself may disappear, bringing darkness when there should be light. But again, all is well and the light returns after a minute or two. Today we know that eclipses are caused by one planet casting its shadow onto another. The moon's shadow obscures the sun, our shadow hides the moon. But to non-scientific people an eclipse is often seen as an animal who eats the sun and then regurgitates it. The animal may be a dog or wolf, as it is in China, among Germanic tribes, and across much of North America. It may be a snake, as in Africa and Indonesia. In South America it is a jaguar. In all these cultures the animal devours the sun, and then returns it.

Animals are invoked to account for all manner of things. Fire, a precious substance that people often award life of its own, is brought by a messenger. In the case of the ancient Greeks the messenger was a man, Prometheus, but to many peoples it is a dog, an animal long associated with the hearth. Sometimes the animal's role in helping man also explains its own characteristics. The bat is

10

black and blind, with naked wings, because the fire it brought to man singed it, and the smoke blinded it. Not just natural phenomena but the world itself may rest on an animal; an elephant, as it does in India, or a turtle, for the Chinese. Animals have always been an integral, and important, part of our world.

It is a two-faced thing, this relationship between man and beast. There is awe, and there is slaughter. There is worship, and there is destruction. And it is not restricted to peoples who subsist on undomesticated nature. Agriculture is scarcely 5000 years old, mankind at least five million, and you do not undo in 5000 years the evolution of the previous five million. The feeling for wild animals is still there. What is not is the opportunity to give vent to that feeling. For the vast majority of people alive today, there is only one place to come close to wild animals: the zoo.

The 1982 edition of the *International Zoo Yearbook* lists those institutions around the world that keep wild animals in captivity and allow the public in to see them. The editor of the yearbook stresses that he cannot vouch for the accuracy of the figures, but even so his assiduous data gathering shows us what the popularity of zoos was at the end of 1980.

In Europe there were some 290 zoos, which were visited by a total of 96 million people during the year. The UN estimates that there are 483 million people in Europe. So one in five Europeans went to a zoo during the year. North America has 181 zoos that were visited by 95 million visitors. With a population of 246 million that works out to almost one in three going to a zoo in the year. And it isn't just the industrialised world that loves zoos. In South and Central America one in ten people visited the zoo, and the Far East has 117 zoos that attract 78 million visitors. Everywhere the story is the same. The global figures are astonishing; something like 357 million people (out of a world total of about 4400 million) visited the 757 zoos listed in the yearbook. To put that figure in perspective, it is equal to the combined populations of the United Kingdom, France, the United States, and Canada. Zoos are popular.

The facts and figures tell only part of the story. Why do people go to the zoo? It will not surprise you to learn that almost a third of all zoo visits are prompted by children, and even when a child doesn't instigate the trip, nearly two-thirds go to the zoo because 'it's a good place to take children'. Even then, however, adults are not there solely for the child's benefit. They enjoy the animals as much, if not more, than the children. The child may decide that he wants to go to the zoo, but once there it is the grown-up who makes the decisions; what to look at, how long to stay, and where to go next.

So at one level you can say that people go to the zoo to take their children. But that begs the question. Why should the zoo be a good place to take children? And wandering around a zoo one can see plenty of people without children. I believe people visit zoos because there is something very rewarding about being in the presence of wild animals. Early people, like the hunters of today, relied on animals for their survival, and their activity reveals a deep-seated feeling for animals. We still carry that legacy with us, and it is one of the reasons we enjoy being close to the animals in the zoo. Not all the feelings we harbour for animals are good: we also go to the zoo to indulge our loathing of certain species, or to expose ourselves to a little gentle fright. As adults we are probably not aware of these two motivations, reverence and hatred, but I believe they are present, nevertheless. Instead we use the excuse of taking the children.

Children have not yet learned to hold themselves aloof from nature. Stories about animals are universal favourites, even in the most urban societies, and in those stories people and animals regularly enter each other's worlds. The child learns about people through animals, and knowledge of and contact with animals is considered essential for his or her education. So we take our children to the zoo, because for urban dwellers that is where the animals are. While we are instructing them we are able to fulfil our own needs too.

Respect for animals, contempt for animals, oneness with animals, all are feelings that we need to express and we can do so at the zoo. To really understand the lure of the zoo you should go to one and look not at the animals, but at the people.

A young mother holds tightly to her little girl, though the fence dividing them from the animals stretches a good metre above her head. Next to her a small boy, perhaps eight years old, is being brave for the benefit of his friends. He is trying to push his little hand through the fence. But when the animals, who could not possibly reach him, start to advance, his bravery evaporates. He turns and tries to displace his sister from their mother's protective hold. Two teenage men have no one to turn to but each other. They spend their time discussing, in voices loud enough to be heard by all around, just how ferocious these beasts are. Stretched along the wire-fencing, like chickens hypnotised by a snake, the public enacts its old drama with animals. On one side are people held in the grip of every emotion from outright fear to admiration. On the other, bare sand, murky water, and a jumbled mass of Mississippi alligators, one of which occasionally breaks loose from the pile to stretch or yawn.

Into the pit, with remarkably little showmanship, steps Bobby Tiger, Seminole Indian by birth and alligator wrestler by profession. He uses a beat-up old public address system to tell us how dangerous alligators can be, holding up the stump of a finger as living proof. And who would doubt him? Of course the alligators are as vicious as they look; if they were not there would be precious little point in our clustering round. Who wants to see a man wrestle a friendly puppy? Bobby is dressed in ordinary jeans and a T-shirt, but despite the 35°C heat he wears over them a colourful Seminole patchwork and embroidered shirt. Grabbing a large pole, with feet bare, he steps into the water to select an adversary.

12

Slowly, and with an evidently practised eye, he begins to poke at the mass of alligators. At first they merely twitch in response, but gradually they liven up and the jumbled mass transforms itself into a seething knot. The big one – Bobby had pointed him out and asked us to keep an eye on him – breaks loose and we sound a chorus of warning cries. Without us to give the shout he would lose a toe, too, and we feel useful. But the big reptile is not after a meal. He has seen all this before, three or four times a day for more seasons than he cares to remember, and he is off down to the other end of the pool where he can resume the endless business of lazing about.

The young ones are not so adept, and continue to seethe. But the crowd has grown weary. The little girl's attention wanders to a couple of birds hopping close by in the khaki dust. Bobby seizes the moment, and an alligator. He reaches down into the grey-green water and gropes about. Suddenly, Bobby Tiger has a 'gator by the tail. No one is watching little birdies any more. All eyes are on Bobby as he drags the alligator out of the water and up on to the sand. He has his opponent.

At this stage Bobby pauses for a bit of a breather. He explains the differences between a croc and a 'gator, tells us again how strong the alligator's jaws are, and asks us not to distract him during the next, difficult part of the show. We will try, but we cannot promise; sometimes the excitement is too much, and little squeaks of fright escape our lips. A quick prod and the alligator obligingly opens his monstrous jaws. Bobby tosses a handful of sand into the animal's gape and the jaws snap shut with a satisfying thud. Another prod, and they are open again. This time Bobby steps forward and, with a speed that surprises the alligator as much as us, he reaches forward and grabs it below the point of that fearsome bite. He pushes forward, swivels, and steps nimbly over the alligator's back. Hauling back, he soon has the alligator's neck arched back, its snout pointed skywards. 'Get your cameras ready,' Bobby advises. Then he leans over the alligator and puts its chin behind his. He removes his hands and spreads his arms, Christlike, chin to chin with a 3-metre 'gator as the shutters click and the mouths gasp. But the show isn't over yet. Now he is going to put the animal to sleep, and having hypnotised it will wake it with a crocodilian love call.

That has us watching again. Bobby sidles warily up to the alligator and begins at last to look a little like a wrestler. He waits for the moment and then throws himself on top of it, reaching for its leg and twisting it over onto its back. The powerful tail thrashes three or four times but then lies quiet. Still prone across its belly, Bobby begins to dismount. Slowly he pulls back onto his knees and rubs sand onto the ghostly green scales that plate the alligator's stomach. Satisfied with his work he shows the crowd how floppy the alligator's foreleg is. And it is. Fast asleep. Bobby selects a volunteer from the audience to come in and stroke the soft underbelly of a Mississippi alligator, and, somewhat gingerly, I approach, not sure what to do. I kneel beside Bobby and put my

13

hand out to touch the scales. I am completely lost, and barely register Bobby's whispered admonition; 'If he moves, go that way. . . . Fast.' Bobby, the other alligators, the crowd around, all of Florida vanish as man feels alligator.

Bobby Tiger gently brought me back to reality, thanked me, and set about doing the same for the alligator. A few seconds later the alligator turned over, blinked once or twice, and waddled back to the water to join the jumbled mass. Bobby Tiger, another show over, left the alligator pit as quietly as he had entered it, switched off the PA system, and retreated to the shade to enjoy a well-earned Dr Pepper.

What had been going on? Why was the audience transfixed? Bobby's show, despite his missing finger, is relatively safe; otherwise he would not have been doing it all these years. Alligators can be vicious, there is no denying that, but it is the tail, rather than the jaws, that inflicts real damage. A swipe would knock an unwary man down, and then the bite might be brought into play. But the jaws, despite looking fearsome, are not too nasty and an understanding of the way they work enables Bobby to do things that appear much more dangerous than they are. Quite simply, the muscles that open and close an alligator's mouth are relatively weak; to take a bite from a large animal the alligator thrashes its head from side to side. That means that a man can, without too much difficulty, open and shut the jaws to order. And the hypnotism is a simple defensive reflex. Turn almost any animal, from a chicken to a croc, over and it will lie motionless until disturbed. Tonic defensive immobility, the scientists call it.

I don't know how much of this the audience knew, and Bobby wasn't telling them. Standing close to wild animals, but safe and assured of their own superiority, they were enjoying the show and secretly, I suspect, some of them, like the people who crowd the corners of the Grand Prix circuits, would not have minded seeing something go wrong. One man, a tourist from afar to judge by his reddened scalp, even sported an 'Official 'Gator Taster' button from Al E. Gator's Restaurant in nearby Orlando. Powerful magic, to eat your enemies; the highest reverence and the final conquest.

The alligators in captivity along the Tamiami trail are probably not in what you would call a zoo. For one thing, they are the only animals there, at least behind bars, while conventional zoos have lots of species. The grackles hopping about in their never-ending quest for food and the paper wasps building their astonishing nests beneath the thatched, shade-giving ramadas don't count. Indeed, most people don't see them; they have eyes only for the alligators, the Indians, and the souvenirs.

What you call it, though, doesn't detract from its appeal. The fact is that people are fascinated by animals, and they will go out of their way to get close to them. As I said, I think this is something to do with our evolutionary past, when we depended on an intimate association with, and knowledge of, animals to survive as gatherers and hunters. Perhaps it goes even deeper than that, to a recognition that, no matter what our religions tell us, we are indeed related to those creatures. We see in them the beast within and having tamed them we may believe we have tamed our own inner beast. Whatever the reason, the lure of animals, especially exotics that may be tame but are nevertheless wild animals, rather than our familiar pets and farmyard friends, is very powerful. For most of the people on the earth a trip to the zoo is the only way to give in to the lure of wild animals. But in the course of our own development the nature of zoos has changed, and will indeed continue to do so.

Over 100 years ago, in 1867, Alfred Vance scored a huge popular success with his music-hall song 'Walking in the Zoo on Sunday', one couplet of which runs:

> The Stilton, Sir, the Cheese, the OK thing to do
> On Sunday afternoon is to toddle in the Zoo.

Overnight the word zoo had passed into the language, though there had been zoological gardens before that and Macaulay had used 'this vulgar but convenient abbreviation' of Clifton Zoo in Bristol as early as 1847; and before them there had been menageries. The idea of keeping animals in captivity goes back much further still. The first captive animals were probably domesticated species, sheep and goats, cattle and dogs, upon which man relied for food. And there were pets too, cats and dogs, kept as much for their companionship as for any economic help they might offer. Some animals were kept for religious purposes, as incarnations of the gods and as sacrifices, messengers to the gods. But these particular aspects of the relationship between animals and man need not concern us because, although the evidence is very sketchy, there seems to have been from earliest times a tendency to keep animals neither as food nor as domesticated pets, but simply for their own sake, as symbols of power or wealth.

Alexander the Great, for example, brought parrots back from India to Greece in the fourth century BC, and Alexander von Humboldt, the German scientist and explorer, reported seeing parrots kept captive in the huts of some of the South American Indians he visited. The lure of parrots continues today, with illegal specimens changing hands for huge sums of money to satisfy the needs of collectors.

South American Indians kept other singing birds as currency, and dogs often played this role too – the Kabaka of Buganda in central Africa measured his wealth in terms of the number he supported. This use of living animals is curious because it requires wealth to feed and house them. Unlike the cattle of the African nomads, which are a measure of wealth because they are a source of food, these singing birds and house dogs confer no material gain on whoever

15

Queen Victoria continued the royal association with zoos when she visited Wombwell's Menagerie in 1847

owns them. They are visible evidence of conspicuous consumption, and perhaps that is why they are prized. Or perhaps it is only because they are rare that they are valuable.

In medieval times wild animals, especially rare ones, were considered fitting gifts for people of power. Pope Leo presented Charlemagne with a lion at the emperor's coronation in Rome in AD 800. In the fifteenth century one of the Chinese emperors was given a giraffe all the way from East Africa. The Emperor Frederick II was a renowned naturalist who swapped a polar bear for a giraffe with the Sultan of Egypt. Frederick also presented a polar bear to his brother-in-law, Henry III of England, and the animal swam in the Thames in 1251. Some animals were thought to be so noble themselves that only royalty could own them; most notable among these were lions and leopards, royal beasts in many palaces from that of Elizabeth I of England to Emperor Haile Selassie (the Lion of Judah) of Ethiopia.

What we know of animal gifts implies that the recipients were well able to cope with them, and such is indeed the case; menageries are almost as old as civilisation. Thousands of years before Christ the Egyptian priests kept menageries at the temples; cats, dogs, baboons, ibises, lions and many other animals were looked after in these collections. On the other side of the world, 1000 years later in the twelfth century BC, the Chinese emperor Wen-Wang (said to be the author of the *I Ching*) built a 600-hectare Ling Yu, or Garden of Intelligence, to house his collection of animals. Such collections seem to have been a feature of imperial Chinese life, and as late as the thirteenth century Marco Polo saw lions and tigers wandering freely through the rooms of one of the Chinese imperial palaces.

Greece, like China, valued learning and knowledge highly, and by the fourth century BC most of the city states probably had their own collections of animals. We know that Alexander the Great, quite apart from parrots, sent other specimens home from his military campaigns and these found their way into the various collections. One of Alexander's teachers was Aristotle, who may well have been responsible for fostering his interest in exotic animals. Certainly Aristotle's own *History of Animals* tells us that he was familiar with many animals that were not native to Greece, and he must have visited these menageries to see them.

In quite another time and place, Montezuma, ruler of the Aztecs, maintained a menagerie in his palace at Tenochtitlán, which Hernando Cortés reached in 1519; this collection was so vast that it reputedly employed 300 keepers to look after the animals. The bird-of-prey aviaries were better than many of today, and along with the hawks, falcons and eagles were kept jaguars, pumas and snakes. One report says that these beasts got through 500 turkeys a day. There was a huge lake, ten ponds for waterfowl, and paddocks for llama, vicuna, deer and antelope. Among the birds and reptiles Montezuma kept, perhaps the most important was the gorgeous and revered quetzal. In Texcoco (often referred to as the Florence of Mexico) there was a large collection of animals that also included among them painted stone sculptures.

Collections of exotic animals, what we would now call zoos, seem therefore to have been a feature of all civilisations. We know precious little about these very early zoos, but they represented a tradition – the association of wild animals with powerful rulers – that was ancient then and yet continues to this day. The primary motive was to demonstrate the power and glory of important people, and this sentiment is still part of the zoo world.

The panda, symbol of conservation, is perhaps the most prized exhibit any zoo can have, and the Chinese not surprisingly use pandas as tools of diplomacy; as the bamboo curtain was drawn aside in the 1970s so the number of pandas in the West increased. Richard Nixon received a pair for the National Zoo in 1972 and President Pompidou's visit to China in 1973 was also marked by the

Animals are still used as gifts and objects of diplomacy. Edward Heath feeding Chia Chia, one of the two pandas given to him when he visited China in 1974

gift of two pandas. Edward Heath's visit in 1974 produced Ching Ching and Chia Chia for London Zoo. Gifts to friends put them under an obligation to reciprocate, and the Chinese are very careful about who they will give pandas to. In the United States the pandas at the National Zoo in Washington are considered a national resource, but the directors of many other zoos in America are not reticent in claiming that they would make more of the pandas than Washington has; as long as the panda remains an item of international exchange, they are unlikely to get the chance.

That animals have long been seen as symbols of power undoubtedly contributes to our fascination with them. But there is another much darker side to the relationship. You show power by keeping an animal captive; how much more powerful are you if you kill it?

In a relatively short time the Roman empire managed to convert the mysticism and reverence for animals of the Egyptians into a bloodthirsty appetite for violent death, an appetite that, as it grew, needed ever greater helpings to satisfy it. We are accustomed to thinking of Roman gladiatorial games as a day's sport at the Circus or Colosseum, but at the height of the empire the games might have gone on for months on end. Perhaps the most excessive were those staged by Trajan to mark his conquest to Dacia (Romania) in AD 106. This celebration lasted some four months, and during the games 10,000 gladiators lost their lives. Of more immediate concern to us, 11,000 animals were slain during those same games – that is, roughly 100 animals each day – killed before a crowd that is most politely described as frenzied. Trajan was only giving people what they expected, continuing a tradition set up earlier. Augustus, who ruled between 31 BC and AD 14, ran through about 3500 animals including, so it is said, a snake 25 metres long. Nero, in the middle of the first century, once set a company of horsemen against a collection of 400 bears and 300 lions. The Colosseum was sometimes flooded so that gladiators could kill hippos, crocodiles, and seals. Titus, in the three years between AD 79 and 81, kept (which means killed) about 5000 animals. The catalogue goes on and on. Trajan was remarkable only for the wealth of records we have about his games.

The Roman appetite for public death was not confined to Rome itself. In every outpost of the empire there was a stadium, and in all of these men killed one another and animals. Gladiators were drawn from the ranks of slaves and captives, and for many it was a way out, but there were also well-born Romans who fancied themselves as fighters, and gladiatorial schools trained pupils in the craft of killing. At least the professionals, some of whom specialised in killing animals with bare hands, stood a better chance of leaving the stadium alive than the Christians, just one of many persecuted strata of society thrown to the lions. But while men might opt to become gladiators, for fame and fortune, there was no rush of animals to be killed. Proconsuls in the far reaches of the empire not only had to supply their own town stadia with animals but were also charged with sending suitable quantities back to Rome for the games there. I find it impossible to imagine how they discharged this duty; the game must have been extraordinarily plentiful, and the shipping very well organised, to sustain the Roman demand, but sustain it these men surely did.

The games continued for centuries, until, in 325, Constantine (coincidentally, perhaps, the first Christian emperor) decreed that they stop. But making a decree was one thing, enforcing it quite another, and gladiatorial contests continued. In fact Constantine's decree was overturned in the sixth century by

19

Justinian, who ordered that games be resumed, but specifically forbade priests and bishops at the spectacle. Justinian was most likely nudged in this direction by his empress Theodora, who was the daughter of the bear-keeper at one of Constantinople's two amphitheatres, and was a strong influence on the emperor. In any event, games, which included the slaughter of animals, resumed in Constantinople and continued at least until the twelfth century.

Massive organised animal slaughter may have died out, but traces of our passion for it remain throughout the world. The Spanish bullfight is an obvious example, one in which the old tradition of man killing animal in front of spectators is maintained. From time to time stories of other forms of similar entertainment find their way into the newspapers. Badger-baiting, in which dogs despatch badgers, is enjoying a resurgence in the north-east of England, and it is still possible to attend dog-fights and cock-fights, but the Roman appetite for animal death as a spectacle seems to have waned.

A contrast to the very public spectacle of the games is the private enjoyment of hunting animals as sport, and in this the Romans, curiously, were quite unlike the civilisations that came before and after them. The Egyptians, Assyrians, Babylonians and Greeks regarded hunting as a noble pursuit, the proper entertainment for those of proper birth. So too did the Teutons, Franks, and other

Assyrian lion hunt. 'One desperate beast, braver than the rest, charges the chariot.'

Europeans. But as far as the Romans were concerned hunting was not a fitting pastime for a gentleman, and was best left to lower social orders.

For early man, as for some people today, hunting was an essential ingredient in the recipe for survival. Agriculture and the domestication of animals changed all that, and it was no longer necessary to track and kill animals in order to eat. Of course there were still those who hunted animals for reasons of survival, generally to sell the product, but agriculture permitted hunting to develop into a sport, one that only the rich and leisured could afford to engage in. Egyptian hunters formed a social class of their own; they might hunt on their own accord but they also spent much time assisting nobles in tracking, killing, and then preparing the game, much as gillies do today in Scotland. The Assyrians and Babylonians, like the Egyptians before them, developed the notion of training predators to hunt for man's amusement. Cheetahs, dogs, and even lions were trained as hunting animals, and the first records of the use of birds – falconry – date from Babylon in 700 BC. The Greeks too were interested in the chase, and wrote at length about it.

But none of this compares with the development of hunting in later Europe, whose peoples, for some reason, have always had a particular enthusiasm for the pastime. At first hunting, mostly for the pot as a supplement to the diet but also purely for sport, was open to everyone except slaves, who were not allowed to carry weapons. Slowly, however, ownership of land came to include owner-ship of the animals on it, and the right to hunt became firmly attached to the landowners. Serfs in the feudal states might be permitted to hunt on their lord's land, or there might be areas set aside for the commoners, but the landowners were the ones who did most of the hunting.

Some of the exploits of those landowners are hard to credit today, but the records show clearly that hunting was a very important part of life. Perhaps the most extreme examples are furnished by the Electors of Saxony, who held the title of Lord High Master of the Chase of the Holy Roman Empire. This, and the land they governed, gave them exceptional opportunities to indulge their passion for hunting. John George II, Elector between 1656 and 1680, killed 42,649 red deer in the twenty-four years of his reign. He turned down the crown of neighbouring Bohemia not for any political reason but because the stags there were smaller than those of Saxony, and he built a high and expensive fence between the two principalities to protect his own, more valuable beasts. The Landgrave of nearby Hesse exhibited the same passion. Not content with his daily bread, he added a codicil to the Lord's Prayer: 'Give us this day our daily hart in pride of grease'; that is, a good stag with lots of food reserves, taken just before the start of the rut.

Elsewhere in Europe the story was the same. In eighteenth-century France Louis XV stopped in the forest of Villars-Cotteret to chase stag on the way home from his coronation. The records show that in one year, 1726, Louis XV somehow contrived to spend 276 of the 365 days hunting. In Russia the Tsars enjoyed unparalleled hunting in the imperial forests and in one twelve-day hunt in the forest of Belovezh the recorded bag was 36 elk, 53 stags, 325 roe deer, 42 wisent and 138 wild boar.

Hunting was clearly very important, but it is hard to assess just what contribution it made to the domestic economy. The Elector of Saxony's 42,649 red deer will have been eaten of course, and doubtless shared among many people besides his immediate retinue. So the nutritional aspects of hunting are far from negligible, but it is impossible to say whether the returns, in terms of food alone, offset the costs of mounting the hunts. Probably not. For modern hunters, it seems unlikely that the meat represents a bargain. The important thing seems to be the chase, and the prevalence of hunting today is yet another manifestation of the fascination with animals that draws people to zoos. There is a more direct link than that, however, because it was from the hunting preserves of the old aristocrats of Europe that the first modern zoo emerged.

Not content with hunting wild deer roaming free in the forests, several noblemen created deer parks around their castles. These were carefully managed, stocked with deer and other game, and offered their owners the chance of more or less guaranteed good hunting. Crown Prince Maximilian of Austria, later to become the Emperor Maximilian II, was no exception, and in 1552 he set about installing a deer park around the castle at Ebersdorf, near Vienna. It was an ordinary enough deer park for the most part, called, like similar parks elsewhere, a menagerie. The word is derived from the same root as mansion, and originally meant no more than a domestic establishment. Maximilian changed all that; he brought exotic animals to the deer park, where he simply kept them on display. Other rulers had done so before Maximilian, but none as thoroughly.

The first of these outlandish animals was an Indian elephant, which Maximilian had brought overland all the way from Spain, stopping the caravan several times so that the people could get a closer look at the new arrival. At one of these halts the crowd was aghast when a little girl, some five years old, was pushed and fell right in front of the oncoming giant. But there was nothing to fear. According to one report, 'without taking another step, the elephant made a wide sweep with its trunk to give itself room, gently lifted the child and, with the air of a gentleman, handed her to her mother Frau Marie Gniger.' No wonder the Viennese people took to the beast. It lived at Ebersdorf, in Maximilian's menagerie, but died within a year on 18 December 1553, the bones of its right leg being made into a stool which can be seen in Vienna to this day.

Ebersdorf was, by all accounts, a successful deer park and menagerie, but nevertheless in 1569 Maximilian, now emperor, purchased an area known as the Katterburg. Here he established another enclave for deer, with facilities for game birds and fish as well. He also created a menagerie at the castle of Neugebäude, now part of Vienna's central cemetery, and after Maximilian's death it was this menagerie that continued while Ebersdorf fell into desuetude. Katterberg, however, is where the story continues, for it was later absorbed into the imperial palace of Schönbrunn and it was there, nearly 200 years later, that the first animal collection that we would recognise as a modern zoo came to be built.

The husband of the Empress Maria Theresa, Franz Stephan, had a great interest in zoology. He found that travelling from the palace at Schönbrunn to Neugebäude to study the animals was very wearying, and in any case the menagerie there was on the small side, and he therefore commissioned a menagerie in his own backyard. The architect Nicholas Jadot de Ville-Issey drew up a design which was clearly based on another famous Austro-Hungarian menagerie, that of Prince Eugene of Savoy at the Castle Belvedere south of Vienna, siting the Schönbrunn menagerie a little way down the hill from the palace at the end of a broad tree-lined avenue. The layout was simple: at the centre of a circle stood a beautiful rococo pavilion, eight-sided, with windows looking out over the animals arranged around it. The outer circle was composed of thirteen wedge-shaped paddocks, with a little animal house at the far end of each. The walls between the enclosures were high, so that the only place from which one could get a good view of the animals was the pavilion itself, and in the summer Maria Theresa and Franz Stephan would stroll down from the palace to take breakfast there. As they did so, they could gaze out on the best collection of animals in Europe, a fitting sight indeed for the rulers of one of its most powerful nations.

The public was admitted to Franz Stephan's menagerie on occasion but it remained nevertheless essentially the private collection of the emperor and empress. Just how private can be seen from a charming anecdote. When the

The little pavilion at the centre of Schönbrunn in Vienna, the first modern zoo

main menagerie was still at Neugebäude, the gardener's daughter was responsible for feeding the lions. One day in 1669, she went in to feed them as usual, but never emerged. Things were not, in fact, completely as usual, for it was her wedding day and she was already dressed up in her wedding finery. Her favourite lion was apparently possessed by a fit of jealousy and killed and ate her. The tragic tale of 'the lion's bride' became well known and Maria Theresa, eighty years later, used it as an excuse to forbid any 'ravenous' animals at Schönbrunn. All the carnivores had to stay at Neugebäude, where they remained until 1781 when Josef II, also a passionate zoologist, closed Neugebäude the year after his mother died and brought the raptors to Schönbrunn.

Josef II set up a Society for the Acquisition of Animals and pestered embassies and consulates for specimens for his collection. He also financed expeditions to the Americas and Africa to bring back animals, and slowly the menagerie at Schönbrunn began to grow. In what was to become a familiar pattern, money ran out. Franz II spent his private funds on buying up travelling collections for their specimens, which he brought to Schönbrunn, and the public, which had previously been merely tolerated there, was now encouraged to attend. The zoo began to have a profound influence on society life in Vienna.

Nothing exemplifies this more clearly than the fuss that attended the arrival of the first giraffe in 1828. The animal was a present from Mehemet Ali, Viceroy of Egypt, and landed at Fiume, on the Adriatic, in May. In Vienna, on 9 May, the theatre at Leopoldstadt gave a benefit performance for the poet Adolf Bäuerle, consisting of 'a modern work of art accompanied by song' entitled *The Giraffe in Vienna* and starring prominent actors of the day. After resting at Fiume, the giraffe began the long walk to Vienna, fitted with special leather shoes and a waterproof cape made of waxed cloth. At Karlstadt the poor animal showed signs of exhaustion, so the authorities decided it would be best to send it on to Vienna by carriage. This was duly done, the giraffe travelling in a modified cart with two cows ahead to supply it with milk, and three coaches behind to carry the accompanying personnel. The procession arrived in the city on 7 August, and the city certainly seems to have been ready for it.

The *Vienna General Theatre Journal* devoted a special supplement, published on 30 August 1828, to a report of the giraffe festival that had taken place in Penzing a fortnight earlier, on 19 August. Every lady received a bouquet of flowers, crowned by the head and neck of a giraffe made of sugar. The report continues: 'Excellent music conducted by Mr Friedl, soon invited the guests to dance, a polonaise followed by waltz, cotillion, gallopade à la giraffe, and others. . . . Beautiful transparencies, executed by Mr Eduard Gurk, depicting the giraffe attended by an Arab, were to be found in a copse at the bottom of the garden. The Arab, Cahi Alli Sciobary, who accompanied the giraffe to Vienna, himself appeared at the ball. Deeply moved with amazement and delight at the transparencies of himself and the giraffe, he indicated by gestures of his

The Egyptian cat goddess Bast, who defended Ra against the serpent Apep

# WALKING IN THE ZOO

SUNG WITH DISTINGUISHED APPLAUSE BY

## THE GREAT VANCE

ENT. STA. HALL

Pr 3/-

"WALKING IN THE ZOO, WALKING IN THE ZOO.
THE O.K. THING ON SUNDAY IS THE WALKING IN THE ZOO;
WALKING IN THE ZOO, WALKING IN THE ZOO
THE O.K. THING ON SUNDAY IS THE WALKING IN THE ZOO."

WRITTEN BY

MUSIC BY

## HUGH WILLOUGHBY SWENY ESQ & ALFRED LEE

*Left* the Great Vance's song popularised the word 'zoo' in 1868. Domination over animals is an important part of our relationship with them, and is still given expression in such spectacles as alligator wrestling (*top left*) and the modern bullfight (*top right*). More blood was shed in Roman times (*above*). *Overleaf* one of the Elector of Saxony's staghunts

Display conditions make all the difference. At Emmen, in Holland, the crocodiles are seen against a lush background, and become much less fearsome than they are in bare cages behind vicious bars. *Previous page* London Zoo in 1835, a fashionable place to stroll and look at the animals

A giraffe, a gift from the Viceroy of Egypt, arrived at Schönbrunn in 1828, and had an enormous and dramatic impact on life in Vienna

hands and feet that the dances were much to his liking and that he would fain tread a measure himself.' The giraffe, alas, died on 20 June 1829, after just ten months and thirteen days at the menagerie. The menagerie, by contrast, went from strength to strength and in 1906 was the site of the first elephant birth in a European zoo.

Schönbrunn Zoo today is not one of the great zoos of the world. The little pavilion is still there, the fresco and painted panels as charming now as they must have been in Maria Theresa's time, and serves as the zoo cafeteria, complete with rococo fridge, gilt-framed mirrors, and lovely chandeliers. As such, it is one of the nicest zoo cafeterias anywhere in the world. The thirteen enclosures still surround the pavilion, though the high walls between them have been taken down and replaced with wire netting. It is an average urban zoo, somewhere for people to go to see wild animals, with all the problems that that entails. What makes Schönbrunn special is its history, the fact that for more than 400 years exotic animals have been kept on that site.

A very different spirit guided the formation of the Jardin des Plantes in Paris, the next great collection to be founded. Where Schönbrunn has its central pavilion with surrounding enclosures designed to give a view of the animals only to those privileged to be inside it, the Jardin des Plantes has broad walkways, avenues down which ordinary people can stroll to admire the animals. This design reflects the origin of the Paris zoo, a royal menagerie appropriated by the people.

Louis XIV, the Sun King, had built a menagerie in the grounds of his palace at Versailles, the first animals arriving in 1665. The collection grew, and with it the number of visitors, until the damage done by the public forced Louis to restrict admittance to members of his court. His successors, Louis XV and Louis XVI, took no great interest in the collection and the menagerie fell into disrepair. In 1789, with revolution imminent, Louis XVI moved to Paris and the menagerie declined further. Nevertheless the collection was maintained at Versailles until August 1792.

The revolutionaries considered it shameful that animals should be well fed while people were starving. A group of Jacobin sympathisers, probably the most ruthless of the revolutionaries, took it upon themselves to go to Versailles and 'both in the name of the people and of nature, to demand that those creatures which God had created to be free, and whose freedom had been denied by the vainglory of tyrants, should be set at liberty'. The director was in no position to refuse, but as he handed over the keys he pointed out to the Jacobins that many of the animals might well, as their first act of freedom, turn and attack their liberators. Prudence overcame principle, and the revolutionaries decided to leave the dangerous beasts in confinement. And in a further display of practicality, those that they did free they sent straight to the butcher, therefore solving two pressing problems; the animals could no longer offend anyone's sensibilities by being fed while people were starving, and some of the people were, for a short time, released from starvation.

In the wake of this the remnants of the menagerie were offered to the former Jardin du Roy in Paris, now renamed the Jardin des Plantes by the revolutionaries, and the offer was sweetened by the promise of a magnificent rhinoceros still in the Versailles collection. Originally a herb garden where plants and their medicinal properties could be studied, in 1793 the Jardin was incorporated into the newly formed Muséum National d'Histoire Naturelle, and the tiny menagerie it contained was expanded. Many specimens came from travelling side-shows that offered people the entertaining spectacle of fights between wild and domestic animals. The authorities in Paris banned these shows and confiscated the animals, dumping them on the unwilling custodians of the Jardin des Plantes. In April 1794 the last remnants of the King's menagerie arrived from Versailles. These included a quagga and a lion and his friend, a little dog, but they were without the rhino who was too ill to travel and died the following month.

Times were not always easy for the young Paris zoo. People were still starving and it was very difficult to maintain the collections, but somehow they were maintained. In the years that followed much good scientific work was done by the professors of the Muséum. But in the autumn of 1870 came the greatest set-back of all: the Prussian army laid siege to Paris. Once again, expediency proved more important than exhibition, and all the edible animals in the Jardin were slaughtered to provide food for the people of Paris.

Unlike Paris and Vienna, London Zoo – the first menagerie to be described as a zoological garden – was founded expressly as a zoo, rather than emerging haphazardly from previous collections. Sir Stamford Raffles and Sir Humphry Davy got together to promote a society that would be devoted to the study of zoology, and in their prospectus stressed that the animals must be brought 'as objects of scientific research, not of vulgar admiration'. These high-flown sentiments continue to plague the Zoological Society of London to this day. The gates of its gardens in Regent's Park were opened to members and their guests

'The elephant (in his bath)', front cover of the London *Mirror*, 4 August 1832

on 27 April 1828 and George IV granted the Zoological Society of London a Royal Charter in 1829. The zoo was an immediate success with fashionable society, much as the one in Vienna had been, and quickly became the place to take the air in London. Soon after the opening the *Mirror* reported: 'The Gardens, independent of their zoological attractions, are a delightful promenade, being laid out with great taste, and the parterres boasting a beautiful display of flowers. The animals, too, are seen to much greater advantage than when shut up in a menagerie, and have the luxury of fresh air, instead of unwholesome respiration in a room or caravan.'

In 1847 members of the public were admitted, for the price of a shilling, on weekdays only, and they too enjoyed strolling around the zoo, but from its very inception the Zoological Society of London, unlike almost every other zoo in the world, was concerned primarily with the science of zoology and only secondarily with the needs of visitors. Where Vienna, Paris, and London had led, other cities were quick to follow. By 1870, shortly after Vance had made strolling in the zoo the OK thing to do, there were zoos in Dublin, Bristol, Berlin, Frankfurt, Antwerp and Rotterdam. More than forty of the zoos that exist today are more than 100 years old. Every city needed its zoo, it seemed. But why?

I have said that people have a powerful urge to get close to wild animals, to be near them and to feel them. The reasons for this are many and complex, and probably involve evolutionary memories of hunting and a sense of power over nature. This was the Victorian age, the height of the industrial revolution, when men discovered that they could do almost anything they turned their minds to, or so it seemed. Engineering brought mastery of the physical world, and the quest for knowledge and understanding brought some mastery of the natural world. Zoos were places where people could go to see, and learn about, the exotic animals of the world, and with the growth of colonial empires the zoo also served to illustrate the holdings of the mother country.

Education, in the formal sense, was sorely lacking. The better zoos had attached scientific societies, modelled on London's, but little provision was made to supply the public at large with information about the inmates. Indeed, little information was needed; to see these animals, alive and an arm's length away, was an education in itself. The ideal zoo contained a wide selection of animals, housed in cages that afforded visitors an unobstructed view and set in beautiful gardens. The animals were on display, and their housing was designed to that end. London Zoo was typical in this regard; its buildings, as one history notes, 'designed more for the pleasure they could give visitors than for the needs of their inmates'. A typical example was the Lion House, opened in 1876 (and only demolished a century later). This gave the animals within no privacy whatsoever, for their dens faced the public walkway.

Zoos catered to public tastes, but they also shaped the public's appreciation of animals. Something as simple as the housing of an animal makes an enormous difference to the way visitors perceive that animal. In Paris, at the Jardin des Plantes, a special building for reptiles was constructed in 1874. It is still there, two large halls housing an aquarium and the crocodilians. Still there, too, are the original bars for the crocs, thick recurved iron spikes that grate and squeak in the reverberating hall as the keepers haul them about to move the animals from one pen to another. The message is simple. These beasts are fearsome and dangerous, and we have put them behind these vicious bars for your safety. It is a message reinforced by the brusqueness and violence of the keepers towards their charges and by the notices screwed to the wall behind: ANIMAUX DANGEREUX in big red letters and below that *Ne pas s'appuyer sur les grilles*. The crocodiles themselves, should anyone bother to look at them, give the lie to this warning, as they lie in torpid heaps, their misshapen mouths unfit even for menacing the keepers. The children who visit the Paris crocodiles today don't really see the animals – but they absorb the message of the Reptile House; everywhere their talk is of how dangerous the crocodiles are. The zoo has shaped their perception.

Of course it does not have to be that way. Elsewhere crocodiles are kept in surroundings that emphasise their special characteristics, not simply their viciousness. At Emmen, a small but very progressive zoo in North Holland, the crocodiles live in an enclosure not much bigger than Paris's cells, but the whole feeling is very different. Lush jungle plants and a waterfall give an impression of natural habitat – one that, incidentally, is as false as Paris's iron bars since the crocodiles are not from tropical forests but from more arid regions of Africa. In the water are fish which escaped from their own tank into the pool while still small fry; they live unmolested by the crocodiles. There are no bars to be seen, indeed no ironwork at all, and a simple wooden bridge, quite rustic in character, carries visitors over the reptiles below. Everything seems more peaceful, more harmonious, less dangerous. Again, the zoo has manipulated our perception of these animals.

This will become a very familiar theme. On the one hand, zoos cater to public demand. On the other, they help shape what the public demands. What is acceptable to one group of people at one zoo is completely unacceptable to another at a different time or in a different place. Nothing makes this clearer than our view of bars. Some people (no good adjectival epithet is available; sensitive, civilised, compassionate all carry unwanted assumptions and are, in any case, often misleading) do not like the sight of animals in cages. It isn't captivity they object to, just bars. And that shift in attitude stems from the work of one man, Carl Hagenbeck, inventor of the cage without bars.

Carl Hagenbeck lived in Hamburg, where he carried on business as an animal trainer and dealer supplying the many zoos that had sprung up across Europe

Carl Hagenbeck, who more than anyone changed the face of zoos, with his celebrated African exhibit (*top*) and absurdly overdecorated gate. The park was pure entertainment

38

in the second half of the nineteenth century. He was, by all accounts, gifted with animals and was a very successful dealer and entrepreneur. He also pioneered displays of people, brought from afar and arranged in tableaux to amuse visitors. This was less offensive then than it might seem now, and people flocked to see the strange persons put before them by Hagenbeck. On one of his European tours it is recorded that on a single day, 6 October 1878, some 62,000 people visited Berlin Zoo to attend Hagenbeck's travelling exhibition. What they saw included Nubians from the Sudan, together with camels, elephants, giraffes and rhinos. But it was the people who were the biggest draw. In addition to the Nubians there were Laplanders, Eskimos, islanders from Tierra del Fuego, Kalmucks and even Buddhist priests. These human zoos helped assure Hagenbeck's fortune, but what he really wanted was a zoo of his own.

He bought a large, flat potato field at Stellingen, outside Hamburg, and in 1900 began to transform it into his vision of a park for wild animals. It was to be a place of beauty and entertainment, as it still is, with no high ideals of science or education. But the real revolution was the nature of the captivity enjoyed by Hagenbeck's animals. Hagenbeck was an immensely clever landscaper, and instead of putting his animals behind bars he put them into moated enclosures. Carefully planted trees and shrubs, artificial rockwork, paths that meandered between the exhibits all conspired to give a feeling of freedom. The animals were still captive, but their captivity was well hidden. And by judicious placement of the various moats and hedges, and a sound knowledge of what people could and could not see, Hagenbeck created the illusion that predator and prey were apparently living together freely.

You can still see it today, the polar bears in their enclosure above the seals in theirs. The two cannot get at one another, as they would do in life, but the moat that separates them is invisible to the public. The result is a great deal of entertaining behaviour from the animals, and a strange feeling in the onlooker that this is somehow better than a cage. You see it even better in the African section, a marvellous confection of enclosures. From the bottom, in front of the little lake with its breeding flamingos, a panorama stretches up and away to culminate in a rocky peak. In the middle distance are zebras and ostriches, feeding peacefully, but behind them is a pride of lions, the cubs clambering over the rocky sides of the outcrop. Of course all the paddocks are separate, the animals kept apart by moats, paths and fences. The point is that from the bottom, when you stand where Hagenbeck intended you to stand, the illusion is complete. The animals look free.

Hagenbeck's zoo was a great success, so much so that the grateful inhabitants of Stellingen changed the name of the street that ran past his monstrously ornate gate from Kaiser Wilhelmstrasse to Hagenbeckallee. His idea was a brilliant one which fired the imagination of the zoo-going public. Cages with bars remained, of course, but soon zoos were ensuring that they had at least one open, naturalistic exhibit. London's Mappin Terraces, which house the bears and sheep, were opened in 1913 and used some of the same principles. And today Hagenbeck Tierpark is one of the most aesthetically pleasing zoos to visit. Under magnificent specimen trees the green lawns curve away, enclosed by beautiful floral borders and paths. Peacocks wander on the lawns and strike poses on the little Japanese bridge. Mara, those improbable long-legged South American rodents, dot the grass and will approach a patient visitor to be fed. The atmosphere is genteel and lovely, eye-catching animals displayed to perfection. But captive.

Tucked away in one corner of the Tierpark is the Afenhaus, with its sad cargo of apes. No landscaping here, just cold tiles and iron bars, and a collection of apes who would not be out of place in a psychiatric institution. They sit there and stare through you, a painful reminder that no matter how you may decorate the bars elsewhere, a prison is still prison.

The 757 zoos world-wide, attracting their 350 million visitors, are proof that animals in captivity are popular. Safari parks, game reserves, aquariums, all are increasing in popularity. The growing trend towards pretty exhibits that put the animals into a natural context has been taken as evidence that people are becoming more concerned about the plight of zoo animals. Equally, that same trend can be seen as evidence that people are showing their customary aptitude for self-deception. We like to see animals and get close to them, but we don't like to be too aware of the ways we prevent them getting away. Inside the 757 zoos, attracting the 350 million visitors each year, are 162,874 mammals, 256,413 birds, and uncountable other animals. What possible justification is there for captivity on that scale?

## Chapter Two

# THE NEW MENAGERIES

**E**xtinction is a fact of life. More than 99 per cent of all species that have ever lived are alive no longer. Those that exist at present will not last forever. As it has done since the beginning of life on earth some 4000 million years ago, natural selection will remove some species and replace them with others.

Just how frequently species go extinct is all but impossible to gauge. In the great disasters, the mass extinctions that grab people's attention, species vanish quickly and in vast numbers. The most famous of these, the death of the dinosaurs, 65 million years ago at the end of the Cretaceous era, was accompanied by the death of many other plants and animals, most notably almost all the plankton that form the basis of life in the oceans. About a quarter of all the animal families vanished completely. Even that great extinction, however, pales into insignificance beside the event palaeontologists call the Permian extinction. About 225 million years ago, at the end of the Permian period, fully half the families of marine creatures died out. Trilobites, ancient corals, ammonites and many other organisms familiar only through their fossilised remains vanished in the blink of a geological eye. Argument rages over what caused the mass extinctions. Some say that the dinosaurs, and the other species whose extinction marked the end of the Cretaceous period, were toppled by the after-effects of a massive meteor that ploughed into the earth. Some say the Permian extinction was caused by all the continents coalescing into a massive super-landmass, thereby considerably reducing the shoreline available for marine creatures to occupy; competition did the rest. Fascinating though these discussions are, for our purposes all that matters is the realisation that species go extinct, either dramatically as in the mass extinctions, or more prosaically in the usual run of things.

It is going on right now. According to Dr Norman Myers, the noted conservationist, 'it is not unreasonable to suppose that we are losing at least one species per day.' And it is getting faster. 'By the end of the 1980s, we could be losing one species per hour.' The result of this accelerating extinction is that by the year 2000 around a million species will have vanished from the face of the earth. Something in excess of a million and a half species have been identified and recognised by science; biologists estimate that there are between five and ten million more as yet unknown. So by the year 2000 we may have lost as many as 20 per cent of the species now alive on earth.

This is extinction on a grand scale, a scale to compare with the Permian and Cretaceous extinctions. But it differs from those in one important way; they were caused by changes in the inanimate environment, while the current extinction is caused by a living species, ourselves. And we have the singular ability not only to be aware of what we are doing, but also to stop doing it. This is not the place for a polemic on humanity's greed and shortsightedness. The rate of extinction is important because it offers zoos their justification. Zoos can save species from extinction. They are stationary arks.

Conservation is now the order of the day. Zoo directors everywhere say that their aim is to conserve species, to halt the decline in wildlife, perhaps even to reverse it and restock the wild with captive-bred animals. That takes money. George Rabb, director of Chicago's Brookfield Zoo, and Bill Conway, director of the New York Zoological Society, estimate that it costs $1600 to feed a single Siberian tiger for a year. That amounts to $1.2 million for the 750 Siberian tigers in captivity in zoos around the world. $1.2 million a year, just for food. Add in maintenance, vet bills and all the rest and the cost rises to $2,432,000 per year, so that by the year 2000 we will have spent something like $50 million on keeping Siberian tigers alive in captivity. Tigers, being carnivores, are expensive to feed, but care costs money too. Okapi work out at about half the cost of tigers, but gorillas, which need more veterinary care, are about $7500 a year each, two and a half times the cost of a tiger. Zoos are expensive.

Many people are willing to give money to support wildlife conservation, but most of those donations go to the organisations that campaign for wildlife in the wild, and not much of it finds it way to zoos. (It is little enough anyway; about £5 million a year for all the conservation bodies in Britain, a sum described by one noted conservationist as 'pathetic'.) People will pay to visit zoos, but they want more for their money than simply the warm glow that accompanies the doing of a good deed. Indeed, very often those who describe themselves as conservationists find zoos anathema, while those who visit zoos have anything but conservation on their mind. So while the modern zoo director may see his job as conservation, he has to get people streaming through his turnstiles, handing over an entrance fee that will support the zoo and its lofty aims. To do that, he needs to provide the zoo-going public with entertainment.

When I was young I used to visit London Zoo quite regularly. One of the best parts of the visit was the chimpanzees' tea party. We would make for the little grandstand by the clock tower early enough to get good seats and wait for the fun to begin. The chimps would come out with their keepers and the ensuing scenes can best be described as lightly controlled pandemonium. Looking back now it is possible to uncover all sorts of motives that made us stare: chimps are so like us, and yet so unlike, that they are a grotesque parody of people. The tea party accentuates the gulf between us and makes it even more enthralling. By putting chimps into a human environment and laughing at their abysmal performance we see how superior we humans are. For the children, wish-fulfilment is perhaps an important factor. Many of them would dearly love to tip jellies over their friends, but they do not. Instead, they watch the chimps do it.

Chimps' tea parties were quite acceptable, and very popular, back in 1966, when *Blue Peter* presenter Valerie Singleton joined in the fun

The children I take to the zoo today do not have the chance to see such a spectacle because in 1972 the zoo stopped the chimps' tea party. There were all kinds of good reasons behind the decision. To perform as they did the chimps had to be removed from their group and raised with human keepers. But when they become adolescent, between six and eight years old, chimps, like human adolescents, can be boisterous and unruly, and so they have to give up the tea party and be returned to the group. There they have problems fitting in because they are so thoroughly humanised that they do not do so easily, and the females, when they breed, neglect their babies. For all these reasons, the zoo decided to abandon the tea party, but with mixed feelings. The great British public enjoyed watching them and the chimps enjoyed performing, but it was felt to be more important to use the chimps as a successful natural breeding group than as entertainment. The drying up of supplies of young wild-caught chimps no doubt influenced the decision.

The change in policy came about through changes in the zoo's thinking. Breeding and conservation were deemed more important than entertainment, and there was a growing feeling that this sort of entertainment in particular was demeaning for the animals performing and for people watching alike. No matter that, with a slightly different emphasis, the tea party could have been used to demonstrate how very clever and adaptable chimpanzees are, able to perform remarkably well in circumstances utterly alien to them. People, for all their cleverness, are very bad at aping chimps, and would probably starve if they had to rely on getting food by 'fishing' for termites, for example. The tea party went, and with it a good reason to visit the zoo and a source of entertainment for the chimps themselves.

The good zoo director serves two masters; he wants the best for the animals in his care and he needs to attract the public to pay for that. This raises a very real dilemma. What is good for the animals – large enclosures, secluded areas, privacy – may not be good for the public. And what is good for the public – cafeterias and toilets, entertainment, easy viewing – may not be good for the animals. The chimps' tea party is odd because public and performers both enjoy it, but in the long term it fosters the wrong ideas in the public and makes social life and breeding difficult for the performers. The zoo director has to get people in to finance the efforts at captive breeding and conservation, but many of those people will not understand the necessity and are hardly likely to pay for it directly. The needs of the people and the needs of the animals are therefore often in conflict.

It was a hot August day, and I had spent the best part of the morning wandering around London Zoo. The place was full, and busy, and I was hardly aware of some of the despair that has surrounded the zoo of late. I had been to the little gift shop and bought some of the less nasty souvenirs there and I had seen all the animals I wanted to on this side of the canal that divides the zoo in two. What I needed was a rest, something to eat and a chance to revive myself, so I headed past the gibbons for the cafeteria. Once there, I instantly regretted my decision. The place was full of people and a long queue snaked back from the counter. The tables were littered with the debris left by previous customers; cigarettes stubbed out in the remains of an oleaginous egg, half-drunk cups of milky coffee puckering under the greenish fluorescent tubes. The bright orange decor, rather than cheering, seemed to highlight the sordid aspects of the place, like a depressive wearing a grin. The queue shuffled slowly forward and rather than focus on how appalling it all is I lost myself to a daydream.

In my mind's eye I was back in the Clore pavilion, with its small mammals above and its moonlight world below. In particular, I was in front of the little marmosets, entranced by their jerky robotic motion and strange wizened faces. Like demented hairy old men they chased one another around and about through the branches. A little door in the cage opened, and in came a dish of food. There was a delicious fruit salad, lovingly prepared by the keepers. Fresh sliced bananas, oranges, the best grapes carefully split in half, chunks of apple, some celery, nuts and raisins, and mixed in with all the goodies were vitamin supplements. How delicious it looked, and not surprisingly the wizened old men fell on it with obvious delight.

'Yes love?' asked the pale acned girl serving time behind the counter, bringing me back to reality. I looked around, and instead of the appetising fruit salad enjoyed by the marmosets there were plates of soggy fried fish, grey burgers, sodden rolls. O to be a marmoset!

Charles Clore, who paid for the pavilion that bears his name, knew a thing or two about people's needs and how to satisfy them; his commercial empire included Selfridges, the hugely successful department store. If another donation like Clore's were to become available, what would the zoo do with it? Would it, for example, renovate the bird-of-prey cages, which certainly need it? Or would the money be used to create some decent facilities for people? An eponymous restaurant, hamburger stand or toilet might not suit the needs of a benefactor's ego, but it would make the zoo a better place to visit, and if that brought in more people the improvement of the animal facilities would be put on a much more secure foundation.

Fish and chips secured and paid for, I made my way through the mess and went into another reverie. This time it was not the marmosets I dreamed of, but Sea World in San Diego. The drive out along Sea World Boulevard ends in huge car parks, where the attendants advised me to write down the number of my patch as it is all too easy to forget. On the way in I collected a map of the park which included a handy timetable of all the shows, and the first thing I did was to book a tour with one of the Sea Maids. Portable loudspeaker in hand, she shepherded a gaggle of visitors around, giving us a glimpse behind the scenes and relaying information that presumably was once of interest to her. After the tour she helped us to plan our day so as to see all the shows we wanted to, for shows are what Sea World is all about. The killer whales do their stuff six times a day in high season. The dolphins, the seals, the sharks, even walruses, perform for the public's benefit. Around almost every corner was a souvenir stand, filled with high-quality goods to remind us of our visit. And around every other corner it seemed there was food for the customers, ranging from simple hamburger stands to slightly more elaborate Mexican fast-food joints. The Hawaiian Village restaurant, looking out over Mission Bay and at the end of the chairlift, is a very fancy restaurant indeed, one that attracts customers who have not even been to Sea World. Sea World makes a profit; London Zoo does not. End of reverie.

What brings people to Sea World is not the restaurants nor the car parks. It is the animal shows; the other things just make it easier. And, of all the shows, it is the killer whale show that the visitors come for. So although most of the other animals, certainly the marine mammals, have to earn their keep as well, I will focus on Shamu and the other killer whales. Show business, cleverly deployed, makes the Shamu show one of the most exciting animal presentations I have ever seen, and it is an excitement that is hard to convey on paper. The best I can do, perhaps, is to describe something that amazed me when I first saw it, and continues to puzzle me.

Shamu performs in a largish pool before a high bank of seats. All the seats have a good view, but those closest to the stage have one overwhelming draw-back, a disadvantage that the staff point out repeatedly before the show begins. When the whales jump, they splash. And when the whales splash, the first six rows get very wet. Sea World could abandon those first six rows, and ensure that nobody gets wet. The public could avoid those rows after hearing the warnings. But Sea World puts those seats there and the people use them, so when the whale leaps, the people get soaked. They scream, they moan about their cameras, but they do not move out of the splash zone.

That tells you something about the attraction of the killer whales, but nothing can prepare you for the sheer excitement of seeing three killer whales, a total mass of about 12 tonnes, clear the water completely. It is an awesome sight. The other tricks the whales perform are impressive too: leaping through the water with a trainer clutching a hoop around the whale's snout; corkscrewing gently along the surface so that the trainer, standing upright on the whale, has to walk around, lumberjack style; cradling a recumbent swimmer between its fins; and perhaps most impressive, coming up to give a small child the experience of a lifetime, a fishy kiss on the cheek. It is little wonder that the Shamu shows are the draw that they undeniably are.

So what is the difference between Sea World's Shamu show and an old-fashioned chimps' tea party? All the world, the people at Sea World will tell you. In the bad old days the animals appeared in contrived skits, like *Shamu Goes to College* or *A Shamu Bicentennial*. Watery tea parties by the sound of it. All that has changed and the new show, *Shamu – Take a Bow*, is said to be 'an educational tribute to the whale and its capabilities'. The killer whales are not performing tricks far removed from their natural behaviour, they are simply having a good time with the trainers and entertaining the crowds almost by accident. 'Not only is the show more dignified, but the audiences seem to enjoy it more,' says Mike Yeakle, manager of animal behaviour at Sea World San Diego. It is a big claim, but one that is supported by the behaviour of whales and trainers between shows. They rest, it is true, but there is an obvious and genuine bond between them, and the whales do seem to play for the fun of it. No two shows are the same either, because if a 1800-kilogram whale doesn't want to play ball there is absolutely nothing a person can do to force it to. So the trainers, who also do the presentation, have to be flexible, recognising the moods and willingness of the stars and capitalising on whatever the whales are prepared to do.

Then there is the question of information. The chimpanzees' tea party tells you nothing about tea parties and less about chimps. Sea World would claim that their show tells you lots about killer whales, and the trainers do impart a modicum of information, though at the time most people are more interested in what the whale is doing than in anything the trainers may be telling them. But sitting back and concentrating on listening to the commentary, I noticed that, despite the showmanship of the presentation and music and the rapid-fire dialogue between the trainers, the information they impart is pretty sparse:

'Of all of the mysteries of the sea, none is greater than the mystery of the animal who reigns supreme.'

'He is a giant.'

'His ability to swim and to hunt equals perfection.'

'Even so, he is not confined to the water alone.'

'He is full of mysteries, and wonder.'

'He is a killer whale.'

At which point the stirring martial music reaches a sort of climax and Shamu appears leaping clear of the water, soaking the front rows to the accompaniment of a couple of thousand indrawn breaths that almost drown the music.

'He is . . .'

'Shamu.'

And the applause is rapturous. But now, as Shamu swims valiantly round, here comes the education.

'We know he's a killer whale.'

'And we call him Shamu.'

'But what do we really understand?'

'Some people say that killer whales are driven by an insatiable appetite.'

'Some people say that killer whales are more intelligent than man.'

'Some people say that killer whales attack for the mere pleasure.'

'We can begin with the things we know for sure.'

'Shamu's weight.'

'Eighteen hundred kilograms, 4000 pounds.'

'His length.'

'Forty-two decimetres, 14 feet.'

'Top swimming speed.'

'Twenty-eight knots, 30 miles per hour.'

'But what is his true potential?'

'We may never really understand, but we can experience all of his strength and agility.'

'Combined with an intelligence.'

'And in it there is beauty, like the finest gymnast or ballet dancer.'

'And there is spectacle. Focus your attention on the centre of the pool.'

'In one fleeting moment – diving, leaping, spinning.'

'Natural grace, beauty, power.'

'Put this all together and it's truly phenomenal.'

'Phew, yeah.'

Then the show begins in earnest. Any more information would probably be superfluous, but even so we are told a little about how people train killer whales.

'How do we create a performance like this? Well, we don't, Shamu does.'

'That's right, and it's different every time too. And boy if it looks like a lot of fun, that's because it is.'

'And what about our relationship?'

'Well, whales aren't people, and sometimes we have to remind ourselves of this, but through our recognition of their true magnificence we can in a very special way become close friends.'

'The ideals of friendship and Shamu seem to go hand in hand, and over the years we've made a lot of friends together, some who live in the water and some who don't. Right now we'd like you to meet some of those who do. With them they've given us a chance to live a dream, a chance to swim with and to play with and to ride . . . the dolphins.'

On with the show. Later on Shamu does his most celebrated trick, making a new human friend, and his introduction to a little girl or boy is always a touching moment. Educational too, in the widest sense.

So Sea World's claim that *Shamu – Take a Bow* teaches something is at least partly true. If they choose not to mention that there is no Shamu – whichever whale appears first in any given show at each of the three Sea Worlds gets the star billing – who can blame them? Nor do they mention that killer whales have never bred in captivity, that they live in a large social group that wanders

Siberian tigers in their element at Minnesota

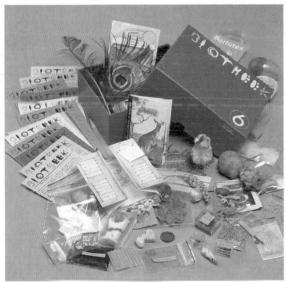

Of course zoos care about the food they give their animals. London Zoo's silvery marmoset (*left*) has his meals lovingly prepared each day, but the public cafeteria is not very pleasant. People must be catered for, sometimes taking precedence over the animals. Emmen Zoo (*above*) leads the way in entertaining education. A child gazes at part of the museum display on reproduction, having been prepared for it by a richly packed box of goodies, supplied beforehand to school parties. The anomalous bird stands in the entrance to the museum and is designed to show how evolution might have proceeded. The label tells you that it is impossible, and that it lays its eggs on All Fools' Day, but many people unfortunately take the bird seriously.

thousands of square kilometres of open ocean. Despite these misgivings, it seems probable that people come away from Sea World with a slightly better understanding of life in the oceans. More to the point, performances like the Shamu show bring the people to Sea World in the first place.

Killer whale, the biggest attraction wherever they are presented

Sea World exists to make money. Although they contribute to education and conservation you can be sure that if they started to lose money their parent company, publishing conglomerate Harcourt Brace Jovanovich, would ditch them quickly enough. If it makes money for Sea World, it is good, and if some of that money does help conservation, so much the better. But the important thing is Sea World's profitability (which is high).

London Zoo, by contrast, is a charity dedicated to advancing zoological knowledge. It therefore faces an enormous problem if it does anything at all to raise money. In 1931 its charitable status was challenged, not for the first nor the last time, over the issue of animal rides. There were those who felt that charging children for a ride on a donkey or camel broke the zoo's charter; perhaps, strictly speaking, it does, but wiser counsel fortunately prevailed. The advantages of being a charity are few. London Zoo gets a 50 per cent reduction on its rates, which probably amounts to some £50,000 a year, but it still has to pay a 15 per cent Value Added Tax on all goods sold in the zoo. No other country in the European Economic Community requires charities to pay VAT. To get around the strictures of charitable status London Zoo, like so many other charities in the UK, has associated companies, Zoo Restaurants Ltd and Zoo Enterprises Ltd, that divert all their profits to the zoo. Alas, in 1982 these companies lost £93,293. (Figures for 1983 show some improvement.)

Times are hard for zoos. If they would dedicate themselves wholeheartedly to entertaining the public, life might be easier, at least financially, but almost all say they exist for purposes of conservation. Dissenters are refreshing for their honesty. Carl Hagenbeck, great-grandson of the original Hagenbeck, admits that his zoo is 'an area of recreation and entertainment. The zoo of the future,' he adds, 'will be a simple entertainment with no endangered species.' But Hagenbeck, like his forebear, is exceptional. Unfortunately for zoo directors, most people do not find conservation sufficient enticement to persuade them to go to the zoo. Entertainment is essential, and so zoo directors provide it and resolve the conflict between two opposing aims by presenting the entertainment against an educational backdrop.

Education comes in a number of guises. There are the formal instructional possibilities inherent in any collection. A zoo, with its strange and fascinating animals, makes a fine excursion for schoolchildren. Another aspect of formal education is the information provided alongside the exhibits. Even the name of an animal may instruct many visitors to an urban zoo. Informally, the zoo harbours a wealth of information that visitors clamour for; any keeper who gets drawn into a conversation with visitors will find they are a very appreciative audience, so appreciative that the keeper's main task of looking after the animals can easily be neglected while he looks after the visitors. This thirst for intimate knowledge, provided by living people rather than labels, is one that a few good

Labels are an important educational tool for zoos, but will be ignored if they are not also entertaining

zoos are exploiting, as we shall see. But even the way an animal is presented is a part of the education on offer.

In Chapter One I pointed out how the housing a zoo provides for an animal affects the way that people think about it. Even if they know nothing about the animal, they quickly absorb a message from the surroundings the zoo puts it in. In the early days of zoos and menageries simply to see the animals was an education in itself, and the cages were designed to give an unobstructed view of the animals within. Zoos vied with one another for the most comprehensive collection and the postage stamp zoo, with one or two of as many species as possible, came into being. People were drawn by the unknown made available. Then along came Hagenbeck, and the presentation of animals in captivity was transformed. Bare cages were no longer enough, and slowly zoos were persuaded to landscape their enclosures to make a more fitting setting for the animals, a technology that will be examined in detail in Chapter Five. All this provided entertainment for the public; having become used to seeing tigers in bare cages, the sight of pretty enclosures, and in them animals free to do more than pace back and forth, was obviously attractive.

At Apple Valley Zoo outside Minneapolis in Minnesota such beautifully landscaped enclosures are immediately appealing. You have to work to see the animals, but when you do catch a glimpse of, for example, the bobcat stalking through its man-made canyon, it is very rewarding. The beaver pond, with a view inside the lodge and beavers at work chopping trees, repairing the dam, swimming about, is charming. But what seemed the strongest draw of all, when I was there, was a very small tank, no more than 1 metre square but perhaps 20 centimetres deep. The back wall resembled an earthen bank, complete with tree roots and tunnel mouths, and on the floor were autumn leaves. Frolicking among them, to the obvious delight of an appreciative crowd pushing in on the exhibit, was a weasel. Now I have seen weasels before in zoos, and they are generally doing one of two things. Either they are asleep, or they are pacing morosely back and forth. This one was having a marvellous time, rushing about the exhibit, sniffing here, jumping there, rolling about in the leaves all over. It was a very entertaining spectacle, and we were having a marvellous time watching it. Then the little animal slipped into one of the black tunnel holes, and the case became still. The crowd began to drift away, but within a couple of seconds the weasel had reappeared and started to frolic again. If anything he had even more energy than before, and a crowd gathered again.

What is the secret of Minnesota's fun-loving weasel? Is it some sort of hyper-active mutant who never tires? No. In fact, it isn't even *one* weasel. There are several of them and, like Shamu the killer whale, each one is *the* weasel while he is on display. Apple Valley runs a shift system. When the weasel popped into the tunnel he was returning to his backstage quarters, opened to him at the end of his shift. And when he reappeared he was a fresh animal, eager to explore these interesting surroundings while he has the opportunity. Every hour throughout the day the weasel display has a changing of the guard, and the visitors are barely aware of it. All they know is that here is a pretty exhibit that contains a lively animal. In a word, entertainment.

It isn't just the weasels either. Many of the animals at Minnesota Zoo are on a shift system, though none has as short a shift as the weasels. The black panthers have two shifts in a day – one lot is on display in the morning, the other in the afternoon. The bobcats, too, are on a similar routine. The idea, simple yet revolutionary like Hagenbeck's, is catching on elsewhere. At Chicago's Brookfield Zoo the same system is used with the cats. Most of the time they are invisible to the visitors, free to enjoy what they like to do and what people hate to see – sleep. But for four hours a day they are on display, and during that time they *have* to display themselves. Judiciously placed blasts of cold air ensure that they don't lurk out of sight in dark corners, and the public is treated to animals behaving in an entertaining way.

The irony is that most visitors would regard the animal's conditions of work as far preferable to its home life. Those weasels that spend an hour a day entertaining the crowd with their high spirits are confined the remaining twenty-three hours in a small cage like the ones used to house laboratory rats. And the cats, when not on duty, live in empty, tiled and barred cages. Education is a fine thing. The public enjoys watching animals behaving naturally in sculptured surroundings, and does not enjoy observing them at rest in barren cages. With

Minnesota's shift system, the public can see what it has come to like and need not see what it dislikes, and what the eye does not see the heart does not grieve over. To the animals, it seems to make little difference; the shift workers are fit and healthy despite their domestic conditions.

Another prominent feature at Minnesota is the Asian house, an example of a new way of arranging the animals in a zoo. A collection is of very little value unless it is arranged according to some informative scheme, a fact as true of animal collections as of stamps. One could, as with stamps, arrange animals alphabetically, the aardvark with the aoudad, eagle with eland, zebra with zorilla, but this would not tell you very much about the animal kingdom. The alternative, one adopted by almost all zoos, is the taxonomic arrangement. All those animals classified as cats, members of the biological family *Felidae*, live together in one location, separated from the members of the horse family, the *Equidae*. This type of arrangement is very good for showing how biological classification works and how related animals are like one another. But there is another way, one that puts the cheetah with the zebra and the mountain lion with the mustang, and this is the method exemplified by Minnesota's Asian house.

In a building that covers half a hectare, and that costs $1 million a year to heat, the animals of South-East Asia are on display. There are gibbons, and pythons, and sloth bears. There are small-clawed otters and clouded leopards, goats and little deer, all displayed in beautifully landscaped cages that line a winding trail. The path curves around and meanders up and down so that you get the feeling of having moved through an enormous exhibit when in fact the Asian house is quite compact. And the animals in it are there solely because they originally hail from one part of the globe.

It is an idea called zoogeographic arrangement – that is, organising the collection on the basis of where animals live. The main benefit is that the zoo can give visitors an idea of how the various animals of an area relate to one another; how the ecosystem works. They can see the animals at the bottom of the food chain, cropping the plants that harness the sun's energy. Then, without having to move too far, they can see the predators that those herbivores sustain. It is a good way for getting the feel of a region. At Metropolitan Toronto Zoo, which was the first collection to be arranged zoogeographically and on which Minnesota was modelled, they have had more time and more money at their disposal, and not surprisingly they go even further than Apple Valley.

Metro Toronto's zoo covers 285 hectares in the north of the city. There are four pavilions and a plethora of paths meandering between large paddocks housing all the usual animals, but it is the arrangement of animals that is most important. Each pavilion was intended to cover one of the world's ecological regions, but financial strictures have meant that the original grand concept has had to be somewhat modified. North America had to be broadened to take in

South America and Eurasia became Australasia; but the original idea remains. The African pavilion, for example, is constructed in two lobes. One represents a dense jungle and the other, laced with lots of small ponds, is a wooded swamp. There, among the traveller's and triangular palms, the screw pines, the figs, bananas and papyrus plants, are the African animals. There is Toronto's famous family of lowland gorillas, the mandrills of the forests, dwarf crocodiles from West Africa, frogs, fishes and bees. In the pool with the pygmy hippos are tilapia, fish growing fat on the hippos' leavings. Elephants, buffalo, monkeys, penguins, pythons, all live in one pavilion by virtue of the fact that they all live in one geographical region. In the half-light is a family of fennec foxes, their enormous ears and deep liquid eyes on the alert for crickets to eat, and next door to the foxes a huge colony of spiny mice scurry about their enclosure.

It is the same in the Indo-Malayan pavilion – this feeling of almost continual surprise as you come across animals of very different biological provenance at every different height. One minute you are looking down at a pied pigeon in the branches below you, the next your attention is drawn up to a mangrove snake in the branches above. White-handed gibbons share an exhibit with Malayan tapirs, slow loris with Indian fruit bats. It is a very exciting place to be.

The American and Australasian pavilions are different in concept, not least because the large animals on display are able to withstand a Toronto winter and so can spend most of their time outdoors. In the pavilions, which blend superbly into the surroundings, are special small exhibits and educational displays. The big animals are outside, best seen from the silent, electrically powered train that runs through the Canadian Animal Domain.

An ostrich, acclimatised to the winter snow in Toronto

58

Judging by attendance, and by the comments of people visiting the zoo, Toronto's approach is proving very popular. And it is being copied, with many zoos around the world actively redesigning their old menagerie-style exhibits, based on taxonomy, to incorporate zoogeographic principles. But it isn't all benefits; it almost always makes life more difficult for a zoo to arrange its animals geographically. It is, says Toronto's head of keepers Lawrence Cahill, 'full of disadvantages'. For one thing, staff tend to specialise on biological families, not regions. So the expert cat keeper has to traipse across from the jaguars in South America to the cheetahs in Africa and the mountain lions of North America. The zoo may have space in one region and overcrowding in another, but is unable to do anything about it without violating the zoo-geographic arrangement.

There are difficulties with the predators and prey in the African savannah; the enclosures are constructed so that the lions can crouch and stalk the spring-bok, sable antelope and gemsbok, although, as in Hagenbeck's zoo, hunter and hunted cannot get together. But while the lions continue to do their stuff, the antelope have long since stopped responding, and quite rightly so as there isn't actually any threat. The public though, says Cahill, doesn't notice that there is no reaction from the prey. Some of the problems are peculiar to Toronto because of its own topography. In the savannah, again, the ground is dominated by little hillocks; the animals, not surprisingly, preferred to avoid the public's gaze by moving round to the far side of the hills. The zoo, also not surprisingly, has responded by making it impossible for them to do so. The result, unfor-tunately, is that large chunks of the enclosure might as well not be there for all the good they do the inmates. But despite the problems, Cahill is all in favour of zoogeographic arrangements. 'For the public,' he told me, 'it's nice for them to look at animals in this way.'

And it is, although in some respects it is possible to go slightly overboard in pursuit of biological verisimilitude. In Minnesota Zoo, the plants in the Tropics house are the usual sort of jungly creepers and suchlike, but they do not all come originally from South-East Asia. At Toronto, even the plants are authentic. Admittedly there are rubber plants in the Indo-Malayan house, because al-though the rubber tree *Hevea brasiliensis* is native to South America it was brought back to Kew Gardens and thence to Malaysia in 1876, and that is good enough. You will also find limes, bananas, figs, and Chinese loquats in the Australasian pavilion, and the coffee bushes in the African have even borne fruit.

Minnesota takes as much care over the plants, but is less bent on accuracy. They say it isn't that important; people are there to see the animals, and in any case plants have been widely distributed by man so it doesn't matter if they don't strictly adhere to the regional concept. At Toronto, where they are sticklers for accuracy, even with the best will in the world you cannot grow acacia trees where the winters are long and hard – the acacia trees by the savannah are apple trees, cunningly pruned to look like the real thing. Both zoos, however, by following a geographical arrangement, offer their visitors extra entertainment and education.

Whatever method you choose to arrange your animals – geographically to emphasise ecology and habitat, or taxonomically to emphasise evolutionary relationships – education is an important aspect of running a zoo. Its collection can be used for more formal educational purposes, too. Almost every important zoo offers children the chance of making a school visit. For some, this means no more than offering a group discount on the admission fee. Others, as we shall see, go out of their way to prepare children and make the visit valuable.

Emmen is a small town in the north of Holland. Its zoo, Noorder Dierenpark, is very modern, right in the city centre, and it is gaining a reputation as one of the most progressive zoos in the world. It wasn't always this way though. In 1972, when she inherited the zoo from an uncle whose more or less private collection it had been, Mrs Rensen-Osting found it 'in an extremely dilapidated condition'. She resented being burdened with the zoo, but nevertheless she set about changing it. 'If we must have zoos,' she says, 'then at least we should do the best we can with them.' Perhaps the best symbol of Emmen's success is the playground just inside the main gate, where children can let off steam and at the same time learn how it might be to move like a mouse or a mountain goat, for this is a zoo dedicated to children and to providing entertaining education.

Modernisation started in 1974, and out went the polar bears and lions and chimpanzees, all of which had been kept in miserable enclosures. In came a huge new African savannah enclosure, in which rhino, giraffe, gnu, zebra, springbok, ostrich and waterbuck graze contentedly. A huge walk-through aviary enables hundreds of birds to wheel freely overhead, and a beautiful aviary at the side holds waders; to provide some spectacle the tide ebbs and flows every fifteen minutes, giving the birds something to do and the people something to watch. There is a small but astonishingly effective display of ordinary brown rats in their normal environment, a lovingly recreated sewer, complete with rusty jerry cans and old boots, but no sewage. As a result of this overhaul, attendance has climbed steadily from less than 200,000 to almost a million, and while all the new exhibits are good, what makes Emmen such a hopeful zoo is its educational programme.

Part of the zoo is a building, the Biochron, dedicated to exploring the complexity of life and its evolution. So-called living fossils, animals that have hardly changed since they evolved, are displayed alongside their petrified relations – living *Lingula* next to practically identical petrified brachiopods almost 570 million years old, horseshoe crabs beside their fossil relatives. There are gemstones, too, and dioramas that depict life at various evolutionary stages. What

Unusual animals on exhibit, sewer rats in an artificial sewer at Emmen

exists is impressive enough, but it is not yet complete. Work continues on a mirrored hall that at the moment is littered with stuffed animals and props and mountains of polystyrene blocks ready to be carved into a landscape, but when it is finished it will greet visitors with a representation of the ecological inter-weaving of different species. And when that is done work will start on an exhibit of man, his evolution and history. The hope is that this will eventually end up in an exhibit of great apes, but until the display can be realised to the same standard as the rest of the animal exhibits no one at Emmen is sorry that they got rid of the chimpanzees.

Good as the exhibits and the Biochron are, Emmen's real pride is its museum and the educational programme that prepares visitors for it. The museum is linked to the Africa house and contains an integrated exhibition of some aspect of natural history, the theme changing every year. When I visited it, the subject was 'The Senses', and a series of cunningly contrived exhibits was designed to show the importance of sight, smell and so on in animal life. The year before it had been 'Camouflage', and next year it will be 'Reproduction', but the museum exhibition itself is only the part of it. Schools can buy in advance a special box of items with which to explore some of the ideas before they meet them in the museum. The kit for 'The Senses' cost 25 guilders (about £6) – 15 guilders of which are refunded on visiting the zoo – and included flower seeds, tasting samples, naval signal flags, a morse code flasher, paints, vegetable dyes, artificial scents, fishing lures – a real Aladdin's cave of stimulating bits and pieces crammed into a brightly striped yellow and black box. The zoo sends out about a thousand of these boxes each year, and well over half of the purchasers turn up, usually at the head of a party of schoolchildren. Holland is small, admittedly, but still Emmen manages to pull them in from all over the country.

Other zoos are looking closely at Emmen to see if its ideas are appropriate for them, and many are paying increased attention to the possibilities for formal education. At the Denmark Aquarium in Copenhagen, school parties get detailed activity sheets, a method of involving children in more than merely gawping. The Aquarium's programme concentrates on getting children to see the animals as adapted products of their environments. The arrow fish looks ugly, with its bulging eyes and huge, scowling, downturned mouth, but that is just a human perspective. In reality those eyes and that mouth enable it to exploit a food supply open to few fish, animals perched on vegetation above the water. Other zoos use similar sheets to foster in children a thirst for knowledge. Roger Wheatear, director of the Royal Zoological Society of Scotland's zoo in Edinburgh, which has long been at the forefront of zoo education in Britain, has a novel way of assessing their value. 'We rarely see any of these . . . sheets littering the park,' he told a meeting of the International Union of Directors of Zoological Gardens. 'This may be a rough way of gauging success,' he continued, 'but I think it is significant.'

As well as providing educational material, some zoos offer classrooms too, where teachers can either supervise their own pupils, or the zoo's own employees, animal and human, are on hand. When I visited Copenhagen Zoo a class was learning all about aggression and dominance in house mice. A short lecture introduced them to the subject and showed them what sorts of behaviour to look for. Then with a ready supply of mice – black, white and brown – they were off, matching the mice in pairs and seeing who dominated whom. This is just one of the classes the zoo offers, each tailored to children of different ages and designed to illuminate different aspects of biology. They could be held in schools, but having them in the zoo is more cost effective and educationally beneficial. As with activity sheets, more zoos are seriously using their facilities to offer classroom teaching. Few, however, go as far as Cincinnati, which has an entire school within the zoo.

Barry Wakeman, director of education at Cincinnati Zoo, is effectively headmaster of one of Cincinnati's high schools. It is equal to all the other city schools, but offers special attractions for children who have a particular interest in animal care and husbandry, and pupils from all over the city can come there. As well as all the normal subjects – mathematics, English, history, geography and so on – they get a thorough grounding in the theory and practice of zoo-keeping, and most of the pupils go on to be keepers, here and at other zoos, or veterinary assistants, or into other jobs connected with animals. The resources of the zoo are put at their disposal, and having a school within the zoo makes a lot of sense.

Cincinnati's director, Ed Maruska, is outspoken on the subject. Despite Cincinnati's contributions – good and bad – to conservation, he sets great store by education. 'I think it's far more important than conservation, even with our breeding record,' he told me, and his policy pays off. In 1981 Cincinnati Zoo snapped up both of the American Association of Zoological Parks and Aquariums' two awards for education.

Formal education certainly has its place in zoos, and school parties form an important group of visitors, particularly as attitudes are much more easily manipulated in the young. But the more casual family visitor is not neglected either. Many zoo directors feel that here the education has to be provided without making it obvious what is going on. For some, signs and labels are likely to be the only way they will absorb information, and even such simple means may not always be effective.

Looking around the wonderful old Reptile House at New York Zoo's establishment in the Bronx I commented on the clear but simple labels. My guide, David Mleczko, laughed. 'Yeah, but people don't believe 'em.' He explained that as he walks through the Reptile House, which is the zoo's most popular exhibit, he often stops to eavesdrop on the conversations. And more often than not, especially at weekends, the following scene may be played out. In front of a cage of menacing, but quite harmless, green iguanas, a young man, out for the day with his girlfriend, explains that these are gila monsters: 'the most poisonous animal in the world.'

'But hon,' she replies, 'it says here they're iguanas from Costa Rica.'

'Yeah, well, they got it wrong. These are gila monsters. I seen 'em in Mexico.'

People, unlike labels, don't lie, and more and more zoos are finding that one way to combat the public's lack of information is to encourage the keepers to talk to the public about the animals they care for. Toronto has regular Meet the Keeper sessions, in which visitors can chat informally with keepers. This policy, though, will lead to an increased wage bill, since more keepers are needed to look after the animals, and other zoos make use of trained volunteers from the local community who are put out into the grounds as so-called docents.

A good docent programme is one of the finest assets a zoo can have. The only requirements are to organise and train the docents themselves, which takes some time and effort, and then to get visitors to talk to them, which doesn't. At Cincinnati a docent stands quietly by the gorilla cage wearing a very odd uniform shirt. Complete with badges and insignia, it is all the same oddly proportioned. The neck opening is huge, and although the sleeves dangle way beyond his hands, the tail of the shirt floats above his own belt. Before long someone is bound to ask what on earth is going on, and that is the cue for the docent to explain that the shirt has been tailored for the big male silverback. He can then tell people about the gorillas, and answer the flood of questions that inevitably follows. In so doing he can help to correct all the usual misconceptions about gorillas, but in an entertaining and amusing way, to people who stay and listen because what they are hearing is fascinating.

Docents will encourage the public to hold and handle the animals, and they are able to devote their attention to small groups of people. They are thus a very powerful tool, and no zoo makes better use of them than the Arizona-Sonora Desert Museum outside Tucson. The training programme is intensive, lasting from after Labor Day in September until Christmas, but is nevertheless oversubscribed. Lily Moore, who organises the docents, explains that Tucson is very community-minded, and that 'the Museum is *the* place to be, *the* place to volunteer'. Tucson is also home to a large number of retired people, attracted there by the sunshine and climate, who have a lot of time to give. Consequently, of the 150 or so docents, something like 70 per cent are retired. The Desert Museum will train and equip volunteers, but requires a commitment in return. 'The younger ones don't stick with it,' Lily says.

The Desert Museum specialises in the indigenous animals of the area, most of which, unfortunately, fall into the class of creepy-crawlies. The docents are most valuable in showing people that by and large these animals are not merely harmless, but positively beneficial. The sight of a little old lady unconcernedly allowing a great hairy tarantula to crawl over her as she explains the spider's way of life goes some way to countering the more lurid type of James Bond presentation of tarantulas. A kindly, white-haired old man has a gopher snake and uses it to talk about the snake's control of rodent pests. An astonishing number of his audience is genuinely surprised, when invited to touch the snake, to discover that it is quite dry, not slimy. Another woman wheels around a little trolley stacked with objects related to the ever-present saguaro cactus, and tells listeners about its important position in the ecology of the desert. They may come away with a slightly better appreciation of the fragility of the lovely landscape around them.

Docents, properly used, are surely where the future of zoo education lies. There are those who doubt that the average Englishman would even notice somebody wearing a gorilla shirt, let alone enquire about it, but I think they are mistaken. Molly Badham, who now uses just such a docent at her Twycross Zoo in Leicestershire obviously agrees with me. More and more zoos are coming to realise that personal treatment is what visitors want, that the zoo itself is a fund of information, and that docents can be used to satisfy the visitors' curiosity.

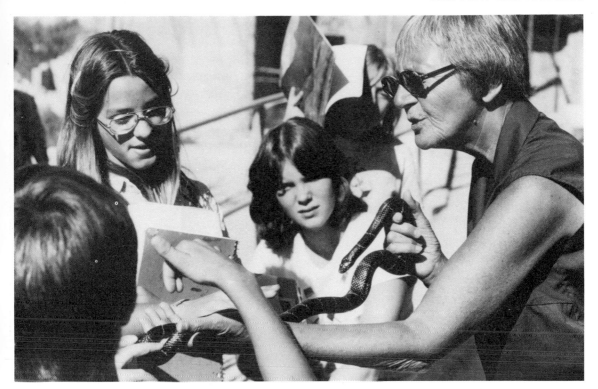

Arizona's Sonora Desert Museum; it's easy enough to raise money for the popular cuddly animals, but the nasties also need help

A collection of animals in a zoo used to be an end in itself. Nowadays, the question most liable to be asked of a zoo director is 'what do you do with your collection?' The answers vary. Kurt Benirschke, director of research at San Diego Zoo, is adamant that conservation is the goal. 'Time is short, the water is rising, room must be made in the ark,' he says. He predicts that there will be no truly free-living large vertebrates within a hundred years, and that all the living specimens will be in zoos of one kind or another. People will still want to get close to those animals, and zoos will be the only places where they will be able to.

Other zoos by and large agree that conservation is important, but many of them are in the business of making money, not of saving wildlife, and what they say does not always match what they do. In any case the public is not yet ready to finance the breeding of animals in zoos for its own sake. It is, however, willing to pay for entertainment. Hence all the shows and hoopla, to attract the paying customers. Chessington Zoo near London has one of the most bizarre arrangements of all, a funfair right in the middle of the zoo. The fairground operator pays a concession fee but keeps his profits for himself, and the sole reason for his existence seems to be to attract people to pass through the zoo's turnstiles. Chessington could get rid of the fair, but to do so without losing money it would need to attract another 200,000 customers over and above the 650,000 that already visit it each year, a formidable task.

The attitude of people to wild animals has changed dramatically over the years, and zoos can take much credit and much blame for this, but there is still a lot to do. In particular it seems imperative to extend our feeling for animals from the easy species, the cuddly pandas and awesome tigers, to those that, while more difficult to relate to immediately, are nevertheless every bit as deserving of our protection.

And the question of attitude brings me squarely back to the chimpanzees' tea party. What has changed to make tea parties undesirable? People still laugh at the antics of humanised chimps when given an opportunity. Is that a bad thing? Perhaps so, if it means that they regard chimps simply as clowns rather than as the well-adapted animals of the broken African forest that we too once inhabited. And if it weren't for performing chimps some of the best primate breeding facilities, notably Molly Badham's Twycross Zoo, would not exist. In the absence of exciting, stimulating cages the tea party was probably the best thing that happened in the average zoo chimp's day. James Fisher, the naturalist and writer, in the late 1950s described it as 'a valuable form of occupational therapy for the chimps. Without them the mammal department would have to design other forms of therapeutic activity.' Are we that sure that chimps now get all the occupational therapy they need?

Treading the thin line between vulgar entertainment and lofty educational aims will always be a balancing act for zoo directors, who somehow have to pay for their charges. Perhaps one day all that education disguised as entertainment will have done its work. People might then derive as much delight from observing a tarantula doing nothing in its burrow as they once did from the riot of a chimpanzees' tea party.

# Chapter Three

# MORE THAN MENAGERIES

Early in September 1914 a bird died in the Cincinnati Zoo. Birds die all the time in zoos, but this was something special. Martha, a hen bird, was the very last representative of her species. When she died, the passenger pigeon went extinct. Despite all the efforts that were made to find her a mate, man had seen to the passenger pigeon's extinction.

Nor was this the only species to breathe its last in the confines of a zoo. Cincinnati has an especially unenviable place in the annals of zoo extinctions, for just four years after Martha died, another bird, the Carolina parakeet, went down the same one-way street. The last remaining quagga, a form of zebra from South Africa, died in Amsterdam Zoo in 1883. And despite tantalising hints, an occasional blurred pawprint or suspicious spoor, it seems probable that the very last thylacine, or Tasmanian wolf, died in Hobart Zoo in 1934. Film exists of this strange beast, gaunt, striped and very wolf-like, pacing relentlessly up and down beside the wire of its cage.

None of these animals, not even the Tasmanian wolf, could be said to have constituted a threat to mankind. So unlike, say, the smallpox virus, which we have successfully exterminated, there was no compelling reason to get rid of them. Indeed, towards the end, when the severity of the situation was realised, Herculean efforts were made to save the passenger pigeon. At one stage the zoo offered $1000 for a pair of passenger pigeons, but although there were plenty of claimants, in the event no one could provide even a single bird.

The real tragedy of the story of the passenger pigeon is that it reflects no more than our ignorance and greed. In the early 1800s vast flocks of passenger pigeons whirred their way across the North American continent, easy meat for the pioneers with their guns. If that had been the only pressure on the bird it would probably still be with us today. Back East, however, the human population of the cities was growing furiously and needed feeding. Passenger pigeons were manna and were blasted out of the skies in unimaginable numbers, then shipped to the hungry hordes on the coast by the railroad carful. The passenger pigeon population crashed, until Martha was all that there was left. Then she, too, went.

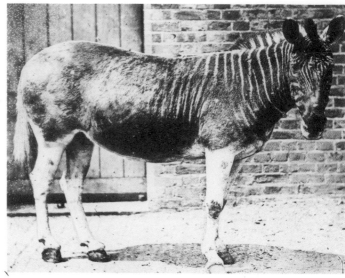

Four species (possibly only three) that went extinct in zoos. The passenger pigeon (*top left*) and Carolina parakeet (*above left*) died in Cincinnati Zoo. The quagga (*top right*) died in Amsterdam Zoo and the thylacine, or Tasmanian wolf (*above right*), may have gone extinct in Hobart Zoo in 1936

Man by his efforts exterminates his fellow creatures, and then, when it is too late, his even more strenuous efforts fail to reverse the decline. Zoos undoubtedly are a part of the problem, with their appetite for the rare, the exotic, the unobtainable. But they are also part of the solution, and to match the list of species that owe their ultimate extinction to the failure of zoos there is a slightly shorter one of species that owe their continued existence to their successes.

In 1865, in a garden of the Chinese emperor, Père Armand David, a French missionary, first saw the deer that bears his name. (Incidentally it was he who, four years later, in 1869, discovered some furs of the giant panda, although a living specimen was not seen by a European until 1913.) At this stage the deer was probably already extinct in the marshes of central China that once formed its ancestral home. Nevertheless, the species was doing very well in captivity, and Père David arranged for specimens to be sent back to the zoos and parks of Europe. This was just as well because during the Boxer Rebellion in 1900 hungry Chinese revolutionaries, in a move as dumbly eloquent as that of the French revolutionaries' a century earlier, ate the last of the imperial deer. The Duke of Bedford, in England, collected at his own imperial park, Woburn Abbey, all the Père David's deer he could find and from those original eighteen animals the current world herd was built up, until in 1981 it numbered 994 (with another 39 unconfirmed), every one of them in captivity.

A similar sort of story can be told of Przewalski's horse, the wild horse of Mongolia. When Colonel Nikolai Przewalski shot his first specimen in 1870 and made the Mongolian wild horse known to the West their numbers were relatively high, dwelling to the west and north of the Gobi desert on both sides of the Altai mountains. But they competed with domestic livestock for food and so, despite a ban imposed by the Mongolian People's Republic in 1926, continued to be hunted. By 1945 there were probably fewer than 100 Przewalski horses in the wild. One was seen in 1968 but since then four expeditions have failed to find any trace of a single Mongolian wild horse. We must assume that in less than a century *Equus przewalskii* passed from being unknown to science to being unknown in the wild.

Fortunately, the rapacity of zoos saved the Mongolian wild horse from complete extinction. Between 1898 and 1903 hunters captured a large number of foals for the Baron von Falz-Fein's new zoo at Askaniya Nova in Russia. By shooting herd stallions and the foals' mothers to get their prey, many of which died on their way to a dealer in Bisk in Central Asia, these hunters must have contributed to the decline of Przewalski's horse in the wild. But they saved it for zoos. Fifty-three animals, 25 colts and 28 fillies, reached the dealer who, perhaps fortunately for us, was a typically unscrupulous member of his profession. He sent only nine animals to the baron who had arranged for their capture; the rest went to fourteen establishments in Western Europe and the United States, all of which had offered a higher price than Baron von Falz-Fein. These animals, with the addition of a single female caught in 1947, constituted the founders of the current herd, but even that nearly did not save them. At first breeding efforts were sporadic and almost random, so that in 1945 there were only three stallions and seven mares left. These were the true founders of the current world herd, which in 1981 was 425 strong.

Père David's deer and Colonel Przewalski's horse live only in captivity and only by dint of our continued care for them. There are many more species that are down to such low numbers in the wild that if they do survive it will be thanks largely, if not entirely, to zoos. And there are very many more that will slip quietly into oblivion, unknown to science and to zoo visitors. The question inevitably arises of why we should make any effort at all to save species that have clearly outstripped their capacity to survive in their environment. Admittedly that environment has changed by the addition of one species – ourselves – but that is the way of natural selection. A few survive, many go to the wall. How can we decide which we should save of those that seem to be heading for extinction?

Dr Norman Myers has recently introduced the notion of triage to the conservation community, with some success. This is a procedure born of the cruel lack of medical resources on the battlefields of the First World War; French surgeons divided the casualties into three categories so that the limited medical resources could be used most efficiently. First were those who were so badly injured that no effort would save them; these received a shot of morphine but no medical care. Next were those whose injuries were not imminently fatal; they could be safely ignored for the time being. Finally came the group whose state was such that medical intervention could provide the difference between life and death; these were the ones who would be attended to immediately.

The logic of Dr Myers' plan is sound enough, but when he outlined his ideas to a meeting of London Zoo's scientific fellows one thing was missing; he had no specific ideas of how we should assess the value of a species and its call upon the limited resources of conservation. Saying that it was essential that we make our decisions conscious, he offered a series of ways to extract 'the best value for each conservation pound', and proceeded to examine the biological, ecological, genetic, economic and cultural criteria that might be applied. We could favour island species, for these are likely to be unusual. But by the same token we could ignore island species, because they are unrepresentative. We could save species that play a key role in the ecology of a region, for example bees in the tropical rain forests, where they are at the hub of a whole web of interdependencies. But if this type of species is threatened then we can be sure that all the others that rely on it are equally, if not more, needy. There just is no easy answer, especially when Myers himself concedes that the most important category may be the one he calls cultural, the pandas and suchlike that are of limited ecological significance but can exert enormous emotional leverage on the public. A little effort invested in pandas can bring enormous returns for conservation in general. Triage worked on the battlefields because everyone agreed that the goal was to save as many lives as possible. It would be fine for conservation if we knew why we wanted to save species, but we do not.

Arguments can be put forward which attempt to link our own survival to the survival of wild animals and plants and these, you might think, would be persuasive because they appeal to base selfishness. Who would have thought that armadillos could be enlisted in the fight against leprosy, or that the blood of capybaras contains compounds that can combat leukaemia? But if you don't know which species is going to provide the next serendipitous discovery,

Capybaras, the largest rodents in the world. Their blood contains compounds that can combat leukaemia

you don't know which to choose, so that yardstick is of little help. Then there are the projected consequences of the continued destruction of, say, rain forest – droughts, floods, famines. But although these are frightening they are not arguments for saving species, at least not in zoos. They are arguments for preserving habitats, replete with as much genetic diversity (that is, as many species) as possible, both for the singular serendipities and the global consequences. Against such a background, what are the points to be made for breeding animals in zoos?

The first is obvious, but important for all that. Zoos will continue because people want to see the animals in them. In the old days all those animals came from the wild and there were dreadful losses at every step of the journey. Whole social groups of gorillas or elephants might be slaughtered to capture a single infant which more often than not died in transit. By breeding their own animals and supplying one another, zoos can ease the pressure on the remaining wild populations.

Gerald Durrell, founder of the Jersey Wildlife Preservation Trust, tells a story that shows how this can work. After years of patient effort his team had succeeded in building up a good captive population of Rothschild's mynah, a beautiful and much endangered white bird from the forests of Bali, and had established breeding groups in zoos around the world to guard against catastrophe. So he decided to sell his surplus Rothschild's mynahs and advertised accordingly. An indignant phone call from a Dutch dealer complained that Durrell had set his price much too low. Would he please raise it because demand for the dealer's wild-caught Rothschild's mynahs had fallen off. Precisely.

The second point is harder to make, but when I see that scratchy film of the last Tasmanian wolf I feel robbed. Why could the zoo not have done a better job of breeding the beast? What opportunities have been missed for comparing the marsupial wolf with its placental analogue? If the Tasmanian wolf were still alive today, the struggle to save the World Heritage Park around the Fraser

71

River in Tasmania might not have had to have been so hard and protracted. Zoos cannot save whole habitats themselves. They cannot even save enough species to recreate the complete occupants of anything but the simplest habitat, although they can and do propagate individuals for later reintroduction. What they can do is save representative species as living warnings of our greed, to educate us, and to open our eyes to our folly.

The success stories are renowned. In January 1982 the gates on their holding pens were opened and a herd of fourteen Arabian oryx was shooed out into an area of Oman called the Jiddat al Harasis. The oryx have done well, the culmination of a breeding effort that began in 1962, when a largely British expedition to the region, organised by the Fauna Preservation Society, captured two females and two males, one of which later died. There being nowhere safe to keep them in Arabia, the surviving three were sent to Phoenix Zoo in Arizona, where the climate closely matches that of their home. A year later a calf was born and the world herd was officially inaugurated. By 1979, supplemented by a few animals brought in from other zoos and private Arabian collections, the world herd had swollen to 322. Forty-eight calves were born that year. Plans could be made to return the Arabian oryx to Arabia.

What had made it necessary to create a world herd, with all the expense and administration involved? Hunting, especially with modern armaments and vehicles. Oryx is good to eat, and its hide, too, is useful, so it represented a considerable prize to the desert nomads of the area. The flesh, unfortunately, was also considered to be a panacea. The oryx used to inhabit the whole of Arabia from Syria and Palestine in the north down to the southern shores of the peninsula, and throughout its range it was hunted, but this was no threat because even the best hunters might have to track an animal for days before they could get a shot at it. However, as rifles replaced ancient firearms, oryx were killed in increasing numbers, until by the end of the Great War only a few animals survived outside the southernmost part of the Arabian peninsula. Arab princes, supported by vast retinues and using automatic weapons, continued to pursue the beasts in cars and Land-Rovers and by the 1960s there were probably fewer than 200 animals left. Countries that had laid waste their own oryx populations crossed the borders and covetously plundered their neighbours' herds. In 1961, for example, a raiding party from Qatar crossed into Aden and killed 28 oryx. In another such incident a Qatari party crossed into the Jiddat al Harasis in south Oman and killed the last remaining oryx in that area. The Harasis, who are not hunters, were furious and today, encouraged by the Sultan of Oman, they jealously and zealously guard the reintroduced herd. From three animals to 300 in two decades is certainly an achievement, and the growing herd of oryx in Oman is testimony to the efforts of conservationists. It is, to all intents and purposes, a success story, an example of zoo breeding put to good effect.

Arabian oryx, rescued from the wild, bred up first at Phoenix Zoo, and now returned to the wild with a constant guard of local tribesmen

So is that of the ne-ne, or Hawaiian goose. The story of its decline contains all the usual elements. Isolated on islands, with no predators on the ground, the ne-ne all but lost the ability to fly and gave up the water completely. Unlike all other waterfowl it does not even mate in the water. None of that mattered, though, for the ne-ne was well adapted to its home; there were 25,000 of them on the Hawaiian islands in the eighteenth century. But with the introduction by western settlers of pigs, goats, sheep, rats and mongooses the ecology of the islands was badly disturbed and the ne-ne's survival jeopardised. The rats and

73

mongooses ate ne-ne eggs and chicks, and the other animals uprooted the plants and disturbed the natural vegetation. By the end of the 1940s there were just thirty ne-ne left in the wild and eleven in captivity. A pair of the captive birds was shipped to Peter Scott's newly-formed Wildfowl Trust at Slimbridge in 1950 to begin the rescue programme.

All went well and as the birds settled down Scott sat back to await the first nesting. To his consternation both birds built nests and both laid eggs; the prospective founders of a captive flock did not include a male, and Scott relates with some glee how the team at Slimbridge sat down to an omelette of one of the world's rarest birds. The culinary pleasures stopped, however, when a male arrived the next year, for nine goslings were hatched the following breeding season.

By 1960 the captive flocks, at Phakuloa on Hawaii and at Slimbridge, were big enough to start releasing birds back into the wild. There are four ne-ne sanctuaries on Hawaii and the neighbouring island of Maui, the first of which received captive-bred birds in 1960. In the beginning the birds' wing feathers were clipped so that as they grew back the birds became more mobile and could gradually shift to fending for themselves. The reintroduced birds seem to be doing all right as far as it is possible to ascertain. The highlands of these young volcanic islands, which is where the ne-ne lives, have sharp-edged barren lava flows that make walking extremely difficult, and it would take considerable effort accurately to assess the success of the reintroduction. There are about 750 birds in the wild, compared to thirty in 1950, but nobody knows how well those birds are breeding. Conservationists are certain that about fifteen goslings have been raised on Maui, which doesn't sound all that successful; the true figure may or may not be much higher. But added to the Hawaiian geese in the wild, there are another 1250 or so in captivity around the world, so it seems that the species has been saved, certainly in zoos if not back on the islands.

Père David's deer, Przewalski's horse, Arabian oryx and Hawaiian goose are four species that owe their continued existence to captive breeding. In each case, the most important factor in the species' successful reproduction was the effort made to breed it. Simply removed from natural and unnatural threats, these animals did very well. Their fecundity enabled the captive populations to grow at a rate that could never have been sustained in the wild, even if there were not the additional threat posed by human activities; and sometimes that is all that is needed to breed animals in captivity – protection from the vicissitudes of nature. More often, though, there is some little trick, some little wrinkle, that is needed to get the animals going. Here are some of them.

Gerenuks are dainty antelopes that live on the arid desert fringes of the African savannah. They have long necks, delicate faces and huge ears, and are best known for their habit of standing upright on their hind legs to browse on the leaves of the thorny acacia bushes. Bronx Zoo got some gerenuks and, in keeping with its avowed policy of breeding as many species as it can, set out to persuade them to multiply. The keepers gave them everything they could want; space, care, fresh food and clean water. Despite the lavish attention, however, the gerenuks would not breed. The problem turned out to be the water. Gerenuks are creatures of dry scrubland; they will drink if they are given the chance, but normally they get all the moisture they need from their food, with only an occasional supplementary sip. In the zoo they drank the water offered and excreted most of it as a dilute urine. Along with surplus water and waste products, however, the urine also contains reproductive signals from the female that indicate her state to the male and help to make him ready and willing to mate. In the zoo, with water freely available, the does' urine was so dilute that the chemical signals were never strong enough to have the desired effect on the bucks. As soon as the zoo restricted the gerenuks' access to water all was well. The female signals were now strong enough to get the males going, and the result was successful captive breeding.

Chinese alligators once thronged the banks of the Yangtze river, but now they are rare, endangered and threatened. A co-operative programme involving Rockefeller University and the New York Zoological Society tried hard to get these animals to breed, but they would not. Eventually it was discovered that the body temperature of the adults needs to fall, so that they become chilled and hibernate, before they will breed. Now they are doing very well at a special reserve in Louisiana, chosen because its climate and that of the lower Yangtze are almost identical.

Flamingos, always associated for me with Alice's recalcitrant croquet mallets, are very popular birds in zoos and gardens. Part of their attraction, apart from their improbably long legs and oversized beaks, is surely their glorious pink colour. However, it isn't natural. The pigment comes direct from the little shrimps and other crustaceans that the flamingos eat. In captivity, fed artificial food that contains all they need to stay healthy, the birds inexorably fade until they are almost white. The keeper maintains their colour by adding the pigment carotene to their diet. But what is interesting for our purposes is that even white flamingos will breed if conditions are right, but the pinkest of birds will not if they are wrong.

In the wild, flamingos build chimney-pot nests of mud, depositing the eggs on the top of the mound. Although these nests may look silly to us, they are very functional for the top is often quite a few degrees cooler than the baking mud surface. In a natural flamingo rookery the nests are packed very close together, and the overcrowded birds are continually bickering with one another, but in many zoos, where preliminary nests were constructed for them out of concrete, well-meaning zoo keepers at first built them a discreet distance apart. Unfortunately, the birds were not in the least impressed by this unaccustomed luxury and steadfastly refused to use the nests. Only when the starter nests were brought much closer together, so that the occupants could bicker, did the flamingos begin to use them, and now young flamingos routinely hatch in captivity.

There is another side to this crowding business, too, that may affect the zoo breeding of flamingos. In the wild, the birds often go in for mass courtship displays, thousands of them marching back and forth along the lakefront, squawking and striding in unison. This display helps to synchronise their breeding efforts so that almost all the chicks are born in the space of a couple of days, providing a glut for the predators and a better chance of survival for the individual chick. The display also seems to be needed to prod the birds into full reproductive condition and it may be that sheer weight of numbers is as important a factor for breeding as crowding in the rookery, for Sydney Zoo's birds, despite being crowded, have never bred. There are now only eleven of them, the remnants of a flock imported in 1947. Since then, such imports have been banned to safeguard Australia's native animals from disease. In an effort to goad the birds into breeding, the zoo authorities this year installed a series of mirrors around the little flamingo lake. It will be interesting to see whether this tactic works, though I confess I have my doubts.

*Above* Flamingos at Taronga in Sydney. Will the mirrors encourage them to breed?
*Right* London Zoo has never matched the attendance it had in 1950 when Brumas the polar bear was born

What is good for flamingos, however, is disastrous for cheetahs. Whipsnade Zoo only started to breed its cheetahs with any degree of success when the keepers instituted a new regime that kept male and female apart most of the time, allowing them to meet briefly when the female was in season. The result was breeding that can now be considered prolific, with almost 100 cheetahs born in captivity at Whipsnade in the past few years.

Just providing the right habitat can be very important in stimulating successful breeding. Birds that build their nests on sandy ground, for example, or in the fork of a tree, are far more likely to breed if provided with the right kind of site. Bronx Zoo displayed its waterbirds in old-fashioned zoo cages for more than fifty years without a single egg being hatched. As soon as they offered them a simulated natural habitat, in 1964, many of these species started to breed.

Often a zoo's breeding programme is a prime attraction for visitors, and they are scarcely aware of the tricks of the trade. Who could fail to be delighted by a busy flamingo rookery or an attentive cheetah mother? Indeed, babies are very good for business; London Zoo has never regained the peak it scaled in the summer of 1950, when Brumas the baby polar bear pulled more than 3 million visitors through the gardens' gates. But breeding can also be a source of conflict between the zoo's needs and the public's.

Take the Congo peacock. This magnificent bird, with its plumage that manages somehow to be both gaudy and quite subtle, is severely endangered in the wild. Nobody knows for certain how many are left in the rain forests of Zaïre, but the number is not large. Captive breeding is thus desirable, the more so as the Congo peacock is an attractive bird, popular with visitors and easily displayed in lush, eye-catching enclosures. But it is also a nervous bird, and simply will not breed while on show, no matter how lush, how eye-catching, how like home its accommodation. Take them out of their naturalistic cage, however, and put them round the back of the zoo in a ramshackle old aviary, as they have at Antwerp, and the birds will breed fairly readily, just as long as they are not disturbed too often. So a zoo must, if it wants to breed Congo peacocks and display them too, have two set-ups. One need be no more than a rudimentary cage, provided it is away from the public eye and undisturbed. The other, in which the birds are seen by the visitors, can be as pretty as the zoo can make it – but it will not assist breeding.

Breeding conditions need not be terribly lovely. The Congo peacock needs privacy, and will only breed, as at Antwerp, when it is not on public display

Off-exhibit breeding, as it is known, is now a feature of most of the world's better zoos. A lucky few, however, have the resources to go even further; they have separate breeding establishments that are geographically distinct from the main zoo and often closed to visitors. Gary Clarke, director of Topeka Zoo in Kansas, has the use of a large chunk of an old army airfield on which to breed some of his prized specimens. The sight of his Przewalski horses, standing atop an old grass-covered bunker on a blustery January day, looking out over helicopters full of troops training, was one of the strangest I have ever seen in a zoo, but it is not one that the zoo's ordinary visitors can enjoy. Similarly, the

National Zoo in Washington DC has a special breeding farm, once used to raise horses and mules for the army, at Front Royal in Virginia, where it now breeds a score or more species, including Père David's deer. But the zoo that takes off-exhibit breeding to the limit, the one that many other zoos envy, is the New York Zoological Society.

Far away from the Bronx, off the coast of Georgia about 30 kilometres south of Savannah, is St Catherine's Island. This small coastal island has been managed by the New York Zoological Society since 1974 as a breeding farm for zoo animals, completely off-limits to the public. At the moment there are about thirty-three species being kept at St Catherine's, all of them threatened, though some less so than others. Most of the space is occupied by hoofstock of various kinds, but there are also birds and reptiles. Many of the species at St Catherine's are closely related duos, like the Arabian oryx and the gemsbok. In the aviaries there are Leadbeater's cockatoos alongside palm cockatoos, sandhill cranes and wattled cranes, and over in the reptile section radiated and angulated tortoises, both from Madagascar, share adjacent pens. The aim of St Catherine's Island, according to Jim Doherty, the general curator in charge at New York Zoological Society, is to breed endangered species for reintroduction and to supply other zoos, and the paired species help to achieve that. Research to improve breeding is carried out on the less threatened species of the two – the gemsbok, the sandhill crane, Leadbeater's cockatoo – and the results applied to the more threatened. That way the research scientists can investigate better breeding without threatening further the most endangered species.

Many problems beset the zoo keeper who is trying to breed animals in captivity, but one that is less than obvious was explained to me by Dr Sandy Friedman, then director of biological programmes at Minnesota's Apple Valley Zoo. It was a bitterly cold day in December, and we had just driven past the musk oxen, in their element in this inclement weather, their long hair skirts flapping unconcernedly in the icy winds. We turned a corner and there were Minnesota's Siberian tigers, looking like no other tigers I have seen. In the deep white snow, they seemed more regal, more magnificent, more commanding. Also more playful, as they wrestled in the cold, rolling and tumbling and sending up clouds of snow to mingle with their frosty breath. But Sandy appeared troubled when I complimented him on how good his tigers looked. When I asked him for an explanation he told me that he thought tigers were going the same way that pigs had done back in the 1950s.

Wild swine, the various relatives of our domestic pig, used to be a very popular zoo exhibit. They still are at a few zoos in Europe, such as West Berlin's. But thirty years ago several American zoos had good collections of these pigs, from hairy little Vietnamese pot-bellied pigs to awesome giant forest hogs from Africa. They were attractive and easy to breed – too easy in

79

fact. Many a zoo director took the decision not to keep breeding his wild swine, and each was confident that he was making the right choice. All was well for a while. Then the pigs, who had been quietly getting older, began to die. The zoo directors looked around for replacements and found that there were none. And they couldn't bring any more in from the wild because of fears that they might harbour diseases that could devastate the domestic pig population. And so, through a combination of bad luck and bad judgement, wild pigs have all but vanished from American zoos.

The same could happen, Friedman fears, to tigers. They, too, breed very well in captivity, and many zoos now give their adult females long-term contraceptives as a matter of course. It is not impossible that one day all the tigers will be too old to breed, with not enough replacements coming up the ladder. Someone needs to keep an eye on the whole tiger population in all the zoos of the world to ensure that the disaster that overtook wild swine does not get tigers (or any other species) too. That body could be ISIS, the International Species Inventory System, which happens to be based at Minnesota Zoo and which I will talk about more fully in the next chapter. It has indeed adopted the tiger for detailed management, but even ISIS is unlikely to be powerful enough to deal with cases like the white tigers.

Although rare, white tigers have been spotted occasionally in China and Korea, and were comparatively common in the Rewa district of India. In 1951 the Maharajah of Rewa caught a young white male. He discovered, when he paired it with a captive yellow female, that all the cubs were yellow, but when allowed to mate with their white father these yellow cubs produced one white tiger for every three yellows. This is the classic inheritance pattern of a so-called recessive gene, and is quite interesting for that reason. The Maharajah, however, was not content with simple tiger genetics. In 1960 he gave a white female to President Eisenhower for the US National Zoo and in 1963 he gave a white pair to Bristol Zoo. Bristol now has eight white tigers, all descendants of the original pair. In the United States things were not so straightforward.

In 1973 the National Zoo in Washington sent three yellow tigers, which carried hidden the recessive white gene, on loan to Cincinnati. What happened next depends on who you ask. National Zoo's Devra Kleiman told me that she was well aware of the white gene and asked Cincinnati specifically not to breed from these three tigers. Ed Maruska in Cincinnati is equally adamant that the tigers had failed to breed in the District of Columbia, and bred almost as soon as they reached Ohio. In any case, Cincinnati Zoo found itself with three extremely attractive and popular white tiger cubs, but returned all except the female parent to the National Zoo. In 1975 Maruska brought in another descendant of the Maharajah's white male to mate with the National Zoo's female, and in 1976 he bought a second white female from Brookfield Zoo in Chicago. After all the breeding loan agreements had been settled and the offspring redistributed to the various zoos involved, Maruska was left with a white pair of his own. These he has used to produce several white litters for his own and other zoos' profit. Fascinating though this history is, it does not answer the question: should white tigers exist?

This is one of the arguments that currently divides the zoo world. Some, like Cincinnati's Ed Maruska naturally, think they are a valuable asset. To others, like New York's Bill Conway, they are anathema. They certainly pull in the crowds and Maruska even rents his white tigers out to smaller zoos as an attraction for the summer. They can be used, at a pinch, to tell people about genetics, inheritance and mutations, although I have never seen this satisfactorily done. Against this must be laid the simple fact that they are eating another tiger's meat. White tigers are no more representative of the wild population than Persian cats or white peacocks are of theirs. They exist because we choose to allow them to, not because they fill some niche in nature. A tiger costs $1600 a year to feed. Is it worth spending that kind of money on the fifty or so freaks when one's stated purpose is to save the wild tiger? Maruska says it is, because the white tigers bring in more than they cost. Conway says it is not. I agree with Conway, not just because of the cost, but because it seems to me there is something atavistic about using freaks to attract visitors.

Tigers, at least in India, are in trouble not because of zoos but because of hunting and changing patterns of land use. In 1939 there were 30,000; records from hunting parties indicate that by 1964 this figure had fallen to 4000 and by 1969 to 2500. The decline was speeded up by the destruction of the forests in which the tigers lived, probably more so than by the direct effects of hunting. At this stage zoos seeking to replenish their stocks from the wild could have been a severe threat to the wild population. Fortunately captive tigers breed well enough so that there is always a surplus of them. Any zoo that wants tigers need look no further than the pages of *International Zoo News* to see who has spares, and it is by supplying one another from captive-bred stocks that zoos do most good for conservation.

On a cold Sunday morning in December, high up on the Chiltern Downs, I watched Richard Kock, a vet at Whipsnade Zoo, preparing a hypodermic. He looked his patient over – a nervous zebra who needed calming before being crated for a long journey – and after consulting a well-worn set of tables decided on the dose. His hands were steady as he drew the required amount of tranquil- liser into the special syringe. He charged it, pumping air into the chamber at its rear: when the needle pierced the patient's skin it would trip a little valve and the compressed air would then force the drug into the zebra's muscle. Everything ready, Kock attached a bright feathered flight to the hypodermic, put the dart into a blowpipe and, with none of the stealth usually associated with this weapon, stepped boldly up to the edge of the pen and let fly. Smack into her rump went the dart, and within minutes the zebra was calm enough to be led into a small but secure wooden crate for her journey.

Whipsnade was acting as the staging post and main supplier for one of the biggest shipments of zoo animals ever to leave Britain. The sedated zebra was joining a herd of her colleagues, as well as waterbuck, rhinoceros, cheetah and many others – more than 200 specimens in all – that were the second shipment to go to a spanking new zoo in Doha, capital of the Arabian state of Qatar. The press attention that morning was focused on the three young Bactrian camels being shipped out to the desert; coals to Newcastle to a news editor in search of a story, except that these Bactrians were the two-humped Mongolian camels from the Gobi desert, rather than the familiar dromedary.

Getting all the animals ready had been a logistic nightmare, but now it was all done. One by one the crates were fork-lifted onto lorries ready to roll down to Heathrow airport where a jumbo jet was waiting to take them to Doha. The flight had been timed to arrive in the pre-dawn cool: 6500 kilometres and less than twenty-four hours from Whipsnade, as the muezzin called the faithful to prayer, wild animals from Africa, Asia and America, bred in Britain's zoos, were unloaded for the benefit of the Qataris. Some – the rhino for example – were reluctant to leave their crates. Others bounded out and were quickly at home. The move was over, and had been a complete success. All would be ready for the official opening of the new zoo on the Emir of Qatar's birthday.

Not quite coals to Newcastle. Bactrian camels supplied by London for a new zoo in Doha

The supplying by zoos of other zoos is a very important consequence of captive breeding. It means that zoos no longer need support the dealers who traffic in wild-caught animals. With no market for their animals, the dealers will no longer buy animals from trappers, and so the animals that once died to supply zoos – the mothers that were shot to get their babies – will live. That is the theory, and like so many theories it is fine until examined in detail. Then it begins to break down.

Individual zoos are remarkably coy about where they get their stocks, but the ISIS computer gives us an insight. Of 58,830 mammals and birds registered on the books at the end of 1983, 38,256 were born in captivity. That leaves 20,576 – a staggering 35 per cent – that were not. About half, 10,085, were definitely brought in from the wild and the rest are classified as 'don't knows'. For the mammals, and there were 4211 of them in that category, this almost certainly means wild-caught, while 'don't know' birds might be wild-caught or they might be from private breeders. Those figures apply to the zoos on ISIS's books, and those are probably among the more scrupulous of institutions. Where the others get their stocks from is anybody's guess, but it is clear that zoos are still a drain on the wild populations and have a long way to go before they are self-sufficient.

High up on a bluff overlooking San Diego Zoo's Wild Animal Park is a large cage. A tall mesh fence stretches higher than I can reach and encloses about a quarter of a hectare. On top of the fence are coils of sharp barbed wired that sparkle innocently in the Californian sunshine, and within the compound stands a row of adjoining inner cages, taller than the fence and shrouded in shade-giving green netting. When I peered through the fence, I could not catch even a glimpse of the inner cages. A massive padlock guarded the gate, and I was acutely conscious that security here is very tight indeed. A dangerous animal was being kept at bay. But this is a zoo in reverse; I represented the dangerous animal, man, and I was being kept out. Inside were Sisquoc and Tecuya, the two inhabitants of what keepers at the Park call the Condortration Camp. Officially it is called the Condorminium and cost $196,000.

Sisquoc and Tecuya are Californian condors. They live here in San Diego as the tangible result of a last-ditch rescue attempt that has cost, so far, $25 million. There are fewer than twenty perhaps no more than fifteen – Californian condors left in the rugged hills north-west of Los Angeles; efforts to protect them have of course been made, but these are judged insufficient to assure the species' safety. We do not know the age or sex of the remaining wild birds and what would be a minor trauma to a bigger population – a few untimely deaths for example – would be a catastrophe for the Californian condor. It was to safeguard the species that – after long debate between the interventionists, who wanted actively to interfere, and the preservationists, who wanted only to

83

increase protection for the remaining wild birds – the decision was made to bring eggs from the wild and raise birds in captivity.

There are sound reasons behind this approach; most notably, there is the phenomenon called double clutching. Birds normally lay a clutch of eggs and then incubate it. If the clutch is destroyed, or removed, the parents will very often produce a second or even a third clutch. Condors normally lay a single egg every two years; by removing eggs they can be induced to lay three in a season, a sixfold multiplication. And removing one egg leaves the parent birds with the opportunity to make their own contribution towards copying themselves for future generations.

While the approach may be sound, the early days of the rescue bid contained elements of farce tinged with a hint of tragedy. At the very start the intervention-ists scored a notable own goal; on 30 June 1980 the five-strong Condor Research Team scaled a cliff face to examine the chick in one of the only two nests known to contain young that season. Two hours later the chick was dead, the victim of inexperienced handling by the scientists. That set the research programme back severely, but it was not just the scientists who were clumsy.

The Condor Research Team eventually got going again and established hides to watch the parents at the nest, the better to learn how to raise chicks if they ever got hold of any. One pair had produced a single bluish-white egg, but seemed to be forever squabbling over who should incubate it. Change-overs between the parents, which should be smooth and swift, were often accomplished only after protracted bickering. But at least they were breeding. One day Helen Snyder, an observer from the National Audubon Society, was watching the nest as usual when one parent returned to relieve the other of incubation duties. The sitting condor, however, was reluctant to go and, as had happened so often with this pair, a tussle ensued. It had happened before, but this time Helen watched aghast as the recalcitrant condor kicked the priceless egg over the edge. It smashed on a ledge and within minutes ravens were on the spot feasting, as Peter Scott had with his ne-ne eggs, on a vanishing species.

The parent birds, not surprisingly, have no notion that they are almost done for. They sit and breed as they have done for hundreds of thousands of years. They were there long before the Indians, who later came to revere the condor as a god, trudged across the Bering Strait into Alaska. They cannot know that the white man, who also wrecked the Indian, has placed them, too, on the brink of extinction and is now trying to pull them back. They showed no hint of distress at the smashed egg. They carried on as before.

Condor Team researchers were thus delighted when, just a month after the accident, the cantankerous couple made up and produced a second egg. Double-clutching showed its evolutionary worth, and there was jubilation among the condor's rescuers. Alas, as one reporter put it, the 'soap opera turned to tragedy'. The ravens had developed a taste for embryonic Californian condor and returned

Père David and descendants
of the deer he found in the
Chinese emperor's deer park.
The Mongolian wild horse,
discovered by Colonel Nikolai
Przewalski. Both species
owe their continued survival
to captive breeding

Armadillo babies are all genetically identical. They are also very useful in research on leprosy.
Conservation will preserve as yet undiscovered benefits, but zoos can help only indirectly,
by fostering an awareness of the importance of all wildlife. The ne-ne, or Hawaiian goose, is
another species that avoided extinction through captive breeding .

St Catherine's Island, where away from the public gaze New York Zoological Society concentrates on breeding endangered species such as the wattled crane

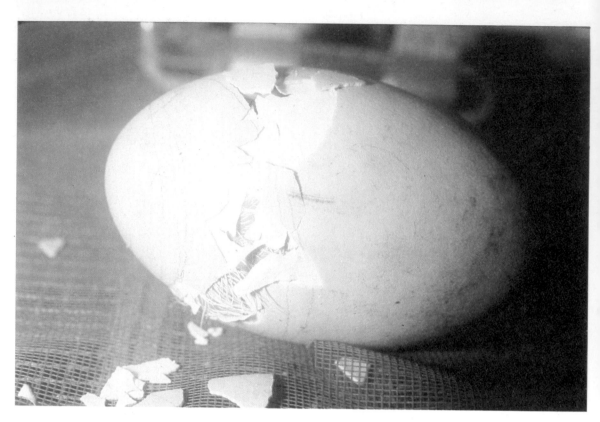

The California Condor Recovery Program has vastly increased the number of condors alive in captivity, caring for the eggs and youngs chicks and raising healthy adolescents, but to what end? Perhaps some species should be allowed to go extinct

91

Andean condors could benefit immensely from a fraction of the money spent on their Californian cousins. White tiger, a drain on resources or a draw for paying customers?

to the nest to harass the long-suffering birds. Accounts of what happened next vary. According to San Diego Zoo officials the incubating condor left the nest for a brief period that was long enough for the ravens to glide darkly in and feast. Another report had the incubating parent lunging out to defend the egg from a raven that had had the boldness to alight on the nest. Solicitous, but clumsy, the condor once again kicked the egg from the nest to smash on the rocks below: 'The raven, showing no regard for conservation, swooped down and ate the embryo.'

All this brouhaha strengthened the interventionists' hand; in August they removed a nestling, later christened Xolxol, spirit of the condor, which was being neglected by its parents. Xolxol first did a nine-month stretch in the Condortration Camp and then was paroled to Los Angeles Zoo, where he was to be the companion of a captured juvenile bird. The intention had been to release the captured bird after it had been fitted with a radio transmitter that would make life a little easier for the scientists studying the birds in the wild. 'Bad weather and poor health' thwarted this plan, so the bird remained at Los Angeles Zoo.

While Xolxol was being transferred, the rescue effort focused on the quarrelsome condor couple in the wild – good at producing eggs but no good at looking after them. The female had laid an egg on 2 February, and three weeks later the people stepped in and removed it, by helicopter, to San Diego Zoo. There, on 30 March, with a little gentle assistance from one of the keepers, the first Californian condor ever to hatch in captivity was eased from its shell. The keepers were taking no chances. They played tape recordings of the calls wild king vulture parents utter during hatching; these sound like a dog barking and make the chick more active. They tapped on the shell as they had seen wild birds do. They used a meticulously crafted leather and plastic hand puppet of a condor's head to provide the infant Sisquoc with food; minced mouse and vulture vomit to begin with, whole mice later. The idea was to prevent him getting used to humans. And for his first few days Sisquoc lived in an incubator designed for human infants. Nobody knows whether all these efforts are needed, but why risk not providing them?

Where Sisquoc led, others quickly followed. A second and third egg were removed from the still-bickering – but fortunately still productive – pair that had laid Sisquoc. Tecuya hatched on 5 April and a month later she and her big brother were moved out to the Condorminium. A fourth egg, laid by radio-tagged parents, thus proving that the tagging was not harmful, was brought in.

All this is splendid. As I wrote the first draft of this book the total population of Californian condors had been increased by something like a quarter, and the teams were out in the hills again looking for more eggs to bring in to the Condorminium. They got eight, and at the end of April 1984 two had hatched and the other six were 'expected momentarily'. The Californian condor population is on the up. The increase, however, is all captive. Indeed the wild population has declined by at least three, the bird captured and kept at Los Angeles Zoo and two chicks brought in last year. But there are undeniably more Californian condors alive than there were a year or two ago. Not as many as there were ten years ago, but at least it is a start.

Or so we are told, loudly and often. As I stood outside the Condorminium, squinting through the fence in the vain hope of a flash of the inmates, my gaze happened to wander up to the top of the cages. A stiff breeze was blowing up the hillside and perched on the pole tops was a group of ten or so turkey vultures. These small birds, relatives of the Californian condor and considered, as the condors once were, vermin, made me think again. Mocking the efforts of the condor team and its $25 million success story, a turkey vulture would open its wings and step on to the breeze, effortlessly soaring away down the slope or simply staying put, riding the air current like a surfer. That, I thought, is where the Californian condors should be, up in the sky.

Lately it has become more and more common to hear the Californian condor described as a symbol; fine, but what exactly does it symbolise? Bureaucratic bungling? Conservationist commitment? The ineptness of parenthood? The programme has absorbed $25 million, money that almost certainly could not have been raised for any other less symbolic cause. But the money might have been spent in other ways. What threatens the condor is not bungling or ineptness but history, the fact that man chose to build Los Angeles where the bird lived. I have no idea how much desirable L.A. real estate $25 million would buy, but it might be enough to extend the condor's remaining refuges. The California Condor Recovery Program is considering the purchase of a 4600-hectare cattle ranch in the San Joaquin foothills which might otherwise turn into yet more housing. That might provide room for another few pairs, but being carnivores and scavengers these birds need a lot of space to provide them with a living. The money might even have been used to introduce Andean condors, which might prove more successful than their Californian cousins. Who but an expert, glancing up to see one of these superlative birds gliding high above, would notice the difference?

The chances of condors returning to wheel and soar above California seem very remote. And that, surely, is where they belong. There are conservationists who have threatened to destroy the captive condors; they argue that if the choice is to be between living in captivity or dying in the wild, these magnificent birds should be given every assistance in the wild, but allowed finally to exit with dignity. The zoo man, dedicated to the idea that his collection is more than a menagerie, cannot accept this. His operating principle is quite simple; better bred than dead.

# Chapter Four

# BETTER BREEDING

During the summer of 1981 a dairy cow gave birth to her first calf, a healthy little bull who weighed in at 33 kilograms and was up on his feet and nursing hungrily within an hour. Nothing special in that, except that the birth took place less than 8 kilometres from Central Park in Manhattan. The calf was not exactly straightforward either, because he was not related to his 'mother' at all. The egg that he developed from had come from another cow altogether; after she had mated with a bull, the tiny embryo had been removed from her womb and placed in the cow who was now protectively licking 'her' calf. That too is nothing special really. Embryo transfer, as it is called, has been routine with cattle since 1965, and in 1980 some 20,000 cows in North America gave birth to calves that were not strictly speaking their own. A humdrum farming tale, however, would hardly merit inclusion in a book about zoos and the future, so there must be something extraordinary about the little calf – and there is. He is a gaur, while his womb mother was a Holstein milk cow. New York Zoological Society had achieved a notable first, the first successful embryo transfer between two different species, the gaur *Bos gaurus* and the cow *Bos taurus*.

The gaur is the largest wild member of the cow family, a resident of the forests of India and South-East Asia. Its numbers have dwindled as its habitat has been taken over by agriculture, so that there are now probably fewer than 2000 gaurs left in the wild. When its Wild Asia exhibit opened in 1977, New York Zoo made a commitment to breed the gaur and put a herd together from specimens brought in from Omaha and West Berlin. In their excellent surroundings the gaur herd quickly got down to breed, managing eight calves in the following three seasons. Gaurs do breed quite well in captivity – there are about 110 in zoos – and their situation is not exactly desperate. But, for a host of reasons, they were still very good candidates for the high-tech experimental medical intervention of an embryo transplant.

What this entails is not so much a single dramatic operation as the successful culmination of numerous little manipulations, each timed correctly and depending on the one before having worked. First, know your species. Embryo transplants are routine in cattle, enabling prize cows to make a much greater contribution to future generations, though not nearly as much as a bull can with artificial insemination. The gaur was an excellent choice precisely because it is so closely related to the cow; the New York Zoo vets, Janet Stover and Emil Dolensek, could be reasonably certain that what worked with cows would work with a gaur.

Next, choose your specimens. Bronx Zoo purchased four Holsteins and checked the health of the surrogate mothers-to-be very carefully. And the gaur was well chosen too; one of the founder members of the zoo's herd had over-grown hooves that hindered her from walking or standing properly. Soon they would have to be trimmed, and the safest way to do this would be to anaesthetise her. Putting an animal out, for no matter how short a period, is always a slight risk and so zoos like to do as many routine examinations as they can whenever an animal has to be anaesthetised. This time, as well as trimming the gaur's hooves and conducting various medical tests, the zoo vets would attempt to flush growing embryos from her womb, and transfer them to the dairy cattle.

Next get your animals ready. The reproductive cycle is controlled by hor-mones that stimulate and co-ordinate the various bodily organs. So, at the same time that an egg is developing, ready to be fertilised by the male's semen, the wall of the uterus is being prepared to receive the embryo. For a transfer to be successful the donor and recipient must be in exactly the same hormonal state, synchronised in their respective reproductive cycles. To achieve this the vets gave the gaur cow and the four Holsteins two carefully timed injections of a substance known as a prostaglandin. The same compound is used as a 'morning after' pill in people; it works by kicking the body into a new cycle of preparing an egg. The second injection came ten days after the first, and to the vets' delight the initial stage of the transfer was working. The cattle and gaur all showed signs of coming into heat on the same day, two days after the second injection. On that day, 8 October, the gaur, who had never previously mated, was introduced successfully to one of the zoo's bulls.

To make the whole effort worthwhile, and to increase its chances of success, the vets had also given the gaur extra hormone injections to make her super-ovulate. This again is a tried and tested technique, used in cattle and people with fertility problems, in which the ovary is prompted to develop several eggs rather than just a single one. After waiting anxiously for six days, after which the fertilised eggs, if there were any, would have travelled down the fallopian tubes but would not yet have attached themselves to the uterus wall, the team moved on to the next step. They had to find the eggs and transfer them to the cows. Dr James Evans, head of the Pennsylvania Embryo Transfer Service at the University of Pennsylvania School of Veterinary Medicine, a man with six years' experience and more than 2500 transfers behind him, was called in. Gingerly he checked the gaur's ovaries and announced that he could feel five burst follicles. She had produced five eggs. Evans rinsed out the gaur's uterus with warm saline solution and carefully collected the washings in a flask. Then, with an electric heating pad to keep the washings warm in the chill New York winter, he carried the flask back to the zoo's hospital, there to search for the embryos, each one smaller than this full stop.

He found one, and pronounced it normal. The relief was considerable; another hurdle cleared. Evans continued to scan the washings with his microscope. He found another embryo, and another, until he had five in all, one for each of the burst follicles. With only four cows ready, this was luxury, an embarrassment of riches. Evans examined the five eggs again and threw away the one that looked least healthy. Then he made a small incision in the side of each of the Holsteins, injected an egg into each of the four wombs, and stitched the cows up again. Another hurdle cleared, four cows carried four gaur embryos. Another wait.

Two weeks after the implant all four cows showed raised levels of the hormone progesterone, a sure sign that they were pregnant. Then came the first setback. Two weeks after the pregnancy test, one cow showed definite signs of being back in oestrus: she had lost the embryo, and had started another reproductive cycle. One down, three to go. Then, on St Valentine's day, five months into gestation, one of the cows aborted her gaur foetus. Two down. Stover admits that she was 'beset by worries' but there was nothing she or anyone else could do except wait. The calves were expected in July; on 24 July one female went into labour. The calf, alas, was stillborn. A little bull, he weighed just 18 kilograms, half the expected weight. It seemed that he had died the day before delivery, but no hint of why emerged. Stover and Dolensek were now left with a single cow, and as July turned into August the team's fears grew. An examination showed that the gaur foetus was alive and apparently well, and after the first week of August had passed the team decided to induce delivery. They injected Flossie the cow with a steroid drug that would normally start birth within 36 hours. A day and a half passed and nothing happened. Had everything been in vain? Only the worrying, for the odds were perfect. And so, on 11 August, after 308 days of gestation, 6 in his natural mother and 302 in Flossie, Manhar was born. His Hindu name means 'he who wins everyone's heart'.

Gaurs, as I said, are not all that close to extinction and breed fairly well in captivity. Why then bother with the fuss, complication and expense of an embryo transplant? Not simply to show that it could be done, but because embryo transplants do offer the potential to multiply some animals much more rapidly than they could manage for themselves, a sort of double-clutching for mammals. The technique has since been applied to other slow-breeding animals and, as I write, a donkey in a field outside Cambridge is carrying a zebra in her womb, and two ponies are each nurturing a Przewalski foal. Whether embryo transfer will ever become a routine part of breeding endangered species I do

Embryo transplantation allows a mare to give birth to a zebra foal, as this one did with the help of Louisville Zoo in Kentucky

not know. Perhaps not, at least not until far more money is available for research into exotic animals; it was no accident that Manhar the gaur was a close relative of the economically important dairy cow, for agricultural interests funded most of the basic research. But despite the seeming ordinariness of Flossie and her calf, it is an arresting example of the many ways in which science is helping zoos to achieve better breeding.

Scientific assistance for zoo breeding programmes comes in many forms, from the glamorous world of embryo transplants to the altogether more routine, but no less important, maintenance of good health. Inevitably a look at the role of science in conservation will seem something of a pot-pourri, but there are some threads that can be followed. Broadly speaking, most research can be put into one of a few categories. There is the question of basic reproductive behaviour, in female and male, which then enables more interventionist techniques such as embryo transfers and artificial insemination. There is the field of genetics and population management, where careful study ensures that breeding programmes are doing as little harm to the species as possible. And there is the prospect of the frozen zoo, keeping species not as living individuals on display but as collections of specially stored cells.

It is this, the frozen zoo, that seems to be the great hope for high science, zoos, and animal conservation alike, although it challenges all our notions of what constitutes a zoo. In a back room of San Diego Zoo's research laboratory is a squat grey chest labelled '20th Century Ark'. Dr Kurt Benirschke, director of research, gave me the singular privilege of examining some of the animals in his special zoo. The fog that billowed forth as I lifted the lid of his ark gave the whole scene a futuristic science-fiction look, very appropriate really as the frozen zoo seems to be more dreamtime notion than practical proposition. But the proposition itself is simple: every species is really no more than a collection of genes housed in different bodies, and every cell in an animal's body contains those genes. Save the cells and you have saved the species, provided you can reconstitute a whole animal from a cell; that is where making the dream real might flounder.

Wafting away the special-effects fog I could see some gleaming stainless steel containers. With fingers made clumsy by thick insulating gloves – the steel is at $-196^\circ$C and would burn my flesh – I lifted one out. It contained row upon row of cardboard boxes, each about the size of my palm. I selected a box and opened it, and there inside were more than a hundred little transparent phials. Each was neatly labelled with a code number, a species name, and the contents. The contents itself were all but invisible, a bunch of deep-frozen cells, suspended in what Benirschke hopes is animation.

The most obvious candidates for storage are obviously the reproductive cells, both as gametes (unfertilised eggs and sperm), and as embryos arrested at an early stage of development. Thawed out and given a suitable recipient, these will grow into whole new animals. The technology certainly works A healthy human infant, and very many calves, have developed from embryos that were frozen. Frozen semen is routinely used in the cattle industry, and frozen eggs have been thawed successfully and then fertilised. It sounds like the ideal solution for most of the problems that currently beset conservation and zoos.

The sample is easy enough to come by. Domestic animals, bulls for example, can be trained to mount and copulate with a dummy. Exotic species are less accommodating, but can still provide sperm samples with the aid of a device called an electro-ejaculator. Less fearsome than it sounds, this is a probe that can be used to stimulate electrically the nerves that supply the genitals. The result is an ejaculation of semen that can be collected for immediate use or storage. It is usually done under anaesthesia, and if for any reason a male has to be anaesthetised the opportunity will then be seized to obtain a sperm sample. There are some fears that sperm collected by electro-ejaculation may be less potent than those ejaculated in the normal course of copulation, but these are minor worries compared to the big problem: that we simply do not know enough about the biology of the exotic and rare species that would make such excellent passengers in a frozen ark.

One headache is the storage medium for semen, the fluid that the sperm are bathed in during freezing. This brew is crucial to the success of the procedure, and makes an enormous difference to the pregnancy rate obtained when the thawed semen is used to inseminate receptive females, but it varies from species to species. Timber wolf does best in a mix of skimmed milk, lactose, egg yolk and glycerol, while elephant semen needs glucose and citrate instead of the skimmed milk and lactose. Brindled gnu sperm thrive in glucose, citrate and yolk. The combinations are as diverse as the animals. Once the correct storage medium is discovered frozen semen can be extremely useful, but getting the best recipe means trying out several, and then attempting to make females pregnant with the thawed samples. With rare species, distributed thinly through zoos world-wide, it becomes very difficult to undertake the necessary extensive research. (A new technique, developed at London Zoo, uses easily obtained hamster eggs to assess the potency of the thawed sperm and should improve prospects for the future.) Benirschke is aware of all these problems, but they do not deter him. 'When we can, we collect semen and store it away,' he told me, 'recognising that for most of these animals the basic biological knowledge is missing.'

If these problems can be overcome, freezing semen is obviously of great benefit to the zoo breeder. Bloodlines can be mixed and mingled without any of the expense or trauma of intercontinental transport. Quarantine regulations can be observed easily. And perhaps most promising, scientists may in the future get fresh supplies of genes from the wild by trapping and electro-ejaculating males in their natural habitat. Basle Zoo has already obtained semen from a wild African elephant in this way. This section of the frozen zoo should make it easier for breeders to follow the dictates of the geneticists.

Semen is only one part of the frozen zoo's contents. Equally important are the eggs and embryos. These are much more difficult to come by, so many fewer species are represented. Washing eggs from the uterus, whether they are fertilised or not, can be a tedious business. Or rather, the washing is simple – it is finding the eggs that can take time. So to make it worthwhile the female is often given fertility drugs to make her produce more eggs than normal. In the case of the gaur, the procedures worked perfectly, but sometimes they do not. Researchers at London Zoo were quite surprised when the zebra mare they were preparing to donate an embryo to a donkey did not respond at all to a fertility cocktail that by all expectations should have worked. The transfer was all the same successfully completed with the single embryo that was recovered, but it would have been preferable to have had a better supply of embryos.

Frozen embryos, even more than eggs, would be an ideal way to preserve the diversity that geneticists say is so important. Zoo populations could be sampled and preserved, like a frozen image of the genetic diversity that exists in captivity today. Zoos would then continue with normal breeding, with its attendant inevitable loss of genetic variability. Then, at some date in the future, when the captive population is too inbred, the embryo bank would be tapped to resurrect some of the old genes, thus restoring its variability and vitality. No one knows how long frozen embryos will last. Many experts say it is an irrelevant question.

If an embryo can be frozen for a week and still develop normally, then it can be frozen for a decade or even a century. I hope they are right.

The third section of the frozen zoo is the largest, but the one least involved in saving species directly. It contains mostly so-called fibroblasts, skin cells. These can be thawed and will start growing and dividing, but they cannot be used to recreate the animal, at least not yet. It might be possible one day to remove the nucleus, which contains the chromosomes that carry a full set of genetic instructions for the construction and maintenance of a particular animal. This nucleus could then be transferred to an egg cell which would develop normally. Indeed, this process of cloning has already been done experimentally in frogs and mice, but it is not yet a practical possibility for the frozen zoo. Still, in the future it might be possible to use the egg of even a distantly related species as the receptor for a thawed nucleus. (One hare-brained scheme that made the news – hare-brained because the cells have not been properly frozen for this purpose – called on scientists to reconstitute the woolly mammoth by transplanting a nucleus from a frozen mammoth cell into an elephant's egg.)

Despite these problems the 'other cells' section of the frozen zoo has a very important role to play in saving species indirectly. As new and improved techniques for working with genes become available it is very useful to have a supply of exotic cells to work with. It means you do not have to run the risks of anaesthesia to knock an animal out just to get a sample of skin to try out a new procedure, but can simply go to the fridge for some cells acquired at some other time.

Many of these new techniques involve looking directly at the DNA of the cell, the long molecule of heredity that carries the coded genes along the chromosomes. The instructions on the DNA determine the sort of animal the embryo is going to grow up into, so looking at the DNA is another way of classifying animals. Oliver Ryder, a research scientist at San Diego Zoo, has pioneered the use of a technique of DNA analysis to obtain information about animals that is not obvious from their outward appearance, and his studies have turned up some surprises. Take the case of the white rhinoceros. White rhinos are found in two locations in Africa, up in the north, around Sudan and Kenya, and down in South Africa. The two populations look remarkably similar, although there are said to be some subtle differences in their teeth, and so they have always been treated as races of a single species, rather than as separate subspecies or species. This is important because in zoo-breeding the white rhino, which is highly endangered, it would not matter very much if two races were mingled, whereas mingling two subspecies would not be desirable. On the surface, then, northern and southern white rhinos are very similar. Ryder, however, decided to look at their DNA.

The methods for doing this owe their existence to the revolution in molecular biology that underpins the new discipline of biotechnology, but essentially the tools are a pair of scissors and a sieve. The scissors are called restriction enzymes. They are made by bacteria, and each restriction enzyme can recognise a specific sequence of code on the DNA. It breaks the DNA at the sequence that it recognises. So if you mix purified DNA with a restriction enzyme you will get a set of fragments, and you will get the same set of fragments every time from the same DNA. If, however, the DNA has changed by mutation (which is the basis of all evolutionary change) then the code sequence will be different and the restriction enzyme will produce another, different, set of fragments. To sieve and measure the fragments you use a technique called gel electrophoresis. The DNA fragments are dumped at one end of a thin slab of jelly and an electric current passed through it. The fragments are electrically charged and so are frog-marched through the jelly by the current. Different-sized fragments move at different speeds, so after a little while the fragments are spread out across the jelly in order of their size. What you see is a ladder of DNA rungs at different positions along the gel and, therefore, if you get different electrophoresis patterns from two sets of DNA, you can measure the differences between them.

When Ryder did this with DNA samples taken from northern and southern white rhinos he discovered that the differences were much greater than he had expected. Races of a single species should have very similar DNA patterns because they have not been evolving separately for long. But the northern and southern 'races' were quite different. In fact they were as different as many separate species are, and it looked as if the two populations had not interbred for about two million years. Any future breeding of white rhinos would do well to take note of this, and avoid mixing northern and southern specimens, not only because they will not breed as effectively, but also because zoos do not want to change the animals they are preserving, and mixing northern and southern rhino would alter two million years of evolution. And if a zoo does not know which group its white rhinos are from, Ryder can use his electro-phoresis technique to tell them.

Having sorted out the white rhinos, Ryder is turning his attention to other species. The owl monkeys of South America are one candidate for study, since they are composed of a number of different breeding populations with very different DNAs. Being able to go to the fridge for samples, to refine the tech-niques, and to expand the study to animals that were sampled long ago or far away is very helpful for this and similar projects – yet another use for the frozen zoo.

The frozen zoo is obviously an exciting idea. It won't satisfy our need to be close to animals, at least not in the short term, but it clearly has a role to play in long-term conservation. Unfortunately, the mysteries of keeping animals on ice are still something of an enigma, and only three or four zoos world-wide are doing anything to penetrate them.

Scientists will continue to explore the possibilities of keeping genes alive outside animal bodies; at the same time, though, they are applying themselves to discovering more about those bodies. Sometimes even something as simple as deciding the correct sex of an animal needs a laboratory full of expensive equipment supervised by a highly trained person in a white coat.

This seems surprising because we ourselves usually have no difficulty in telling men from women, unisex notwithstanding. But we are fortunate. There are many species in which male and female are outwardly indistinguishable. Nearly a third of all bird species are monomorphic – that is, they have sexes that look almost identical – and so are many reptiles. The animals themselves may be able to tell with ease which is which, but the zoo keeper cannot. So if a pair is not breeding, while this could be because they are incompatible, it could also be because they are not a proper pair at all. It used to be that the only way to tell was to open the birds up and have a look at their gonads, or reproductive organs, but a new technique can sex birds reliably with no need for any interference. The raw material is something most bird keepers simply throw away: excrement.

The theory behind the exercise is simple. The reproductive organs, in addition to producing the gametes themselves, also manufacture sex hormones. Ovaries and testes both make so-called male and female steroid hormones, but in different amounts. Ovaries produce lots of oestrogens, the female hormones, and not so much testosterone, the male hormone; testes the reverse, high levels of testosterone and lower oestrogens. The hormones are excreted via the kidneys and find their way to the outside world in the droppings. By measuring the ratio of oestrogen to testosterone in a sample the scientist can decide whether the bird that produced it is male or female. If the ratio is high the bird is female, if low male.

Faecal steroid analysis, as this method of bird sexing is called, was pioneered at London and San Diego and has several advantages over other ways of sexing birds. Looking at the gonads directly is a surgical procedure and so, even when carried out by experts, carries the risks of anaesthesia. Careful research into techniques, particularly at London Zoo, has admittedly brought the risks right down to less than one in a thousand, but the danger remains measurable, and the one that dies might be a Californian condor. Faecal steroid analysis holds no risks whatsoever. Direct examination on the other hand gives an immediate answer and needs only a skilled practitioner to provide it. Steroid analysis takes time and needs a technician and expensive laboratory equipment. A gram of parrot droppings contains less than one thousand-millionth of a gram of oestrogens. The sensitive techniques used to measure that minuscule amount – the most common is called radio-immuno assay – are beyond the means of most zoos. But samples can easily be sent through the post; San Diego Zoo will do the analysis for zoos it is co-operating

103

with, and in the United States sexing by steroid analysis is available to the general public through a commercial laboratory, at a cost of about $50 a bird.

The method, initially devised to sex parrots, the largest group of monomorphic birds, has proved immensely valuable, and has been extended to other species as well. When the Californian condors hatched the San Diego Zoo was swamped with letters telling them of infallible ways to sex the young birds. Most involved suspending a needle over the bird and watching which way it spun, but the writers were about equally divided on the significance of the spin; half said that clockwise indicated a male, half that clockwise indicated female. In the event the birds were correctly sexed by steroid analysis within weeks of hatching, information very valuable to their subsequent rearing.

Faecal steroid analysis has also found applications in other aspects of bird breeding. The amount of hormones in the droppings reflects the amount removed by the kidneys, and this depends on the amounts made by the sex organs. When a bird is in breeding condition its gonads are more active and secrete more hormone, so by tracking an individual's faecal steroids over a period of time one can discover when it comes into breeding condition.

Arden Bercowitz at San Diego has been looking at bald eagle excrement with this in mind. Dickerson Park Zoo in Springfield, Missouri, has an Intensive Bald Eagle Propagation Program that is using a two-pronged approach; suitable pairs are given every encouragement to breed, and non-breeding birds are being studied as potential subjects for artificial insemination. Bercowitz measured the droppings of four birds, two males who were physically disabled and two females who were behaviourally abnormal and would almost certainly never breed if left to themselves.

Monthly values for the ratio of oestrogen to testosterone revealed that both sexes, despite showing no obvious outward signs of breeding behaviour, had an annual reproductive cycle. The males were able to produce semen only during the month of March. Their ratio of oestrogen to testosterone had been declining for the two previous months; Bercowitz interprets this as greater activity in the testes, producing sperm and more testosterone which lowers the steroid ratio. The females showed no signs of breeding – neither completed nest building nor laying. But their hormone ratio was very revealing. In March, just when the males were most active and at their lowest steroid ratio, the females too were most active and had their highest oestrogen to testosterone levels. They did not breed, but they were clearly primed to do so.

Analysis of excreted hormones thus offers the zoo scientist a window, albeit a sometimes cloudy one, onto the inner workings of an animal's reproductive machinery. That is important because it allows the breeder accurately to track an animal's reproductive state – a *sine qua non* of all the more complicated breeding procedures. There is no point inseminating a female who is not fertile, or waiting for nature to take its course and reveal a pregnancy the usual way.

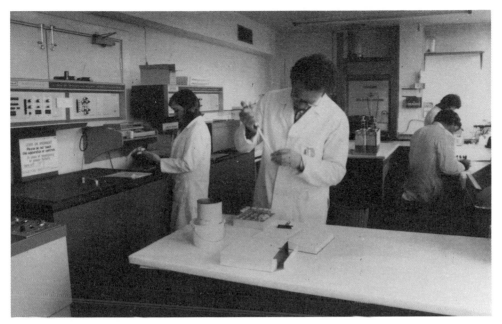

Keith Hodges' laboratory in the Institute of Zoology in London Zoo

Science must step in. Keith Hodges, a researcher at the Zoological Society of London's Institute of Zoology has devoted his work to the female, and in particular to investigating the reproductive status of female mammals by looking at the hormones in their urine.

The trouble with exotic animals, a by now familiar lament, is that so little is known about them. The dairyman can consult published works that will tell him the significance of the hormone levels in his cows. He can buy a simple kit that will detect the time of peak fertility, which enables him to make the most efficient use of an expensive bull's semen, and pregnancy testing kits so that he can do it all again if he needs to without wasting a valuable season. For most zoo species, the basic data are missing, and much of Hodges' time is spent gathering them.

At night, before the Przewalski horses and pandas are brought in, their keepers put a plastic bag into the main drain of their quarters. The bag will collect the animal's urine, freely and without imposing any stress on the unwitting subject. In the morning the keeper sucks up a few centilitres of the fluid into a clean syringe and takes it to Hodges, who labels it and stores it in a fridge. Next will come a whole string of chemical processes designed to measure accurately the tiny amounts of hormones in each sample; rather than go through all the stages every day Hodges tends to wait until he has a whole batch worth doing.

The technique is essentially the same as that used to measure hormones in faecal samples, radio-immuno assay followed by scintillation counting. Those are complicated terms for a series of measurements that use the exquisite sensitivity of the body's natural defence mechanisms to find the hormone molecules and then very accurate physical measurements to see how many molecules there are. The immune system, which protects you from invaders like bacteria, works by recognising certain proteins, antigens, on the surface of the invader. It makes another protein, the antibody, that detects the antigen and binds tightly to it, alerting the white blood cells and other defence mechanisms so that they can destroy the invader. The relationship between antigen and antibody is like that between a lock and key, and so the antibody can be used to separate out its antigen from a mixture of all sorts of different compounds. And because the antibody is so sensitive and finds its antigen so accurately it can be used to collect all the antigen molecules in a mixture, even if there are only a very few of them.

The first part of Hodges' assay therefore consists of preparing the sample and mixing it with an antibody that binds with the hormone he is interested in. The second part requires him to measure just how many molecules of the hormone antigen have become bound to the antigen. Hodges loads all the samples into the snake-like conveyor belt of a machine called a scintillation counter. The sample contains a compound called a scintillant, which gives off a tiny flash of light every time it is hit by a particle of beta radiation. The antigen has been radioactively labelled and so emits beta particles. The scintillant converts hard-to-measure beta radiation into easily measured light, and all the machine does is to count the flashes and convert that into a concentration of hormone. It remains only for Hodges to plot the figures on a graph and then – the hard part – decide what they mean.

He moves always from the known to the unknown. If ovulation in the well-known animals – cow, sheep, woman – is associated with a change in the ratio of oestrogen to progesterone, can he find a similar change in exotic species? If he can, does the date of the change match the date of behavioural changes? Do the various hormones show cyclical ups and downs that indicate the normal reproductive cycle of the female? Not all species are identical; if they were very little research would be needed, but the exceptions can usually be slotted into the existing pattern of knowledge. In this way the zoo scientist moves along from racehorse to Przewalski's horse to Hartmann's mountain zebra, uncovering the basic reproductive biology. Only with that information can an embryo transplant, for example, be attempted. Even a routine mating, male and female in the time-honoured way, will be successful only if the female has produced an egg, so the information is worth having.

After mating, if all goes to plan, comes pregnancy. Again, with well-known animals the bodily hormonal changes, mirrored in the hormones excreted from the body, are also well known. Progesterone, in particular, goes up and stays up, but there are earlier changes still involving hormones called chorionic gonadotropins. These are the ones detected in the very earliest pregnancy tests, and obviously the sooner a zoo knows that a female is pregnant or not, the sooner it can take appropriate management steps. The early pregnancy detection kits were developed because there is a market for them among cattle breeders and women; not many people want to know when an okapi has conceived, but those who do want the same simple and reliable way of testing if possible, and that is what Hodges is striving to provide. Measuring hormones in urine is thus a very productive pastime, both in itself and because without it none of the other approaches to breeding would be possible.

Most of the research into basic breeding biology is directed at females. This is because the female's contribution to successful breeding is more involved and, in a sense, more important. The male has to provide sperm, of course, but most male mammals are only too willing to do that. The female, who invests so much in each of her offspring, is choosier than the male, and does not mate as readily. Encouraging motherhood is more profitable, and that is why most zoo research seems to be designed to take full advantage of the female's parental investment. Sometimes, though, a closer look at the males has shown why breeding programmes fail.

Benjamin Beck, while at Brookfield Zoo in Chicago, started to ask why his gorillas were not all breeding properly. At first he thought it might be something to do with being from incompatible sub-populations from different areas of Africa, as revealed by the shapes and wrinkles of their noses. In Chicago the pairs that bred had similar shaped noses, those that didn't had noses that differed. Unfortunately a survey of other gorilla pairs in other zoos ruled the nose idea right out. But the survey did reveal that many male gorillas who had been presumed to be capable of siring offspring were sterile. In fact about half

Gorillas; nose shape is not the key to compatibility, but many males are sterile

of the male gorillas in captivity turned out to be infertile. Further investigations revealed that this seemed to be the result of an infection, reminiscent of the effects of human mumps, that had attacked the gorillas' testes. What the disease is, whether it gets them in the wild or in captivity, how to prevent it, these are questions that need further research. The important discovery is that many males are infertile and so of no use to the breeding programme.

Even with male and female reproductive biology fully understood, there is still the problem of putting them to work. Animals in the wild do not simply mate at random with the first suitable partner they stumble across. They can be very particular, and we are usually profoundly ignorant of the basis for their choice. In evolutionary terms the most desirable will be a partner that will give the joint offspring the best chance of surviving to breed themselves, and that tends to weed out those individuals that make an inappropriate choice; inbreeding offers the clearest example. Animals often harbour harmful mutations of some of their genes, but are protected from the mutation's bad effects by a so-called dominant correct copy of the same gene. It is only when two mutated copies find themselves in the same body, usually as an accident of birth, that the harmful effects are manifested. Close relatives are likely to have many of their genes in common, including the harmful ones, so when they mate with one another the chance of their offspring getting two harmful mutations is much higher. In the wild the offspring of inbreeding die out, and with them vanishes the tendency to choose a closely related partner. Many animals thus have in-built mechanisms that enable them to avoid inbreeding by choosing unrelated partners. In zoos, however, choice is a luxury. Inbreeding is rife.

Despite the theoretical objections to inbreeding, many zoo keepers have denied that there are any bad effects in practice. There are, as we shall see; but it is interesting to ask why they have not been given due consideration. Perhaps the most important reason is the existence of captive populations that are known to be very inbred but are also apparently healthy. The classic example is Père David's deer, rescued from just three or four pairs. Nothing could be more inbred, but the species does not show any gross abnormalities. Captive breeders also cite the way laboratories produce pure-bred strains of, say, rats and mice, by repeatedly mating brother and sister or father and daughter, without ill effects. Finally, their optimism seems supported by the lack of published reports of the harmful effects of inbreeding.

The facts, however, tell a different story. Katherine Ralls and her colleagues at the National Zoo in Washington examined the breeding performance of sixteen species of ungulate for which they could get information, simply comparing the survival of infants born to related and unrelated parents. In fifteen of the sixteen, an infant was more likely to survive beyond six months if its parents were unrelated. The effect could even be shown with individual females; when

The first stages of an embryo transplant, collecting the gaur embryos

The end result, Flossie the dairy cow and her gaur calf Manhar. *Right* Kurt Benirschke with his frozen zoo in San Diego. Frozen samples are increasingly important in research and conservation, but will never replace conventional zoos

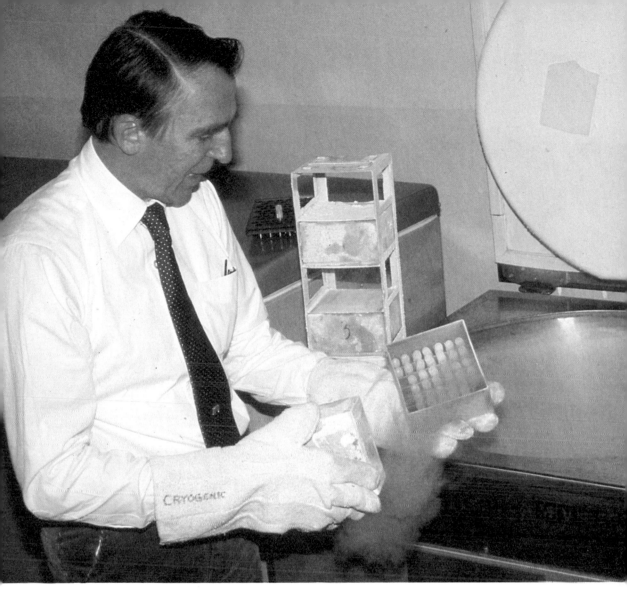

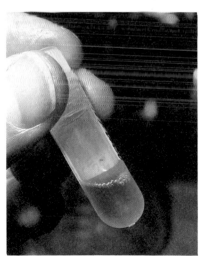

111

Like so many bird species, males and females of the orange-flanked (grey-cheeked) parakeet are outwardly identical. Sexing these birds is now easy with the aid of highly technical scientific measurements

Dorcas gazelle, a species in which inbreeding has been proved to be harmful

the sire was unrelated to the female her offspring survived much better than when the sire was related to her. Inbreeding hurts.

It is not always easy to know *why* inbred animals die off. Usually the vets say that it is a question of being less able to cope, of succumbing more easily to diseases and environmental stresses. For one species, Dorcas gazelle, there were enough medical records for Ralls to attempt an investigation, and this proved very revealing. Outbred young Dorcas gazelle calves are remarkably sturdy. Once they make it beyond the crucial perinatal period – the four days after birth – they survive. Only five calves died after reaching their fourth day, and in every case this was the result of the trauma of being captured or transported. Inbred calves were not only twice as likely to perish, they also did so throughout their first six months as a result of succumbing to all sorts of medical problems.

I believe the facts to be incontrovertible; inbreeding is possibly the most dangerous pitfall in captive breeding. So why do some so-called experts in captive breeding continue to deny this? Because their justifications are mistaken. Père David's deer are indeed highly inbred because they are derived from just a few founder animals. But the number of founders is far less important than the size of the final breeding population, and Père David's deer were allowed to multiply rapidly, which offsets the disadvantages of inbreeding. It is true that laboratories produce pure-bred strains by very close inbreeding, but most of their attempts are doomed to failure. Of every twenty strains begun by breeding labs, nineteen go extinct for unknown reasons connected with inbreeding, a fact often overlooked. Finally, there is the claim that there is no published evidence of the bad effects of inbreeding; but as Ralls and her colleagues have pointed out, this is due more to the fact that zoos have not hitherto kept adequate records or taken enough interest in the question, than to the actual absence of bad effects. Where the data exist, the ill-effects of inbreeding can be found.

Ralls is quite forthright about her survey and its implications. 'The evidence that inbreeding often leads to increased juvenile mortality and other deleterious effects in ungulates is at hand and the time has come to institute sound genetic management of small ungulate populations wherever practicable, without waiting for evidence of such effects in each species or population.' But what does sound genetic management entail, and how is it to be instituted?

In theory it is easy. You decide how many animals you are going to have in the population. The fewer there are, the more quickly you will lose genetic variability; somewhere between 100 and 500 is generally considered acceptable. Then, following a few simple rules, you quickly breed up from your founder population to reach that total as soon as you can. The primary rule is that in every generation you pair the most unrelated animals, which preserves the population's genetic diversity as long as possible because the most unrelated animals will have the most diverse offspring. A corollary of this is that males and females should make an equal contribution to each generation. In nature a few males usually father most of the offspring, but if one male in captivity is allowed to father more than his share, then the genetic diversity represented by the other males has been wasted. Together these two rules not only preserve as much genetic diversity as possible but also ensure that the zoo breeders do not unwittingly select animals for certain qualities, such as the ability to reproduce in captivity. Finally, when the population has reached the number agreed upon you must manage it so that it remains in what demographers call a steady state. The number joining the population by birth must equal the number leaving by death, reintroduction to the wild, or some other form of removal such as medical research. If no surplus is wanted for, say, reintroduction, then each animal must replace itself, and that is all.

These rules have emerged from studies by population biologists, studies that threaten to change the way captive animals are bred, for the better. No longer can zoos simply get on with breeding their own animals; if they genuinely do want to preserve species then they must get together and co-operate to ensure that they can achieve their goal. This realisation has allowed the emergence of a new kind of population biologist, one who specialises in zoo animals, and with it a whole new organisation. The American Association of Zoological Parks and Aquariums was instrumental in setting up the body called ISIS, the International Species Inventory System, which is based at Minnesota Zoo outside Minneapolis. ISIS began, as its name implies, as an inventory system, a computerised stockbook of all the zoos that chose to belong to the system. It catalogued the animals and enabled zoos to find the ones they required, for example to make a mate, much more speedily. But as it has grown it has incorporated more data, for example the parentage of each animal, its breeding success, and so on, and with these data the scientists have been able to examine different breeding programmes and see how best to serve the interests of conservation.

One of ISIS's first projects was to look at the breeding of the okapi, the strange relative of the giraffe that lives in the forests of Central Africa. Okapis are beautiful animals, with long necks and sloping hindquarters, and a glossy purple-rufous coat marked with horizontal white stripes. So secretive is the okapi that it was not until 1901 that the species first became known. It is probably still relatively common in Central Africa, but it is extremely rare in zoos. Very few animals have been brought out of the wild, and a look at the pedigrees from the okapi studbook revealed that there was an enormous imbalance in the bloodlines. In America almost all the juveniles owed their existence to just one male, while in Europe two or three males dominated the pedigrees. This was a potentially dangerous situation and so ISIS worked out the consequences of various alternatives. They decided that the best plan would be to move a male from Rotterdam to Dallas. This was duly done and the American bloodlines will be much improved. The okapi is still not assured of survival in zoos; infant mortality is very high and the fertility of the adults is very low. These are the classic signs of inbreeding, but everyone hopes that with more sensible management this lovely animal will flourish in zoos.

One of the outcomes of the development of ISIS has been a series of Species Survival Plans, or SSPs. These cover about thirty species to date, including the okapi, and are intended to be an embodiment of all the best principles of sound genetic management. Each species is controlled by a committee of ten or more members who take collective decisions regarding the fate of each of the animals. Zoos that subscribe to a plan agree to abide by the decisions of the committee and see to it that all that can be done for captive breeding is done. It is too early to tell yet whether the SSPs will work, but they certainly show every sign of

115

Okapi, bred up from a very small population, need active scientific management

doing so. In the early stages much of the work consists of righting the wrongs of the past, but as each plan progresses, and as new species come under ISIS's consideration, hope for the future of species in captivity becomes ever brighter. There remains, however, one big problem: putting theory into practice.

The rules are easy to formulate, but almost impossible to act upon. The question of population comes first. As I said before, somewhere between 100 and 500 seems optimal, enough to preserve genetic diversity but not too many to strain resources. How much of the animal kingdom would that enable us to preserve in zoos? To find out we have to treat zoos as we might any other environment, and ask how many animals can be supported in it. This is called the carrying capacity of the environment; in the wild it depends on such things as food availability, while in zoos it depends more on other resources, especially money. The carrying capacity of zoos will determine how many animals can be kept in captivity, and the news is not good. One survey of North American zoos discovered several disconcerting facts about their collections. There were, in the early 1970s, about 32,000 mammals (which, remember, are important to us out of all proportion to their biological role) in the 146 US zoos. Of the 885 species represented, the average number per zoo was just under four and the total in all zoos about thirty-six. That is considerably below 100, the figure deemed barely adequate by geneticists. And yet, if we assume that 32,000 is the total number of mammals that US zoos can carry, then for each species that is offered the minimal security of 100 berths in the ark, two others must be pushed overboard. Without a huge increase in resources, US zoos can preserve fewer than one-tenth of all known mammal species.

Pairing the least related animals would be easy if accurate records have been kept, and if the animals are easily moved around. Unfortunately the truth is that few zoos kept accurate records of the pedigree of their stock until recently, and although attitudes are changing there is still a dearth of information. If the two animals to be paired are in different establishments, then one has to be physically moved to the other. One answer might be to have the entire captive population of each species at a single zoo, but that is asking for trouble. Visitors would not like it and the species would be left open to capricious disaster. Far better to spread the population among a few, say three or four locations. Animals will still have to be moved. Carrying semen and performing artificial insemination will make this easier in the future, but successful AI is as yet limited to a fraction of species.

A planned breeding programme requires the involvement of several zoos, each holding a portion of the population and each prepared to subjugate its own will to that of the programme. Zoos are becoming more co-operative, but they still retain some of the jealousies, idiosyncrasies and animosities from the times when they were one man's private collection, and sometimes, less so now than in the past, rivalries and power politics take precedence over protecting animals. Gary Clarke, director of Topeka Zoo in Kansas, told me a story that exemplified the problems of the bad old days. A West German zoo decided to sell one of its Przewalski horse stallions to an American zoo, an occasion for excitement because the animal, Rolf, was of proven fertility and would be an excellent addition to the rapidly stagnating US bloodlines. Duly paid for, Rolf was shipped over and set to covering mares. Time passed, but none of them came into foal. This happened season after season, and no one could understand what had become of Rolf's much-vaunted fertility. Eventually he had to be anaesthetised for some other reason, and someone thought of conducting a thorough examination. There, tucked neatly away in a fold in the stallion's scrotum, was a tiny scar. Rolf had secretly been vasectomised, and although the German zoo had been paid, no US zoo would gain any of his precious genes. Clarke took pains to assure me that the collective consciousness of zoo directors was now such that this sort of thing would never happen again.

Przewalski's horses illustrate another problem in carrying out the idealised breeding programme. As with so many mammals, the usual social structure involves a single male having reproductive rights over several females, so a successful male has more offspring than a successful female. The ideal breeding programme requires each sex to have the same number of offspring. To achieve this in a polygynous species like Przewalski's horse means moving the males around very often indeed. And what is one to do with the surplus males, those that are not actually breeding at any given time but are still needed for the breeding programme? In nature these males often group together, and zoos will have to mimic this. Already some zoos are willing to have all-male groups on show, taking indirect credit for successful breeding. The black-and-white colobus monkeys that frolic in Brookfield's Tropic World are all males, stored there and available to other zoos. With no females at all the group is remarkably docile and provides an excellent display.

The studbook of Przewalski's horse, which covers a longer history and is more complete than that of any other mammal, has enabled biologists to compare real breeding with the ideal programme, and what has emerged is not very good. Considerable inbreeding has had the classic noticeable harmful effects – Przewalski's horses that are more inbred than average are far less likely to breed, and if they do reproduce they have fewer offspring during their lives than less inbred animals. Most important, much of the harmful inbreeding happened because too few stallions were used. Some mares were allowed to have about eight times their 'share' of offspring, which is bad enough, but some stallions, and this is what has made the stock so inbred, had had more than twenty times their share. Only about one in every four or five stallions ever breeds at all, a horrifying waste of genetic potential.

All that, the people at ISIS hope, is now in the past. Recognising the problems is a big step on the road to dealing with them successfully, and as the various

118

Species Survival Plans are implemented and experience is gained, the preservation of species in zoos should become easier and easier. But it is a dreadful irony that the easiest part of the ideal programme, technically speaking, is without doubt the hardest to implement, because it is socially unacceptable. The fact is simple; if we are to save species, we have to sacrifice individuals, and that means deliberately killing animals.

In the wild, death is a way of life. Animals succumb to other animal predators, they fall ill, they starve. What Charles Darwin called the 'checks to increase' keep numbers down, both by removing animals from the population and by ensuring that few animals survive beyond their reproductive prime. In captivity, most of the checks to population growth are removed. Animals are seldom preyed upon in zoos, although foxes and stoats do account for some. Schönbrunn's director once complained to me that one of his biggest problems was urban foxes. It doesn't much matter when a fox takes a couple of ducks or geese from a farmer, but when the geese are, say, rare red-breasted geese, the fox is more than a nuisance. Zoo animals do contract diseases, but veterinary science comes to their rescue and they are often nursed back to health. And, times of war and siege excepted, no zoo keeper is going to let his charges starve to death. The result is that zoo animals that are breeding, an ever-increasing proportion of the whole, threaten to overwhelm the capacity of zoos to support them. If we are to manage captive populations properly, then having removed all the natural checks and balances, we must replace them with artificial ones.

There are just two ways to regulate an animal population, prevention and removal. Prevention, which is essentially birth control whether it is achieved by physical separation, contraception or sterilisation, might seem morally to be the easier option, but there are good reasons why prevention alone is not the entire answer. First, even if the method is reversible, the reproductive condition of the animals may decline, so that when you want them to breed again they are less capable. Secondly, even the best-laid plans can go awry and random events – an epidemic perhaps, or an error in 'reversible' birth control – could destroy the breeding population. Finally, blocking reproduction can destabilise the breeding population. If birth control is effective no new animals join the breeding group, which gets inexorably older and less able to breed. It may even go extinct through old age, as happened with the wild swine population in American zoos, and is threatening to happen again with Siberian tigers.

Prevention, then, has a place in managing of populations, but it cannot be the only tool. A truly effective policy must include the removal of animals that are surplus to the breeding programme. In the early stages of a programme this might entail moving animals to other qualified zoos, and if a reintroduction programme is successful, then the surplus can be released to the wild. But under most circumstances removal of surplus animals means killing them.

Killing healthy animals is simply done, and is far less traumatic than a natural death. An overdose of drugs, a well-placed bullet, both can despatch an animal more quickly and with less pain than ever happens in nature. But because of the public's misplaced feelings killing surplus animals openly is almost impossible.

It is important to realise that surplus, in this context, does not mean that an animal will be killed because it is hard to manage, or less handsome, or for any other capricious reason. Animals will be surplus to a rational breeding pro-gramme if they are from bloodlines that are already over-represented in the population, or if they are too old to reproduce, or if they have already success-fully produced their share of offspring. And being surplus to a breeding pro-gramme is not what condemns an animal to death, it is only the harsh reality of limited resources that often makes euthanasia the only option.

As with so much else, an investment of more resources can help to alleviate the problem. Obviously if zoos could be expanded so that more animals could live in captivity, the number that would have to be killed would be lower, at least until the new expanded capacity has all been filled. Technology, too, could spare some animals by preserving genes as frozen eggs and sperm and thus freeing space for a greater number of living animals. But even these sol-utions would ultimately be useless. When the expanded zoo is full, more animals than before will need to be killed to keep populations under control. And while the frozen zoo may preserve living genes, the animals that bore those genes are no longer alive. Euthanasia is an inevitable and essential part of population management.

I hope I have convinced you that to save species requires us to sacrifice individuals. The question is why zoo directors have such a hard time implement-ing this essential part of good zoo management. Euthanasia goes on all the time, at all good zoos, but it is done on the quiet, as if there were something reprehensible about it. London Zoo, for example, in its annual report buries the figure for culling in a category that counts all animals 'disposed of . . . by presentation, exchange, deposit, sale . . . as well as culled animals and those killed by vermin or vandals'. In 1983 the total was 1514; of course not all of those were culled, but there is no way to find out how many were. That, I suppose, is why the cull is hidden in that column.

When the sheltered public does find out that euthanasia is going on, there is always a terrible brouhaha. In Detroit, in the autumn of 1982, three tigers were, in the overemotional language of one newspaper writer, 'sentenced to death'. A housewife, Krescentia Doppelberger, brought a $1 million suit against the zoo and succeeded in deferring the death of the animals. The zoo director, Dr Steve Graham, had explained that the tigers were old, with rotten gums and bad teeth, that one had a dislocated hip and was in so much pain that he used the wall of his cage as a crutch, that another had kidney and liver damage and vomited repeatedly, and that the third also had a bad hip problem. None of this counted with Mrs Doppelberger, who perversely seemed to think that because 'animals cannot speak for themselves' they can endure *more* pain.

An almost identical performance took place at Minnesota Zoo outside Minneapolis in March 1984. Again, tigers were due to be destroyed and again there was a public outcry. The worst of this is that Minnesota Zoo is the home of ISIS, which has done so much to explain the need for euthanasia to zoo directors. I find it a dreadful irony that Minnesota Zoo should be prey to the same irrational demands from the public.

London Zoo suffered appalling publicity over one of its elephants, Polé-Polé, who, after years of difficulty, was finally put down in October 1983 with an injection of the drug etorphine. Polé-Polé who as a calf starred in the film *An Elephant Called Slowly*, was a casualty of London Zoo's policy not to train animals. She was difficult to handle, neurotic and bad tempered, qualities that are obviously harder to manage in an elephant than in many other species, and the zoo had been criticised about her condition for many years. Rather than admit that it had failed with Polé-Polé, and that both would be better off without one another, the zoo stonewalled. After long delays it was decided to move her to Whipsnade, where she would enjoy more space and the company of other elephants, but when the time for the move came she sat down in her crate and could not be transported. She finally got up, but subsequently walked with a limp, and was anaesthetised to examine her leg. As the effects of the anaesthetic wore off it became clear that Polé-Polé refused to stand up again, which in a four-tonne animal is a disaster. She was therefore given an overdose of etorphine. In finally taking its responsibility for Polé-Polé's life seriously, London Zoo triggered a storm of protest and probably launched the protest movement that is currently trying to close all zoos in the UK. But the staff there still refuse openly to discuss the important role that euthanasia has in zoo management, judging that the public is ineducable in these matters.

In these three cases there were additional reasons beyond just the require-ments of a breeding programme that indicated that the animals in question should be killed. Not only was it probably the best for those individual animals, but it would also free resources in the institutions to care for the species as a whole. But the unobtrusive putting down of animals for the very good reason that they are surplus to needs will necessarily increase as zoos become better at breeding. The problem here, as identified by the professional associations of zoo people, is an uneducated public, but who should be responsible for educating the public?

In the course of my research I talked with scores of zoo directors, all of whom agreed that euthanasia was a valuable management tool. Chatting scientist to scientist, we were able to accept the necessity for controlling populations both by prevention and removal. But few of those zoo directors are willing to come out in the open and tell ordinary people, the ones who visit and support the zoo, why it is necessary. Nor would they allow us to help them by filming euthanasia being carried out. They are scared of the uneducated public, but refuse to contribute to the public's education. As long as this continues, muddled public outcry will thwart their efforts to preserve species.

We destroy millions of cats and dogs each year, not because they are surplus to planned survival programmes but because they are simply unwanted. Why should zoo animals be any different? Perhaps it is because they have names and personalities, a practice that many zoos are beginning to realise can backfire. Or perhaps the zoo animals are a sort of token to salve our consciences. We feel guilty about the way we treat animals, as food, as pets, and as objects of entertainment, but rather than improve our dealings with animals in general we reserve our loudest objections for the particular animals that, numerically, matter least – those in zoos.

The fact is that if we are serious about saving species then we have to accept euthanasia as an irreplaceable strategy in achieving that end. What is worse, there are bound to be more animals killed at the start of a rational breeding programme as we try and sort out the mess of previous efforts than later when all is working smoothly, and euthanasia is employed only to make up the small deficiencies of birth control. 'In the long run,' the American Association of Zoological Parks and Aquariums counsels its members, 'an honest and open approach to the problem, with assurances that euthanasia would be employed as the last resort, is in the best interest of zoos, the profession and, most importantly, the species.' Zoos could, in fact, take pride in the fact that they have to kill animals because it is a sign of success.

We have to decide. If we want zoos to be more than menageries, if we want them to harbour self-perpetuating collections of species, then we have to accept that individual animals are subjugate to the species as a whole. We give the species continued life, and to do so we must deprive certain individual animals of life. It is not a pleasant thing to do, but matters of life and death are seldom pleasant.

Chapter Five

# TECHNO-ZOO

**P**enguins, vast crowds of them. They fly beneath the water, twisting and turning and then bobbing up to float high like corks. They toboggan over on their bellies and stand on the ice next to me, the bolder ones tugging fearlessly at my jacket. Back in the water some are streaking along, leaping in and out in imitation of porpoises. From time to time, with no warning, one shoots vertically out of the water in front of me, landing on its feet and surveying the surroundings with disdain. Over on the rocks pairs are calling raucously together. The place is a riot of penguins. The air temperature is well below freezing and my breath forms little clouds in the air. The water in front of me is a chilly 7°C. Under my feet there is ice, and my nose is assailed by the stench of fish. I could be in the Antarctic, having the time of my life among the penguins; stately emperors and kings, hyperactive Adélies, rockhoppers hopping as they ought over the rocks, macaronis with their absurd crests, even a stray gentoo.

The list, however, gives the game away. Penguin experts would know that of the six species only Adélies and emperors are found together on the ice; the others avoid the Antarctic continent. So the scenery and atmosphere must be contrived, and this must be a collection of captive birds in a zoo. It is the Penguin Encounter at Sea World, an astonishing example of the way that technology enables us to do almost anything we like for animals, including creating an Antarctic exhibit in the year-round sunshine of San Diego.

The engineering and technological expertise that have gone into making penguins feel at home in San Diego is remarkable. The air is cooled to $-2.2°C$ and passes through filters that remove most of the bacteria which could be harmful to the birds. The exhibit covers 465 square metres, and each day 5000 kilograms of crushed ice are blown over the floor to create a suitable surface for the birds. The pool is 30 metres long, long enough to enable birds to get up the speed necessary to porpoise, and it extends beneath the ice shelf to give them plenty of swimming space. The 560,240 litres in the pool are completely filtered every 39 minutes, keeping the water clear despite bits of old fish and the penguins' best efforts to cloud it. The lighting mimics the Antarctic cycle, so that in the middle of the San Diego summer the lights inside are low, as they would be down south. It is a remarkable zoo cage.

On the other side of the glass things are no less impressive. A moving walkway transports the viewers past the penguins, giving them a view of the birds underwater and on the ice. As you approach the end of the walkway an insistently repeated 'Be prepared to walk!' ensures that you won't be too enthralled to move along. Behind the walkway is a darkened viewing area in which the visitor can sit and watch the inmates without being hurried on. And in case the living birds are boring there are TV screens everywhere, showing a selection of six-minute videos about aspects of penguin life.

At a cost of $7 million, I think that the Penguin Encounter is one of the most extraordinarily satisfying zoo exhibits anywhere. The reasons are not hard to find. The cage is aesthetically pleasing. It allows the birds to go through a whole repertoire of behaviour patterns that are fun to watch. It offers information if you want it. And the goal of giving Sea World a self-sustaining breeding colony of penguins is close to being achieved. Sea World bred the first ever emperor penguins to hatch in captivity, and the Adélies are doing very well there too.

Of course much of the Encounter's set dressing is just that, architectural touches that make the visitor feel good about the exhibit rather than provide necessary items for the birds. In fact, before the Encounter was built the penguins were content enough to breed in a gloomy refrigerated shed. But that is no reason not to include the human touches, and the result is an exhibit that not only pulls in the crowds – attendance was up 25 per cent in the three months after the Penguin Encounter opened – but gives those crowds an experience that they are unlikely to forget. And none of it would be possible without very advanced technology.

In this chapter I want to look at the way that human ingenuity has been applied to the problems of keeping animals in captivity. There are really two aspects to the techno-zoo, both of which can be encompassed by the phrase 'engineering for animals'. First there is the provision of a suitable environment both for the animals and their visitors. As I have said, the creation of a stage set very often goes beyond what the animals strictly need. I doubt, for example, that the penguins at San Diego are fooled by the painted mountains that adorn the rear wall, and they certainly don't need the whale bones that lie in the pool or the fibreglass icicles that fringe the water. They did perfectly well in the old freezer room. But people have moved beyond being satisfied by animals in bare cages, and prefer their subjects in a naturalistic environment. In this sense the Penguin Encounter is no more than the logical continuation of Carl Hagenbeck's pioneering work.

The other side of 'engineering for animals' concerns the performance they give on the stage we have created for them. I know of few sights more dispiriting than that of an animal looping through the same endless movement over and over again, filling a bare environment with its repeated tracks. It does not matter whether it is a patas monkey pacing up and down in Paris, or a polar bear going through the same sequence of loops in Lincoln Park, or a tiger ambling aimlessly in Bristol; stereotyped behaviour, as it is called, is a sign that all is not well. We recognise that, and, having been spoiled by television, we want to see our animals going through their normal behaviour patterns, something that they find hard to do in a sterile environment. Sometimes a decent set can inspire the actors in it, and giving animals a more natural environment evokes more natural behaviour. If not, there are things we can do to ensure that the animals are on their best behaviour.

Psychologists in their laboratories have spent a lot of time investigating a process called operant conditioning. It is a form of learning in which something the animal does is closely followed by the appearance of something the animal needs. This reinforcer, as it is called, has the effect of making it more likely that the animal will repeat whatever it was that it did in the future. I have made this description purposefully vague because the range of behaviour, or operants, and reinforcers is vast. The classic laboratory examples are the rat and pigeon at work in a Skinner box, an automatic operant conditioning device developed by B.F. Skinner at Harvard University. The rat will press a lever for a small pellet of food. The pigeon pecks a special panel to get access to grain.

Those are the simplest examples of what are called contingency schedules – one peck delivers a reward. Schedules can be made much more complex, so that, for example, the reward does not come every time. The animal has to repeat the behaviour several times to get the reward. Or the reward may only be available at certain times. If there is a signal that the reward is available the animal will learn to perform the behaviour only when the signal is on. If there is no signal it will try the behaviour from time to time just in case. Or things can be fixed so that the animal has to go through a whole chain of different behaviours in order finally to get the reward. Each link in the chain is itself a little reward and gets the animal to perform the next link. Operant conditioning is not restricted to simple rats in Skinner boxes; Skinner himself saw it as the basis of almost all learned behaviour, even outside the laboratory, saying that animals would do anything to get a reward or avoid a punishment. And, of course, those animals might just as well be in a zoo.

Animal trainers have long known about the power of rewards and punishments for shaping the behaviour of their charges, and this is something I will return to later. In zoos, however, it took a long time for people to realise that operant conditioning, otherwise called behavioural engineering, could be used deliberately to provide the animals with something to do and the visitors with something to watch. The strange and aberrant behaviour that so many animals use to beg for food from the public was almost certainly learned through an unwitting form of operant conditioning by the public; the animal does something cute so it gets a titbit, and learns to repeat the cute behaviour to get another. But operant conditioning can also be used to shape more natural behaviour. The man generally credited with starting this trend is Hal Markowitz, who at the time was assistant director of the zoo in Portland, Washington. He began with white-handed gibbons.

There were four white-handed gibbons at Portland, and they lived in a typical enclosure: concrete floor surrounded by wire mesh with haphazard bits of scaffolding for the animals to swing on. Their food was placed on the floor each day and about all the gibbons ever did was to descend to the floor to quibble over the choicest items. Gibbons in the wild are consummate aerialists, hurtling through the jungle canopy in a display of acrobatic ability that is second to none, but the ones at Portland were pretty lethargic. Mama, her infant Squirt and her older son Kahlil just sat around all day. The exception was the second juvenile, Harvey. He enjoyed swinging about in the cage, and when showing off would swing as many as seven times around a low bar before hurtling up 4.5 metres to another bar. On the way up he usually slapped the wall, which gained him the nickname Harvey Wallbanger.

Markowitz knew that the crowds far preferred the gibbons when Harvey was doing his thing. He also knew that gibbons frequently spend as much as 40 per cent of their day in the wild flying through the treetops in search of food. The problem was to engineer their behaviour so that they would be acrobatic in their home cage. The solution was a pair of operant stations, 7.5 metres apart and high up on the rear wall of the cage.

Each station comprised a globe with a light inside and a lever. One of the stations also had a chute through which a piece of food could be delivered. When the light came on at the first station a press on the lever would switch on the light at the second station and activate the lever there. A press on the second lever earned a piece of fruit. So to get the fruit the gibbon would have to travel between the two stations. All four gibbons learned to get food from the second station within two days. Teaching them to make the first response in the chain took a little longer, a few weeks, but they learned that too. Eventually Harvey, who had been the most athletic of the four to begin with, could complete the entire sequence, hurtling from wherever he was when the light came on to the first station, pressing the lever there, flying over to the second station and pressing the second lever to get his piece of fruit, all in under two seconds.

With the apparatus and the gibbons working well, Markowitz sat back to watch the behaviour and collect some data. The system was set up so that any animal could collect the reward just by being at the second station when the light came on. This had some interesting social consequences, because although Harvey was perfectly content to work for his mother, allowing her to take the

One of the first pieces of behavioural engineering, the gibbon cage at Portland Zoo. Harvey Wallbanger has just touched the lever with his foot

food that he had earned, he would do no such thing for his brother Kahlil. If Kahlil was at the feeding station when the signal light came on, Harvey would go to the first station but refrain from pulling the lever. He would wait until Kahlil moved at least halfway across the cage. Then he would pull the lever and the two would have a spectacular race to the food. To Markowitz's surprise, there was no fighting over the food; to the victor the spoils.

It is hard to convey the difference between the old exhibit and the new. Where once there had been lethargic gibbons there was now an entertaining display of acrobatics and intelligence. The gibbons were much more active and the public was staying in front of the gibbon cage for longer than before, both signs of an improvement. Markowitz then installed a coin-in-the-slot machine that would switch the apparatus on whenever someone deposited 10 cents. (The gibbons never had to wait more than two minutes for a piece of food. If nobody decided to contribute within two minutes of the previous trial the machine took over.) The public gave more than $3000 in dimes in the first year, money that went to further behavioural engineering projects.

As those projects were completed visitors to Portland Zoo were treated to other, even stranger exhibits of engineered behaviour. There were Diana monkeys that operated a token economy, working for plastic poker chips and then putting the chips into a vending machine to get food. Two polar bears learned to sing for their supper. When a tone sounded a bear would approach a little window and roar. A microphone and switch would activate a catapult that threw a fish into the bears' pool, and the bears would dive in to get it. Harbour seals, gibbons and orang-utans all solved discrimination tasks to get their food, by distinguishing left from right or light from dark. The exercise was not limited to food either; the orang-utans had a system that enabled them to turn on a shower when they wanted one.

Portland even offered a chance for the public to match their wits against the animals. A mandrill called Blue learned to play a speed game that required him to press a button as soon as the light behind it came on. There were three buttons on a panel inside his cage and an identical panel outside for the visitors. If a visitor chose to play he put a dime in the machine. The computer then illuminated one of the three buttons on both panels, one for the mandrill and one for his opponent. The first to press the button scored a point, and the first to reach three points won, the man a verbal reward, the mandrill a piece of food. Most often the monkey won. Visitors would respond to losing their first game with shock, concentrate hard only to lose the second game, and occasionally beat the monkey on a third game. In free competition the mandrill won seven out of ten games.

All this came to an end in 1977 when a new director came to Portland and halted all the behavioural engineering projects. He felt that these exhibits, although they gave the animals something to do, were unnatural and fostered the wrong impression in visitors. He claimed, too, that the animals sometimes responded inappropriately to the machinery, citing an instance in which one of the female mandrills presented herself for copulation to the speed-machine, thereby indicating that she perceived it as Blue's superior. In his defence Markowitz could point not only at the interest of animal and human in the apparatus but also at the beneficial effects of the behavioural engineering. The polar bears became less aggressive towards one another and the exercise that the male enjoyed made him noticeably healthier. Blue's interest in beating the public diverted him from harassing the females and their infants. All the animals whose behaviour had been engineered were said to be healthier. Other zoos had flattered Markowitz by imitating his techniques, but still they were halted at Portland.

Looking at the photographs that accompany Markowitz's reports one thing is striking. All the cages were horribly sterile, nothing but bare smooth concrete, fencing and bars. The behavioural enrichment started from a baseline of zero. From this perspective the artificiality of many of the behaviour routines that he chose to reward is understandable. Anything would be better than the cage as it was. Had the funds been available, Markowitz says, he would have preferred to build spacious naturalistic enclosures, but they weren't, and the behavioural apparatus was in his view a successful stopgap.

Some of the imitations Markowitz spawned at other zoos used exactly the same principles of operant conditioning but camouflaged the apparatus. At Chicago's Brookfield Zoo visitors saw a tiger gnawing at the carcass of a fibre-glass sambar deer. One of the deer's ribs was connected to a lever and when the tiger had moved the lever several times a meatball was delivered into the carcass. Brookfield's pumas were trained to stalk, pursue and capture simulated prey to give an impression of hunting. There were two sets of apparatus in the two puma cages, each slightly different but working on the same principles. To start the sequence the puma climbed out onto a rock ledge. The weight of its body on a panel started a timer. At the end of a random interval, which varied between five seconds and ten minutes, and during which time the puma had to stay still as if stalking, the timer released the prey. An artificial animal (an epoxy woodrat in one enclosure, a steel yellow-bellied marmot in the other) scuttled out of a pile of rocks and across the floor of the enclosure before vanishing again into the rocks. If the puma was successful and managed to catch the prey a chunk of ground horsemeat was dropped into the vicinity. What visitors saw was a very lifelike simulation of a hunt.

The effect of the disguised operant equipment at Brookfield is exactly the same as the gibbons swinging on their levers at Portland, but doesn't look so obviously artificial. Perhaps the major obstacle to the widespread acceptance of behavioural engineering by zoos was the question of apparatus. It was expensive, and it needed dedicated staff to keep it in working order. Further-more, the animals frequently surprised the researchers by discovering ways to get round the requirements of the machine. A kiwi in Chicago learned to block up a sensor hole with leaves instead of probing with its beak, thereby fooling the machine into coughing up an endless supply of worms. An elephant in Portland short-circuited its machine with water, again ensuring itself a better supply of rewards. Animals may be even smarter than we expect, as these instances show, but that is no help when their cleverness defeats our intentions.

For all these reasons there has been a trend away from straightforward operant conditioning and towards more naturalistic behavioural engineering that is part and parcel of the move to more naturalistic displays. Once again food is the primary motivation, but the approach nowadays is to provide it and allow the animal to run through its normal patterns of eating behaviour.

In Zurich the chimpanzees have a couple of very realistic-looking termite mounds in their enclosure. Ever since Jane Goodall published her despatches about life among the chimpanzees of Gombe Stream we have known that termites are an important part of the chimpanzee's diet. More interesting is the way they get the termites; they fish for them, using specially constructed tools. A thin pliant twig will be brought to the mound if there are none nearby and carefully stripped of its leaves. The chimp then finds one of the flight holes buried beneath the surface of the mound and exposes it. She inserts the twig and deftly twiddles it round, then waits a while before pulling it out, now loaded with termites. She tugs the twig across her lips to remove the tasty and nourishing insects and carries on fishing.

This is a marvellous piece of natural behaviour, one that demonstrates the intelligence and dexterity of our closest relatives, and apparently all that is needed to elicit it is a mound full of termites and a supply of twigs. Unfortunately, as one insect breeder told me, it would be harder to set up a self-sustaining colony of termites than chimpanzees. So the mound at Zurich is loaded with various kinds of sloppy foods, yoghurt and honey, mashed fruit, porridge and so on. The chimps still prepare their fishing rods, and poke them through the

Chimps fishing for food at their 'termite mound' in Edinburgh Zoo

holes in the mound to the cups below, and suck off the food, but the food is not termites. It certainly keeps them occupied, but more than that, this innovative display, based on a very simple structure, gives the public an opportunity to see chimps at their finest, doing something that they excel at, rather than sitting around morosely.

The bear pit at Copenhagen Zoo doesn't look all that extraordinary, a large enclosure with three shambling brown bears and a couple of artificial trees. But like the chimp termite mounds, the trees hold a secret. Buried within them is a thin plastic tube which runs underground to a back room where there is a pump and a reservoir of honey. At random times during the day the pump starts up, forcing honey through the tubes so that it dribbles out of the top of the tree. As soon as they hear the pump begin to whine the bears are over at the trees. They climb up and spend a considerable time delving in them and licking their honey-smeared paws. Again, it gives the bears something to do and the visitors something to watch, and all for the sake of a little extra equipment.

In Antwerp the equipment is slightly more complicated. A multi-chambered barrel reminded me of a gatling gun, and for good reason. Each of the chambers can be loaded with a live cricket which is then blown by a puff of air into the cage below. Some of the crickets are fed to lizards, but in one cage is a fennec fox, its huge ears designed to detect the smallest squeak. If the fox is hungry, and the cricket chirps, it won't be long before visitors are treated to a display of superb hunting skill. The fennec fox swivels its head, listening intently, and stalks towards the cricket. It pounces in a flash and contentedly gobbles its prey. Like the honey pump, the cricket gun is on a random schedule so that, just as in life, the fennec fox never knows when the next cricket will appear. It can hunt if it wants to, or it can ignore the cricket. Either way, it is able to express itself through natural behaviour.

These three examples each requires some apparatus, but for many animals all that is needed to elicit interesting behaviour is the right kind of food. Given a dish of completely nutritious but otherwise uninteresting food, most animals will eat it and sit back. But many species have specially developed behaviour patterns designed to obtain them their meals in the wild, and providing them with the right food will unlock the behaviour.

Sea otters can be fed on frozen fish, but at Seattle Aquarium and Point Defiance Zoo in nearby Tacoma a bucket of clams makes a far better display. The clams are dumped into the water and immediately sink to the bottom, where there is also a heap of stones. The sea otter dives, trailing silvery bubbles, and picks up a stone and a supply of clams. Back at the surface it floats on its back, the stone resting on its belly as an anvil. Then, turning its face away to avoid the splashes, it smashes the shells down on the rock, pausing briefly to gobble up the clam inside before moving on to the next one. It doesn't bother to discard the broken clam shells, which soon litter its furry tummy, but when

Antwerp Zoo's locust gun provides live food for animals such as the fennec fox. Sea otters at Seattle Aquarium need neither technology nor training to provide an entertaining performance, just a bucket of clams and a supply of stones. A mongoose at Basle prepares to break an egg; again, the right food produces completely natural behaviour

there really isn't enough space left the otter grabs hold of its stone and the remaining unopened clams, and does a neat roll. The clam shells fall off and flutter down to the bottom and the otter resumes its meal. It is a delightful sight, easily accomplished as long as the zoo has a supply of clams.

Breaking things to get at the food within is the basis of another superb display, this time at Basle in Switzerland. The colony of mongooses there is always interesting because they are extremely social animals and something is always going on among them. But an occasional egg makes all the difference. The mongoose has a special way of cracking an egg. He grabs it with his front paws and backs up towards a hard surface – the wall of the enclosure, or a handy rock. Then he lifts his back legs in a little leap and hurls the egg backwards between them, rather as in a rugby scrum. With luck, the egg will break and he can enjoy the contents. But it is a frustrating business; sometimes he loses his grip at a crucial point, or the egg doesn't crack, and he has to repeat the process several times before he gets what he is after, much to our delight.

It isn't surprising that food is so important in promoting natural behaviour among zoo animals. In the wild by far the greater part of most animals' time is spent either finding a meal or avoiding becoming one. Making them work for their food is, then, only natural. But where is one to draw the line? The public has no objection to vegetarians being made to work for their food, and a handful of grain scattered in the gorillas' straw provides them with something to look for all day. Many of the best primate exhibits include this kind of provisioning, not as an important part of the diet but as a source of stimulation.

With carnivores things become a little more difficult. Zoos that feed their snakes on chicks or mice, even dead ones, tend to do so out of hours rather than risk offending visitors, but we don't seem to mind otters being given live clams, or fennec foxes crickets. In Toronto the fennec foxes live next door to a very prolific colony of spiny mice. Keepers have to remove individual mice from the colony to prevent overcrowding. How nice it would be, the director told me, if he could drill a little hole in the wall so that the occasional spiny mouse would find its way into the fennec foxes' enclosure – but the public wouldn't like it. As far as live food goes we seem to care only about warm-blooded creatures. Nobody minds the fisher cats at Brookfield being given the opportunity to practise their skills on some minnows, but apparently we wouldn't like to see a serval cat make its spectacular leap to catch a little quail in mid air.

I think that is a pity, the result of misplaced sentimentality. We regard it as cruel to let animals live and die as they do in the wild, but nevertheless keep them in captivity. We are prepared to watch wild animals hunting on television, but not in the zoo. Why not go all the way and allow some of the big carnivores to exhibit their natural behaviour? I can think of few finer sights than that of a cheetah at full tilt after a gazelle, so why not let me see it in Regent's Park or Whipsnade?

Giving animals food to elicit interesting behaviour needs no obvious training; the animals simply get on with it. Training, however, can be very important in helping the keepers to give the animals the care they need. Nobody wants all zoo animals to be completely tame, but it is useful if animals are willing to co-operate with the keepers, especially when the animal is as big as an elephant. The way to achieve that is through training. The animal is taught that if it does something – for example lifts up a leg, or even just stands still – it will get a treat. This enables veterinarians to conduct routine examinations and minor procedures without having to run the risk of anaesthesia. Elephants will stand still and obligingly lift up a leg for their toenails to be trimmed, and at Windsor Safari Park the killer whale would even come to the side of the pool and lift her tail fluke out of the water so that the vet could take a blood sample.

The elephants at Hamburg Zoo have been trained to lay on a very special session. Most afternoons they and their keepers line up at the edge of their large enclosure. On the other side of the moat, just a trunk's reach away, are crowds of visitors who are invited to feed the elephants. Although it is stressed that fruit and veg are preferred to cakes and sweets, by the staff if not by the elephants, some people will always try and give them something inedible, like a coin. The elephants have been cleverly trained to discriminate coins from comestibles. They take both, but whereas they guzzle anything edible, the coins they pass to the keeper. He sometimes trades a peanut for it, which keeps the elephant interested in giving up the coins. The public are able to enjoy the feel of an elephant's trunk, and the elephants are protected from objects that might harm them.

A killer whale co-operates in having a blood sample taken

For a time this kind of training was considered wrong. Trained animals were degraded, just as chimps at tea parties were degraded. To an extent this is true, particularly if the training is capricious and inappropriate; I certainly don't like to see animals being cute for food rewards. But with animals like elephants, training is essential. As we have seen, one victim of the anti-training fad was Polé-Polé. She was a product of the permissive sixties, when elephants, too were encouraged to do their own thing. Her thing was to be mean and unpredictable, and in the end she was uncontrollable. London Zoo has now changed its attitude again and the new baby Indian elephant, Dilberta, is being carefully trained to improve her relationship with her keepers and the public.

The other side of training, which I have already touched upon, is training animals to give a show. This is distinct from the continuous show that animals will provide if they have a rich environment to behave in, and should be seen as a specific performance. The trend, as I discussed in Chapter Two, is away from frivolous and demeaning animal acts towards providing vehicles that allow the animals to demonstrate their natural talents. These shows are not as common as I think they should be, because they take time and money and need dedicated staff, but an interesting mixture of the old and the new is provided by the trained bird show at San Diego's Wild Animal Park. There they show talking parrots, a vestige of the old kind of animal act, and free-flying hawks, old in the context of man's relationship with animals, but new in a zoo.

The bird show begins with a flutter of fancy tumbling pigeons, falling through the sky in a display of aerobatics. Then the various parrots, who talk to their trainers and one another and even sing. The star is Poncho, who manages a fair rendition of such old favourites as 'I Left My Heart In San Francisco'. A rose-breasted cockatoo flutters through hoops on command, introducing another rose-breasted cockatoo that is in a cage below a helium balloon 150 metres above the arena. The trainer selects a volunteer from the crowd and asks him to hold a folded dollar bill in an outstretched hand. Beneath the balloon a door swings open and out steps Rosie. She flutters down, slipping from side to side like an autumn leaf, takes a look around the arena, spies her target and flaps up to the volunteer's arm. She gently takes the dollar bill and returns with it to her trainer, Sonny, who gives a short talk about cockatoos and how to train them before Rosie returns the money to the volunteer and flies back to her home cage.

So far the show has been interesting and the birds clever. It is not, however, what you might call spectacular. But still left in the balloon gondola are two birds of prey, a red-tailed hawk and a Harris hawk. Both are magnificent hunters, capable of going into a powered dive and pulling up at the last moment to catch their prey. First to go is the red-tailed hawk. Sonny has said that the hawk will fly to her fist. Those of us with binoculars raise them to the balloon, where we see a second door flap open. Nothing happens for a while, then we see the hawk standing at the edge. After a slight delay she steps out and spreads her wings into a glide. She slips about up there, effortlessly keeping her height in the breeze that blows up the valley while she gets into position. Hovering almost motionless, it seems that something has gone wrong. She is going to fly off. But glancing down at Sonny, I noticed her raise her gloved fist high. The hawk has seen this signal, and only now prepares to dive. She hunches her left shoulder forward, tucking the wing behind. Then the right wing is folded back, and finally she seems to draw her neck in as she tilts down into the dive. It all seems to take place in slow motion, as if the hawk is trapped in treacle. Scant seconds later, though, she has pulled out of her 160-kilometre-an-hour stoop to alight gently on Sonny's upraised fist.

Next it is the turn of the Harris hawk. We have been told that this bird will catch its prey in mid-air, barely pausing to pull out of the stoop. Those who haven't seen the show before are sceptical, those who have are smugly antici-patory. The door opens and out steps the hawk. It glides for a moment, getting into position downwind of the arena. Then it folds its wings and begins to plummet in a very steep dive. As the hawk hurtles earthwards a trainer hidden in the rocks behind the arena throws a leather lure out above the crowd. The hawk adjusts its path fractionally and is now falling straight at the centre of the crowd. At what seems like the last possible moment it brakes, extends its claws, and snatches the lure from the air, flying back to the trainer for a morsel of meat and rapturous applause.

Something few people ever see in the wild, a hawk stooping, has been demon-strated twice to order, and will be repeated three times a day. One hopes, after all the hidden effort that goes into creating a show like this, that the audience will leave with a slightly better appreciation of the animals they have seen.

A trained hawk comes in, part of the bird show at San Diego Wild Animal Park

Sometimes, though, there is no need to teach the animals any tricks, nor provide them with any special equipment, in order to achieve a fantastic display. For very sociable animals all that is needed is a fairly interesting enclosure that is large enough to let them get on with their everyday lives. Their companions are the most rewarding and challenging environmental enrichment they are ever likely to come across, and to stand back and watch a well-adjusted social group going about its business can be enormously satisfying. The finest example of such an enclosure I know of looks out across sail-studded waters to the Sydney Opera House and Harbour Bridge. Of all zoos, Sydney's Taronga does chimps best, and all it takes is space.

The enclosure is big, about 90 metres long and 30 metres wide, sloping down from a high red-brick wall around three sides to a moat in front. It is planted with grass, and a stream runs down to the moat, where fish swim and papyrus grows. To one side are rock outcrops, some real and some fake with doors let into them. A tangle of dead branches sits by the side of the stream but over on the other side of the enclosure are live palms and upright dead trees for climbing in. You can spy on the chimps from any of three glassed-in viewing areas, one high above them in a corner, the other two lower down nearer the front. Or you can stand along the moat. This is the only bad aspect of the design, that as a visitor you can always see hordes of other visitors, but it is unavoidable because it also gives the chimps one of the finest views in the world, out across Sydney Harbour.

Once you have feasted your own eyes on the harbour below, and turned them to the chimps, you see a wonderful display of animal behaviour. Trying to count them I came up with three different figures; seventeen, eighteen and then finally the correct number, twenty. There are many juveniles, perhaps five, who were going in for a great deal of play, rolling around together on the grass and then taking off for a game of follow my leader through the tangle of branches. As they settled down for the day after the exuberance of being released they formed little family groups, quietly grooming one another, the mothers nursing their infants. Food is scattered throughout the enclosure and from time to time one of the chimps wanders purposefully along looking for something to eat. A little one approached the glass of a viewing area and began to play with his reflection. I thought he might be hamming it up for the crowds, but in fact the area was empty and he was just having fun. Everywhere I looked the impression was of a cohesive social group doing what chimps do in the wild. There was no sign of any abnormal behaviour at all, so common in captive primates, save for one old grey matriarch who sat hugging herself by the stream. She was old and set in her ways, the zoo staff told me, and had never really adjusted to the bustle of social life or the wide open spaces of the new enclosure. Elsewhere, everything was pleasingly normal.

The chimp enclosure at Taronga is a good exhibit because it allows an extremely sociable animal the freedom and space to relate with lots of companions, but it looks nothing like the natural habitat of chimps in Africa. Other exhibits strive mightily for complete accuracy, down to copying specific bits of natural rock in fibreglass. I have mentioned before the setting of the stage on which the animals perform, and how the set can encourage the actors. I want to return to this now, and ask for whose benefit the new exhibits are constructed.

To an animal such as an orang-utan it surely does not matter what the 'trees' in its cage are made from, as long as they give it ample opportunity for exercise, encouraging it to climb, swing and stretch as it does in the wild. From the point of view of function there is no difference between the stainless-steel scaffolding that makes up the jungle gym in Stuttgart and the lifelike reinforced concrete trees of Topeka Zoo in Kansas. Indeed, the stainess-steel tubes are in one sense better because they are easier to clean and are stronger. (Topeka Zoo's director Gary Clarke was mortified when, on the day he opened his new orang-utan house, complete with concrete trees, Djakarta Jim, the big male, strode over to a branch and bent it like a straw. The branch was of 15-centimetre-thick concrete around a core of reinforcing rods.) In most cases the design element must be for ourselves, not the inmates.

That this should be so is not hard to understand. Education, in the broadest sense, has given people a different attitude towards animals. They have witnessed the intimate details of animals' lives as portrayed in wildlife documentaries on the television screen and so are not content with bare cages, even with big bare cages. Hagenbeck's park was first and foremost a pleasant place for people, and it is Hagenbeck's vision, aided by new technologies, that is finally sweeping through all zoos today.

One of the more interesting developments is an extension of Hagenbeck's ideas about the line of sight. In Hamburg, the exhibits are arranged so that the effect of many species living together is best appreciated from one place and by looking in one direction. Cast your eye about and you will see lots of other visitors, which tends to destroy somewhat the illusion the exhibit is trying to create. The new architects of zoo design have taken this principle still further, by enclosing the people within very specific viewing areas so that as they look out they see the animals and scenery, but not other people.

For some reason the zoos along the Pacific north-west of America are leading exponents of this type of exhibit. The savannah exhibit at Woodland Park Zoo in Seattle is a prime example. The site is gently rounded, which means that as you look out over it you see a horizon but not the other side of the exhibit. So you are oblivious to visitors on that side. Different species mingle on the savannah, giraffes, zebras and springbok graze among secretary birds, crowned cranes and guinea fowl. An enclosure within the enclosure houses a troop of patas monkeys. To one side are hippopotamuses, with the rest of the savannah as a backdrop, and, in their own separate enclosure, a pride of lions.

Viewing is restricted to a few areas, where there are also explanatory signs.

Elsewhere at Seattle is evidence that you do not need to start from scratch to achieve an excellent display. From three old bear pits Woodland Park has made the largest naturalistic exhibition for gorillas in the world, a valley with running water, tall grass, and huge trees. Like Taronga's chimp enclosure, it provides enough space and vegetation for the gorillas to relax and interact with each other, rather than worry about the public.

The vegetation is lush, quite like the gorillas' home in the lowland forests of Zaïre, and offers the inmates many opportunities to vanish from view. That may frustrate some visitors, but it delights the rest, who have learned to take their time to observe the new zoo exhibits. The stream running through the converted pit has bridges across it, and these often attract Kiki, the young male. He is subordinate to Pete, the big silverback, and spends a lot of his time down by the water's edge gazing at the reflections. Nina, a pregnant female, tends to sit in the warmth of a shelter opposite a glassed-in viewing area. The people there have a good view of her bulging belly, but they cannot see the other visitors who are hidden at another outlook. Pete has not yet adjusted fully to his new surroundings and trails a burlap sack around with him for security, and little Binti, a new female on loan from San Diego, keeps to herself on the edge of the enclosure. As in Taronga, the troop seems enviably normal.

Down the road from Seattle, in Tacoma, is Point Defiance Zoo. In a revitalisation programme that started in 1977 this little zoo is rapidly becoming one of the most realistic zoos anywhere. The sea otters diving for clams are one example. Close by is an exhibit of alcids, the northern diving birds that fill the same niche in the northern hemisphere as penguins do in the south. It is astonishingly lifelike. The rocks are made of gunite, a concrete-like substance, pressed into moulds taken from real rocks where real alcids live. Nothing is left to chance, not even the streaks of artificial guano carefully placed on the artificial rocks. The walruses and seals at Tacoma also live in richly landscaped environments that contain water as an integrated feature, rather than in blue concrete swimming pools that contain nothing but water. But the pride of Point Defiance is its polar bears.

Visible only from two enclosed viewing areas, the spectacle is breathtaking. These areas contain a range of interpretative material to prepare you for the exhibit; a recording of an arctic wind plays endlessly to put you in the right frame of mind as you walk past the tapestry of an upstretched bear on the wall, which gives some idea of the size of these beasts. As you approach the viewing window you see a sloping hillside covered with firs, gently steaming after the recent rain. A stream curves through a meadow and on to a little gravel beach which in turn leads into a deep pool. To the left of the beach is a cliff, and further on round the pool another beach. And in the middle of this landscape, three glorious shaggy white polar bears.

They growl, they leap from the cliff into the water, they bat one another round the head playfully. They swim up to the window to see who is watching them, their shiny fur undulating gently underwater. They chase after fish thrown in by the keeper, roll on the grass, have a good time. Again, the most noticeable thing is that there is none of the repetitious stereotyped behaviour so common in polar bears elsewhere. Polar bears can be a very distressing sight as they ritually perform the same movements over and over again, but not here. These bears seem to me to be behaving normally, and it is hard to escape from the impression that they appreciate the scenery as much as we do. There are good polar bear exhibits elsewhere, of course, but what they lack is Tacoma's setting. It is the landscape that makes the exhibit, but while the firs and grass are real everything else – the stream, the cliffs, the view – is artificial, made of concrete and cunning.

Elsewhere in North America there is an exhibit where all the techniques of zoo design have been brought together to create a place that is unlike anything the zoo world has seen before. It is a place that shows the depth of one zoo's commitment to providing an experience that is as natural as artifice can make it, and it is a place best visited in the dead of winter. Chicago, on the shores of Lake Michigan, deserves its nickname of the Windy City. Snow blankets the ground and icy blasts freeze your face, but if you venture out to Brookfield Zoo you will be transported from the depths of a Midwest winter to somewhere altogether more pleasant.

From the outside there is nothing remarkable to see, a vast aircraft hangar of a building looming over the snow beneath a galvanised sky. Step through the automatic doors, however, and you are in Africa. In front of you is a crude hut, home of the anti-poaching squad, filled with confiscated trophies and yellowing clippings that tell of the threat of illicit hunting. The hut is a nice reminder that while man can by his ingenuity save animals, it is also as a result of his ingenuity that they need saving. Go through a beaded rope curtain, and the view is astonishing. Fully 60 metres away a waterfall thunders out of the cliffs, tumbling down to a broad stream 12 metres below. Leaves and fallen logs litter the ground, and thick bushes grow in profusion. Bare trees stretch 20 metres to the blue-painted sky, and ahead runs what looks like a dirt track. Over in the distance is a rickety suspension bridge, and behind it more giant trees and a bamboo forest. As a backdrop to the whole scene are gaunt sandstone cliffs, rimmed with a profusion of plants.

In the trees sits a group of seven black-and-white colobus monkeys, thoughtfully chewing on pieces of green vegetation they have brought up from the ground, gazing around at their magnificent cage. Sharing the trees with them are little talapoins, spot-nosed monkeys and sooty mangabeys. Down on the ground a troop of mandrills forgathers, the male with his absurdly colourful face and posterior. Kolb's monkeys, their white ruffs a frame for their delicate faces, harass the mandrill, who although he is much bigger than them allows himself to be chivied into a corner. In a pool off the main stream floats a pygmy hippo, and scattered through the foliage are birds: weavers, orioles, white-eyes and finches. Perched on the railings are hadada ibises, magnificent glossy birds that, being hand-tame, will approach visitors and demand to be tickled.

Up the path, bounded on one side by the suspension bridge, which is not nearly as rickety as it looks, and on the other by cliffs, is the gorilla enclosure. It is, quite simply, magnificent. Samson, the 200-kilogram male silverback, used to live in a barred cage that measured 5 metres by 5 metres. Now he has the free run of about 20 metres by 20 metres, not to mention 15 metres up and down, complete with rocks, trees, vines and water. There are lookout posts, from which he can glower at visitors just 3 metres away on the bridge, and hiding holes for when he feels shy. He has become much fitter as a result of having to climb around the exhibit, which has few entirely flat surfaces, and presents a stirring sight. Sharing the enclosure with him are two females, Babs and Alpha, each of whom is bringing up an infant.

The gorillas' enclosure is, I think, the finest in the world, catering as it does both to the animals and their visitors. There are plenty of places to sit quietly and watch, and although one may not have quite the thrill of seeing gorillas in the wilds of Rwanda, one is privileged to watch a troop behaving very normally indeed. Because their environment, including one another, is so interesting, the gorillas all but ignore the visitors, the occasional exception being when Samson chooses to glare across the divide. They go through their daily routine quietly and with a measured confidence, each showing his or her own character. In just half an hour or so I was able to distinguish Babs, the younger of the two females, from Alpha, her mother, simply by the way she behaved. Babs was shyer, less confident, and tended to keep her baby close at hand. Alpha was more open and allowed her infant, who was younger than Babs's, a freer hand. Watching them feed, groom, simply sit quietly together, it was hard to avoid the impression that they were happier now than they had ever been before. I was certainly happier than I have ever been in the presence of captive gorillas.

Africa is part of Tropic World, built by Brookfield Zoo to give visitors a 'total immersion' in the world of the rain forest. The animals are real enough, and so is the water flowing through the enclosure. Some of the plants, the ones out of reach of the animals and close to the visitors, are genuine too. But all the rest is man-made.

The rocks are gunite, sprayed onto a framework and painted to resemble the real thing. The trees have concrete bases, but the tops of the taller trees are made of lightweight epoxy. The leaves that litter the forest floor have been painted on, and the bushes are made of stainless steel with each leaf welded in place. The smaller monkeys scurry up and down very lifelike vines that depend from the trees, and these too are not real. They are made of rope dipped in epoxy resin and twisted, with a coating of sand to discourage chewing. The fallen logs are concrete too, and if you look closely you will see that they form the limits of the hippo's pool, preventing her from straying round the exhibit but allowing the monkeys in to steal her hay and generally annoy her. The effect, from the moment you step through the beaded curtain, is wondrous.

Tropic World is the largest indoor exhibit in the world, a very important consideration, given Chicago's appalling weather. Africa is just one section, the first to be opened; Asia is now also open and South America due to be ready in time for the zoo's fiftieth birthday in May 1984. The intention from the start has been to cater for all three interested parties – animals, visitors, and the zoo itself – so that each gets the maximum benefit.

The animals come first, with the zoo director's belief that the most natural setting possible will encourage natural behaviour which in turn will encourage the animals to reproduce. Not surprisingly, it took a little while for primates that had previously been confined to cages 3 metres cubed to get used to the space and complexity of an exhibit that offers them nearly 150,000 cubic metres to explore. At first they were ill able to judge distances, and the little spot monkeys often fell, fortunately not hurting themselves, as they learned to leap around the exhibit. There were even occasions on which the monkeys tried to walk on the water, never having seen a pool before, but that is all over now and the exhibit provides a magnificent opportunity for the animals to exercise and explore. Some of their methods may be a little unconventional – using the steel branches of the bushes as springboards, for example – but despite this the inmates are doing very well. They are breeding, but an unusual measure of how content they are is their reluctance to leave the exhibit at night. Each species has been trained to associate a particular whistle with food. They ought to come when the whistle blows, but they don't, and sometimes have to be gently moved along with a high-pressure hose.

Next come the visitors, most of whom will never get to see a genuine tropical rain forest. By giving them this kind of experience, zoo director George Rabb hopes to enhance their appreciation of these precious areas of the earth: the people who visit Tropic World will go away with a better understanding of our dependence on rain forest and so will in the end help to conserve it. It is a sentiment with which His Royal Highness the Duke of Edinburgh certainly agrees. After visiting the zoo in his capacity as President of the World Wildlife Fund International he said that it was 'through exhibits such as Tropic World that people in metropolitan areas such as Chicago will be able to relate to what we're losing in rain forests'. That may ultimately be true. In the meantime the visitor appeal of Tropic World is such that 200,000 people a month pass through its doors. They are learning to stay longer, to be still and watch the animals, and to absorb the atmosphere so lovingly created for them.

The final element in the equation is the zoo itself. Rabb is clear that zoos have a crucial role in the long-term survival of a huge number of species. Tropic World was conceived as a way of using the zoo's space and facilities to create viable breeding groups of animals and at the same time provide for the more effective education of the visitors, nudging them towards conservation, by offering them the opportunity to immerse themselves in the exhibit rather than simply see the animals from afar. Ludicrous though it may seem, a tropical exhibit, with its enormous heating bills, was a good way to extend the appeal of the zoo so that people would come all year round. There are few nicer places to be on a bleak Chicago winter's day than in the calm warmth of Tropic World.

The most astonishing aspect of Africa, and the rest of Tropic World, is the attention to detail. Following the path round the big enclosures you might notice tracks set into the gunite. Most obvious are the jeep tracks, evidence of man's encroachment on the environment. This is a consistent theme in Tropic World, represented by a rice paddy in Asia and a logging camp in South America. But look more closely and you will see animal spoor. A leopard pads up to a small waterfall, pauses at the edge of the pool for a drink, and then scratches the earth to scent mark his territory. Baboon prints also litter the mud around the waterhole, and further on up the track the prints of the gorillas mark the path. Getting those prints was no picnic, according to the zoo's director of planning, Paul Joslin. He told me how they set out a pan of clay between two cages and then used food to entice Omega, a 200-kilogram male, to walk through it. On his first approach he effortlessly crumpled the pan. The second time he left a lovely set of prints, but just as designers and keepers were beginning to congratulate themselves, he turned round and erased the impressions, almost as if to spite them. Finally they got their tracks, and these now cross the path by the side of the gorilla enclosure. It is these little touches that make a visit to Africa so rewarding.

I cannot praise Tropic World too highly. It has cost something like $10 million to build, but that is not such a great price to pay for such a stimulating exhibit. Every major zoo could have something like it, and many are indeed building similar exhibits that offer an experience of wildlife rather than a look at it. Cynics may say that captivity is still captivity, that no matter how you pretty it up a gaol is still a gaol. They are right, but they miss an important point by insisting on talking about captivity. Zoos are the only hope for many species, which are therefore inevitably captive. But if an animal can go through its normal behavioural repertoire as a result of the zoo's efforts then it is leading as normal a life as possible, and it is up to the zoo to do whatever it can to provide that normalcy.

Zoos also have an important educational role to play. For people who will never experience nature in the wild a cunning simulation is an excellent reminder of what we all might lose forever. By spending money on this sort of hi-tech exhibit, zoos exercise a kind of leverage, such that the amount invested in Tropic World will be multiplied many times in terms of genuine conservation. That is why technology in the service of animal display is so valuable, not just because it allows penguins to breed in California and gorillas to do likewise in Chicago, but because it allows people to share the animals' world.

It is easy to stay in Tropic World for a long time, once you have accepted the fact that there is more to be seen than the bare flesh and blood of the animal itself. But even when you've been there an hour or more, and observed almost all the behaviour, and learned something of the hierarchies both among species and between species, Tropic World still has some surprises. A low distant rumble sounds faintly familiar, like an approaching thunderstorm. It *is* an approaching thunderstorm, recorded in the jungles of equatorial Africa by George Rabb. The thunder comes nearer, and the animals begin to react. The gorillas saunter down to shelter below the bridge. The colobus leap from treetop to treetop in a blur of black and white, finally settling beneath an overhang in the cliff. The mandrills and mangabeys wander to shelter too, and so do the Kolb's monkeys. Only the little talapoins and spot-nosed monkeys stay out, climbing to the tops of the trees and sitting there looking very pleased with themselves, because normally the bigger monkeys keep them away from these choice sites.

There is a sudden very loud crash, and it begins to rain, a torrential downpour gushing forth from sprinklers set almost invisibly in the ceiling. Visitors unfortunate enough to be on a little sidepath in front of the monkeys get drenched, a deliberate feature of the storm, for otherwise the rain falls only on the exhibits and not on the paths. It rains for two minutes, the little monkeys in the trees apparently enjoying their exposure, and then stops as the thunder dies away again. The air is sweet and clear, and the animals emerge to resume their natural existence. It is a glorious piece of showmanship, a fitting climax to a superb exhibit.

The worst of the zoo world, a lone macaque in a cage that really is a cell. *Overleaf* the best of the new, Sea World's Penguin Encounter, the Antarctic in San Diego

A serval cat hunting, a cheetah at full tilt, two examples of natural behaviour you could not see in zoos today. But why not?

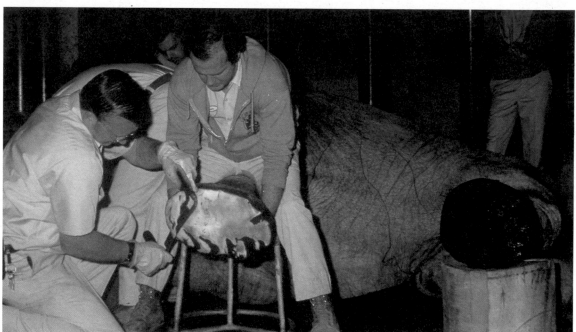

Training allows the elephants at Hamburg to separate harmful coins from choice tidbits.
A trained elephant is also more manageable, like the one above which is having its feet attended
to. The honey tree (*right*) at Copenhagen Zoo gives bears and visitors alike a treat at intervals
through the day

Sydney's chimpanzee enclosure. All you need is space

Technology failed: Djakarta Jim (*top right*) and the concrete branch he broke at Topeka.
*Above and right* the gorillas at Woodland Park in Seattle live in renovated bear pits

Tacoma's polar bears, perhaps the best single species exhibit in the world.
Tropic World in Chicago is a bold attempt to recreate the rain forest experience, and it works

# Chapter Six

# ON SAFARI

**O**utside São Paulo in Brazil, at the Simba Safari Park, a man stops his car 5 metres from a group of lions. He gets out and starts checking an engine that hitherto had been working perfectly. Machismo gone mad. In Florida, at Jungle Larry's Safari Park, a family of lions gorges on a side of beef, watched closely by a family of humans gorging on ice-cream. Conspicuous consumption. In England, within sight of a lovely stately home, a baboon playfully rips the aerial from a car. The aristocracy and its passion for animals. All are seeking to recreate the safari experience, and all are failing. How can they match the snow-capped cone of a volcano towering over big game and a specially laid-on exhibit of genuine Masai dancing? But wait, even that is fake. This mountain is Fuji, not Kilimanjaro, and we are outside Tokyo, not Nairobi. A safari park again.

Almost all cities now seem to have a wildlife or safari park nearby. The one I'm going to take you to is no exception. You get there by driving out of town on one of the main roads, a well-made highway that curls gently up the hills outside town. Past the busy private airport with its hangars and discarded hulks of burned out helicopters, past large housing estates, areas of which are still under construction. On the left as we drive is a military base with the high-wire fence and drab buildings of military bases world-wide. Then we turn off the road, through a grove of eucalypts, and we are at the front gate of the park.

It is an imposing gate, the black silhouette of a lion guarding the thick bars, set into an imposing gatehouse, with high red-tiled roof and lower buildings stretching away on both sides. Facing the gate is a ticket booth. A uniformed guard collects our entrance money and returns with a stamped permit and valid ticket. We can go in. Once through the gates, we quickly leave the neatly trimmed lawn with its ornamental shrubs behind and are soon in quite thick bush. The tunes of a military band on the base are carried incongruously to us on the breeze. Before we have gone too far we spot our first animals, a bachelor herd of impala with their elegant lyre horns. They aren't too scared, but make their way slowly off between the bushes. Some ostriches stand warily by the roadside, and a family of warthogs trots towards us with a purposeful air. We even see a lioness walking through the grass beside us. She is alone, and calls repeatedly, perhaps to find the rest of her pride. We count ourselves very lucky that she crosses the dirt road just a few yards ahead of us.

A little further on, in a valley with a stream and trees along the bottom, there are giraffes. Looking beyond the animals I see, somewhat disconcertingly, the outlines of city skyscrapers. To one side is the flash of the drive-in cinema's big white screen, and in the middle the unmistakable round outline of the Conference Centre. The illusion has been shattered. I had thought we were on safari in Africa, what with the animals and the flat-topped acacia trees punctuating the grass. But we can't be, not with a modern city intruding on the landscape.

Well, actually, we are in Africa, and this safari park is not the whim of a wealthy landowner. It is Nairobi National Park. Seventy square kilometres in area, but only 6 kilometres from the centre of Nairobi, the park encompasses a wide range of habitats, and the game to go with them. There are open plains, highland forest, a river with its fringe of yellow-barked acacia, the fever tree. Deep gorges cut across the park too, and dams have attracted birds not previously recorded in the area. Only elephants are missing.

For many visitors to Kenya it is their first glimpse of wild Africa, a dress rehearsal for the safaris to come. Indeed, for many it is their only glimpse, and depending on their past experience and current attitude it is either terrifically impressive or a great disappointment. There is something thrilling about seeing animals in large groups, more or less unconfined. It is the sensation modern zoos try to give, not always successfully. In the game parks you have the large groups, they appear to be free, and you have to stalk them, all of which add extra enjoyment for anyone who likes looking at animals. The park outside Nairobi provides some of these elements (but none in as good measure as the other Kenyan parks) and so if you have never been on safari, it is likely to be exciting.

Nairobi National Park provides an interesting bridge from the extended zoo of a safari park, where the animals are quite obviously out of place and managed for the visitors' convenience, to a real game park, such as Amboseli or Masai Mara, where the animals are at home and the visitors are managed.

Fences, for example, are obvious at Woburn Abbey. Nairobi National Park is also fenced, but only around its perimeter and most of the time you are too far away to notice it. The animals, however, are still out of place, for most of them would never choose to live this close to a big city and many are transported here specifically to restock the park. But they are not caged in the same sense that the baboons of a safari park are caged. They have to earn their own living. Or do they?

I heard some strange tales in Nairobi. It was said that every Tuesday and Friday morning at 6 am, just before dawn, a team of park rangers stands by, ready to go hunting. At first, before I expressed any interest, the story had a direct simplicity. They went out of the park in their truck, shot a wildebeest or buffalo, loaded it on to the truck and drove back to the park. There they went in, found the lions, and dumped the carcass for the lions to feed on. A fine plan, one that I certainly would not find fault with. Wildebeest and buffalo are too numerous anyway and often have to be shot by park rangers to stop them damaging crops. Lions often scavenge. Why not feed one to the other, before opening hours if necessary so as not to offend the visitors? I could see no objection.

Then, as I tried to witness this provisioning, the story changed. The hunters went out only in response to a specific request from someone whose crops were being damaged, rather than on a regular basis. Still reasonable not to waste the carcass. But even that, it seems, was not the whole truth, and in the end I witnessed nothing; 'It would make us look like a zoo,' was the park warden's comment. The final recipients of the handout, I was eventually told, are not the lions in Nairobi National Park but the lions, cheetahs, leopards and tiger (yes tiger) of the Park's adjacent orphanage. They get this handout, according to Mr J. O. Ochoki, deputy director of the wildlife conservation and management department, 'to keep their instincts'.

I hesitate to write about this orphanage. In bare barred cages, painted a bilious green, are some primates: a chimpanzee, perhaps seven or eight years old, hunched over in a ball; a celebes monkey picking aimlessly at itself; a de Brazza's monkey who finds me much more interesting than his empty surroundings; three vervets, who at least have one another, and next to them five or six Sykes' monkeys; a pair of deranged-looking olive baboons. The carnivores, munching that day on their instinct-preserving buffalo cuts, are off to one side. Elsewhere there are pygmy hippos and Grévy's zebras, completely out of place, and three bear pits, each housing a single disconsolate chimp, one of whom looks easily old enough to be drawing a pension. I suppose we all become orphans if we live long enough.

I have seen some bad zoos, but in every respect this is one of the worst. It turns out, however, that I am misguided, for Mr Ochoki explains that all these animals were sick or orphaned, and they will be returned to the wild as soon as possible. For many, I suspect, that will be as a corpse, and not before. Indeed, I am doubly misguided, for there right by the gate where it can correct the misapprehensions of any visitor like myself is a sign that reads, in its entirety, 'This orphanage is not a zoo.' To which I would reply, 'No, and it isn't much of an orphanage either.'

What puzzles me is why there should be such fear of zoos. Just because Kenya is the home of the best-known and most popular game parks does not preclude her from having a good zoo too. The orphanage could be easily remodelled to make it a much better place for the animals, which would probably

*Above* The orphanage at Nairobi, not a zoo. Mount Kenya (*right*) is seldom this clear

improve the animals' standing with the Kenyans who visit the park. For many of these people the orphanage is the only chance they have to get close to the animals that once wandered their land, and I suspect that seeing them in this condition does little to engender any feelings of respect for wildlife. I appreciate that Kenya is not as wealthy as some countries, but a little money spent on the orphanage would bring enormous returns. There is no stigma attached to a good zoo, and Nairobi could easily have a good little zoo rather than an appalling orphanage. I hope it will not be too long before those in charge of Kenya's game realise that zoos can help them in their task.

But this is a detour. One comes to Kenya not to see caged animals in zoos, no matter how good the zoo, but to admire animals in their natural state in the wild. Nairobi National Park, with its adventitious non-zoo, is essentially a carefully managed collection near a city, a one-cage zoo in effect. And that prompts me to wonder about the other animal experiences to be had on safari. Are they as free, as wild, as natural as I would like to believe? To answer, we must go on safari.

We leave Nairobi on the Thika road to the north, en route for one of the most popular destinations on the safari circuit. A drive of a couple of hours on a surface that is sometimes very good, sometimes jarringly poor, winds past plantations of pineapples, sisal plants with their tall flower spikes, and, of course, glossy green coffee bushes. We are heading towards Mount Kenya,

home of the world's best coffee. Home also of Treetops, the game hide on stilts where animals come to drink each evening.

After two and a bit hours we reach the municipality of Nyeri and The Outspan Hotel, staging post for many of the game lodges in the Aberdare National Park. It is an elegant and gracious hotel of the old colonial sort, where tourists can enjoy lunch and a rest on the wide red-tiled verandah, sipping drinks at the shaded tables that look so much like roofed church gateways. Neat lawns sweep down to flowerbeds and trees, and if the weather is clear there is a superb view of the mountain, its two sharp peaks protruding from the broad cone of a base. Throughout the morning little knots of visitors arrive, some dressed in loud check bermudas, others in crisp new safari suits. There is a general air of expectation, and a lot of testing of long camera lenses. Pied wagtails and yellow-vented bulbuls flit between the tables, gleaning a living and ignoring the lenses and their owners.

Lunch over, some of the visitors are attracted to an exhibition of native dancing. Five tall men, dressed in assorted bits of skin – colobus, zebra, a scrap of leopard – their bodies decorated with ash-white lines and with the shakers and rattles that mark their passage, file through the verandah and lead the tourists back to the arena. Soon the crowd is taken up in the leaping, stamping dance, the leader calling and the chorus returning his call in a very rhythmic chant against a background of joyful ululation.

As we stroll back down from the dance floor no one notices that the scene they have come to Africa to witness is being enacted on the front lawn of The Outspan. A tabby cat is poised motionless, staring into the edge of the flower-bed. A leaf moves. The cat strikes. A lizard dies. The tourists walk by oblivious; Nature may be red in tooth and claw but tabby cats are not what they want to see.

Buses arrive and take us the ten minutes' journey to Treetops, where we pour out and wait like a school party, about to be addressed by teacher – in this case, a white hunter, armed with a double-barrelled rifle. 'I don't know if it is Corbett's actual gun, but it is like the one that Jim Corbett used,' he tells us, assuming that all of us are familiar with the hunter who immortalised the man-eaters of Tsavo. He warns us, first, about the baboons that plague Treetops. Then he points out the blinds along the path, into which we are to run if danger, most probably in the shape of a buffalo, threatens. 'One came for us just two weeks ago,' he says, 'and I had to put a bullet over its ear to turn it away.' At last he gathers us together and shepherds us the 200 metres to Treetops.

It is impressive, and the people who arrived in Nairobi that morning don't know whether to look down at the family of warthogs on the edge of the waterhole or up at the four-storey building atop massive stilts. We climb on up to the bar, people get their bearings and find their rooms, and begin drifting up to the roof terrace. Behind us, the sun is setting. In front of us is the waterhole, the papyrus island in its centre alive with chrome-yellow weaverbirds. Off in the distance beyond the water is Mount Kenya, which we are lucky to be able to see so clearly. Tea is served, a classic English cuppa with scones and a jam sponge, but also refreshing and un-English slices of fresh pineapple. Alerted by, I think, the flash of silver and the white tablecloths, the baboons advance on the terrace.

A mother and her infant, who is old enough to ride jockey-style on her back, are the first to arrive, and the barrage of camera shutters is something to hear. People are fascinated, and faintly repelled, eager to get close but still mindful of the hunter's warning. There is much discussion of the ugliness of another female baboon's immensely attractive swollen bottom, and slowly the people begin to relax. They pull chairs up to the railing at the edge of the roof terrace and sit to watch the animals coming in to drink; buffalo, bushpigs, warthogs, bushbuck, all make their way to the water. The big dominant male baboon has arrived and although the hunter, armed with a big stick, keeps a wary eye on him, most of the people are content to sip their tea and watch the waterhole.

Suddenly all hell breaks loose. The baboon with her infant has struck, snatching a scone from the plate of a woman who had become just a little too interested in the waterhole. Again the shutters click, and there is considerable relief that the woman wasn't bitten and that it happened to her, not us.

There is always an altercation, every day. Last time I was here I watched in horror as a woman, dressed in tight and tasteless leopard-spotted jeans and stiletto heels, walked towards a mother and infant. The woman had a fancy sound movie camera, one of those with a microphone that sticks out in front, enclosed in a bright orange windshield. The baboon was being good as gold, sitting quietly in the sun and attentively grooming her infant's head. The woman was getting the film footage of a lifetime, and the baboon just glanced up at her from time to time. Lulled by her star's good behaviour she clicked closer on her absurd heels. In a trice the baboon whipped out, grabbed the microphone, and bit into it. The woman shrieked, dropped the camera, and ran. Fortunately for her, the baboon decided that the camera was inedible and left the scene. The woman salvaged what she could of her pride and her equipment and turned to the hunter for sympathy; he didn't exactly say 'I told you so,' but then he didn't have to. All the lodges are subject to abuse by the extremely clever, and opportunistic, baboons. Most take care to keep the monkeys at bay, rather than risk damage, but baboons seem to be part of the Treetops experience. They could be kept away, but then Treetops wouldn't be Treetops.

Down below us now a troop of Sykes' monkeys warily approaches the water to drink. Three yellow-billed storks flap lazily in and begin to feed, methodically quartering the water. A flock of glossy starlings buzzes up to the roof to pick for crumbs, and although all of the food has been cleared away the baboons are still very much in evidence. Mother and baby cruise the large ashtrays around the perimeter, efficiently checking each of them. In one they find a discarded cup of tea and a soggy cigarette. Delicious. She of the swollen bottom flaunts herself just in front of one lucky tourist, much to his evident disgust. And much to the liking of the dominant male who strides boldly over and with no ceremony mounts her, ejaculates, grunts, and dismounts. It is over too quickly for most people to snap, but if this isn't Nature in the raw, what is?

Night falls, the floodlights come on, and we retire below to the bar to keep a lookout for more animals and wait for dinner. Nothing much to be seen – just the usual succession of buffalo, bushbuck, warthogs and bushpigs, and a lovely herd of waterbuck. After dinner we again repair to the bar to wait for the elephants and other exciting animals. Unfortunately we are a bit too noisy, and although two hyenas and a white-tailed mongoose put in an appearance no new big game come. Downstairs on the lower balcony the hunter takes a plate of left-over duckling to a tree that adjoins Treetops and conjures a genet out of the foliage. The delicate cat, fearless despite the camera flashes that freeze it in the night, seizes scraps hungrily from the hunter's fingers. The genet slips off and a bushbaby takes its place, wide-eyed in the darkness. Slowly, Treetops begins to quieten down as people drift off to their rooms, leaving just two diehards sitting in the bar, each nursing a cold Tusker beer. Treetops groans and creaks as it settles down, an ark on stilts.

Lying awake, trying to decode the sounds of the night outside my window, I am disturbed by an urgent banging and a repeated cry. It is six minutes past midnight, and at first I cannot make out the meaning of the cry, but the noise approaches down the corridor and is soon at my door. Bang bang – rhino – bang bang – rhino – bang bang – rhino. The sleeping Treetops comes alive as people scurry from their rooms to the viewing windows to spy on the rhino. He walks in front of the lodge, circles round once, urinates into the waterhole, and disappears into the blackness on the other side of the water. The two old diehards haven't stirred. Having perhaps moved on to yet another Tusker, they are more interested in an attractive little blonde woman, whose enthusiasm for wildlife is such that she hasn't stopped to change out of her sheer nightie, than in any old rhino. They've seen it all before. But we haven't, and the ark takes a while to settle again.

In the morning, with Mount Kenya sharp against the rapid dawn, a baboon tries my window, just in case. The night is over, and we are bussed down from Treetops back to The Outspan for breakfast before we go our separate ways. We have all had a memorable experience, a privileged glimpse of wild animals that are absolutely free. At least, that is the predominant impression, although it is an impression that owes as much to myth as to reality.

The animals are free to wander, it is true, but they are not free to leave the park. A 450-volt electric fence and 3-metre ditch see to that. So how big does an enclosure have to be before we stop calling it a cage? All the same, they are free, to ignore the watchers perched at Treetops, but there are powerful incentives for them not to. Water is an obvious one. Animals have to drink, and most of them go to a waterhole once a day; that is why Treetops was originally sited above a waterhole. In the normal course of events waterholes dry up from time to time; the animals simply move to another one, if the drought is not too bad. But that would be no good for Treetops, so they top up the water. When I was there the edge of the water was already some distance from the rim of the hole, and the hunter told me that within a week or so they would have to borrow some irrigation pipes from a nearby coffee plantation and pump in water. They do it during the day, between one lot of visitors leaving and the next arriving.

Almost more than water, animals need salt. So the management puts out salt, about two buckets a week. Most animals will travel miles to a good salt lick. You can see the white salt encrusting the ground just below the windows, which naturally is where the management puts it. That brings the animals close to the lodge, which is good for the visitors, but it isn't doing the plants any good, and excess salt leaching through the soil has certainly contributed to the death of the trees around the waterhole.

The animals are not in a proper ecological balance; there are too many prey and not enough predators. In the park as a whole they ought to cull animals regularly, and around Treetops the numbers and concentration of grazers, attracted by the salt and water, is harming the ground. Worst offenders are the warthogs, which crop the grass very close and then dig up the roots. It is because of the too plentiful warthogs, and the salt, that there is so little ground cover around the waterhole, which perhaps explains why the shyer species don't come to Treetops any more. The hunter is acutely aware of the problem, and the solution, and the reasons it can't be implemented. 'We could lose a hundred warthogs,' he euphemistically explained to me, 'and it would do the grass a lot of good, but the tourists wouldn't understand. They like to see a lot of animals.' And a lot of bare earth?

Treetops is the best-known of the waterhole lodges, and it has a flavour all of its own, but it is not unique. Other places offer the same opportunity to over-look animals watering themselves. In an 11,330-hectare private game sanctuary on the road from Nairobi to the coast are two of the most luxurious lodges imaginable. A short section of unpaved road heightens the sense of civilisation in the bundu when you finally arrive at Taita Hills and Salt Lick Lodge, which operate like The Outspan and Treetops. In fact, given the high standard of construction of the lodges themselves, I would not be at all surprised if that bit of dirt road had been deliberately left unmade to add just a touch of roughness.

Salt Lick Lodge, like Taita Hills Lodge, is sybaritic in the extreme, offering unparalleled comfort as you watch the game. The wide shady verandahs are well served by attentive bar staff and the individual rooms, built like little

165

Salt Lick Lodge, with its neat waterhole and water's-edge viewing chamber

round African huts, are as well appointed as any fine hotel. The lodge half encloses a pair of adjacent waterholes, and off to one side is more water and the natural salt deposits that draw the animals there.

When I visited there was little going on at the main waterhole; some storks, herons and other birds, a lone waterbuck. But at the supernumerary waterhole to the side were large elephants, cooling off in the mud, skittish zebras and gazelles, a warthog, and a group of waterbuck hinds. It was a bustle of animal activity, a shame because most of the visitors were sitting around the bar, where they had a fine view of the empty waterholes before them. A shame, but one with a certain ironic justice. The waterhole in front of the lodge is completely man-made, with a neat sharp concrete edge and no mud. It is filled by a constant piped supply from a dammed lake on the nearby Bura river. There is a cunningly built underground tunnel that takes you to an observation post sunk at the water's edge for a worm's eye view of the game, and from which I could see nothing of interest. And, in the face of all this provision for their needs, the tourists watched an empty scene while around the corner the animals made use of a temporary mudbath and waterhole that owed their existence to the vagaries of nature: unusually heavy rains.

The reality of Treetops and the other waterhole lodges is that the entire experience depends on a great deal of manipulation, of tourists and animals alike. That is not to detract from the value of the experience itself. Few things can be more pleasant than an evening, even an elephant-free evening, sitting in the moonlight perched above a waterhole, swapping tales and watching the wildlife. But it is a romantic delusion to imagine that you are eavesdropping on Nature untrammelled and unfettered.

Mzima Springs is another place that blurs the boundary between the zoo and the wild. It is in Tsavo West National Park, a good two hours' drive from Taita hills along bumpy roads and past spectacular lava-strewn hillsides. Getting there is at times a little like getting round Milton Keynes, an endless succession of numbered roundabouts that all contain the same direction signs. When you do reach Mzima you find a laagered circle of vans like your own, their drivers resting in the shade of a huge fig tree. This is one of the few spots in a National Park where you are allowed to get out of your vehicle. Indeed you have to get out if you want to see more than the parking.

More than 200 million litres of sparkling clear water spring out of the lava each day and form a broad pool before splashing away down the valley to join the Tsavo river. Around the edges of the pool the vegetation is lush and green, with swampy reedbeds and dense growths of bushes. A path winds through the greenery and a sign tells you that it was worn by the hippos that frequent Mzima Springs. Everywhere there are signs of their activity, most noticeably blankets of dung scattered by that peculiar flagellant tail, but no sign of the hippos themselves. Along the path, past a lookout point, you come to a rickety wooden bridge that leads across the water to a little thatched hut a few yards from the shore. Cross the bridge, climb down into the hut, and you are underwater in Mzima Springs.

The hut is like a section of sewer pipe standing on end – indeed it probably is a section of sewer pipe – and let into its circumference are thick glass windows, every one of which is cracked, but no matter. Fish, mostly barbel, circle the windows endlessly and the water, although full of detritus, is clear and blue, at least nearby. You can see the undersides of the papyrus islands, also sheltering a cargo of fish, and off in the distance the fish are poking at a denim hat that must have blown from someone's head. Beyond the islands, 5 or 6 metres away, there is little to be seen through the murk; peer though we might, we cannot see the vast bulk of a riverhorse.

The underwater viewing chamber is a remarkable facility to find in the depths of supposedly wild Africa. It offers a chance to see the hippos in their element, to see the rush of hungry fish swarm over as a hippo clouds the water around it with partly digested grass. But because the field of view is so restricted, compared to the expanse of pool that the hippos wander through, all that most visitors ever see are the circling fish. The hippos spend a lot of the day up at the other end of the pool, where the springs tumble in, looking for all the world like boulders most of the time, with an occasional twitching ear that gives their game away. Sometimes, if you are lucky, one will gape and yawn, and on occasion they may even move.

Fortunately, there is more to see at Mzima than the hippos. All manner of game use the water and a troop of baboons is usually in residence. Signs warn you of crocodiles, although these are generally in the reeds and invisible. Bright red dragonflies dart above the reeds, seeming to flip into hyperspace as they flash from station to station. In one clearing a mist of butterflies – little white ones, yellow ones, big orange and black ones – streams over the flowers. The underwater viewing, however, is what makes Mzima Springs so special, neither wholly natural nor wholly a zoo. That you cannot always see a hippo under-water adds to the wildness, that you sometimes can to the zooness. If there were lots of little huts out in the pool, so that no matter where the hippos rested they were always in view, that would spoil Mzima. As it is, the underwater viewing adds an exciting extra possibility to an already lovely habitat.

These fixed attractions – Treetops, Salt Lick, Mzima – are part of the Kenyan experience, but they are not the whole story. If safari parks are an attempt to capture the spirit of safari without leaving home, what is the real safari like? Strings of native bearers following behind the white hunter and his guide, carrying everything needed to create a comfortable camp in the wilderness? That is certainly the image we are sold; the surprise is that it can, partially at least, be had. Most of the accommodation within the parks system of Kenya is in lodges, purpose-built hotels in the bush. Often these incorporate local styles of architecture but they are essentially hotels, with all modern conveniences. Here and there, however, there are hotels with a difference. These are the tented camps and they aim to offer some of the romance, but none of the discomfort, of an old-fashioned safari. Of these, the most famous – it is com-memorated on a Kenyan stamp – is undoubtedly Governor's Camp.

Opened twenty years ago, on a plateau overlooking the Mara river, Governor's Camp is not like any other game lodge. It is stark; rows of green canvas tents facing out over plain lawns, with no electricity and the only permanent structures a bar and the administrative offices. It looks like the real thing, a temporary camp in the wilderness, but that carefully preserved illusion conceals perhaps the most luxurious accommodation available anywhere in the bush. Certainly it is the most expensive, and the facilities rival those of the big international hotels in Nairobi.

Take the tents. They are as far removed from the average camper's tent as that is from a mountaineer's protective shell. They are really chalets built of canvas rather than wood or brick, erected on secure flat foundations with sturdy supports all around and protective flysheets covering an ample verandah. Inside are comfortable beds, not at all rickety, and wardrobes and tables. Behind each tent is a smaller bathroom tent, again not so much a tent as a bathroom with canvas walls and roof. The floor is tiled, there is a handbasin and, extremely welcome after a hot and dusty game drive, a large shower with copious hot and cold running water on top. Most impressive of all, every tent is equipped with a flushing porcelain WC. No holes in the ground for the intrepid explorers camped at Governor's. The food is sumptuous and plentiful; like most of the visitors, it arrives by air from Nairobi and Mombasa. Dinner at Governor's Camp is a strange sight; in this little enclave carved out of the African savannah, and with buffalo and hippo looking on, people dress for din-ner and sit down to a five-course candle-lit meal, a home from home in the bush.

Governor's Camp is spartan luxury. There are other tented camps, such as Kichwe Tembo just along the Mara which also boasts soi-disant tents, but is more relaxed, with lovely flowers, mostly bougainvillaeas in purple and a profusion of other shades, and giant honeysuckle rambling all over the buildings. Elsewhere are the proper lodges, where your bed is shrouded with mosquito netting, not canvas, but where the sounds of the dark are every bit as audible as they are in a tent, and that, for me, provides much of the romance of safari. Whatever the nature of the roof over their heads, the people in the parks are there for one thing: to see wild animals. They do so on game drives.

The transport is varied. In Nairobi National Park family saloons jostle with big four-wheel drive Landcruisers from the safari companies. In the more remote parks cars are almost never seen, but there are Jeeps, Land-Rovers, Landcruisers and all manner of rugged vehicles, together with the ubiquitous microbuses, some of which really are zebra-striped. Once, in Masai Mara, I was left in a cloud of dust by a convoy that protected, at its centre, a white Range Rover that obviously concealed a very important person. Anything that can make the journey will be used, and the passengers are equally varied, although, perhaps as a result of the natural flocking behaviour of the human species, one kind of vehicle tends to carry one type.

In the neat green trucks of Governor's Camp there are often elderly but spry Englishmen and women, the sort of people who perhaps saw service in Kenya or India when those places were part of an empire. They seem keener than any other identifiable group, and always carry binoculars and guidebooks in addition to the obligatory cameras. There are Americans too, some old and genteel, like the English, others old and not at all genteel, like Americans. The brash Americans often show little understanding of, and less interest in, the wildlife. I wonder why they subject themselves to the few discomforts that remain. They may be on safari, but they still expect cold beer wherever they go.

High point of a game drive, a cheetah and its kill

169

There are other groups too. Germans, generally younger and more obese than any other nationality, and more likely to be sporting a movie camera. Unlike the others, they come for a beach holiday at Mombasa and make one brief glorious safari. And of course there are a few French and Italians, usually the most inappropriately dressed, some thorough Swedes, and one or two others.

No matter what language they speak, clothes they wear, vehicles they ride in, all tourists share almost identical experiences on their game drives, whichever park they are in. The scenery varies, as do the species, so that the doum palms and Grévy's zebra of Samburu are replaced by grass and buffalo in Masai Mara and thorn trees and elephants in Amboseli. But there is a pattern.

The climate on the uplands of Kenya is marvellous, hot during the day, cool at night, and never very humid. Being on the equator, it gets very warm at noon and the animals, as much as the people, tend to rest. For this reason the tourists leave their lodges early in the morning and in late afternoon. The driver, often the same one for a circuit of several parks, helps his customers into the micro-bus. A park ranger climbs in beside the driver, and they're off.

The ranger adds verisimilitude to the hunt. He speaks seldom, and generally in Swahili to the driver, who usually does his bidding. Down the dirt road and onto the plain, in search of game. The first is a herd of Tommies, Thomson's gazelle, their tails windscreen-wipering nonstop and their handsome horned heads held high. If it is their first drive the tourists will be enthralled, they will talk in whispers and use feet of film. Soon they will be bored with the simple pleasure of a herd of gazelle, but not yet. Leaving the Tommies and bouncing over the grasslands it is not long before we have spotted almost all the grazers: Grant's gazelle, impala, common zebra, all munching on the still dewy grass. There are buffalo, massive-horned and mean, in vast herds numbering several hundred. There are elegant chestnut topi, standing absurdly on the anthills keeping a lookout, just as the guidebook says they should. Warthog families are down on their knees grubbing up roots. Sometimes the bus can approach quite close, but more often the animals run off, their tails whipping up behind them like radio aerials.

So far the game has been quite easy to find. Now we start looking harder. Everyone in the bus is scanning the horizon keenly, hoping to be the first to spot something interesting. All the species that were so fascinating just an hour ago now barely rate a mention. An odd shape among the trees turns out to be a monstrous bull giraffe, ill at ease in his wrinkled skin as he picks the leaves of an acacia. We drive on, and in the shade near the river pick out a herd of waterbuck, their distinctive white rumps visible in the gloom. The sun has climbed high, and the day is becoming uncomfortably hot. We have seen an awful lot, but the driver knows that we haven't seen everything yet, and so do we. Maybe next time we'll find lions, he tells us, and we who were so happy with a herd of Tommies begin to hunger for carnivores.

Back at the lodge it is time for breakfast, a rest by the pool, and swapping stories with other visitors. Now we learn disappointment, for another bus saw a leopard, lions, and much more. The leopard was in open country, moving down a river-bed, when a bus intercepted it. It kept on going, as the bus followed behind. Bus drivers keep an eye on one another as well as on the plains, for the surest sign that there is something to be seen is a cluster of buses on the horizon; soon the leopard and its bus were joined by two more buses. The leopard reached the safety of a thorn tree and sprinted up it, the three buses laagered below. Up came three young male lions to add to the spectacle. They clawed at the base of the tree and growled at the leopard, but could do no more and so retired behind some rocks and bushes a little way away. The leopard was perfectly safe in its tree, despite all the commotion below, but it was clearly not at ease. It urinated from the tree, which leopard expert Jonathan Scott, who is living at Kichwe Tembo camp while doing research for a book on leopards, told me later was very unusual indeed. Scott takes that as a sign that the leopard was being harassed, not merely spied upon. In any case, what the leopard did next surely indicates derangement. It hopped down from the tree and loped off past the watching tourists towards the bushes where the young lions had vanished. They sprang out and the leopard was dead.

The tourists telling this tale were distressed and impressed in equal measure. On the one hand, they had seen a leopard, a treasured sight not granted to many. On the other, they had seen the leopard killed, and almost certainly had some inkling that they had themselves been a contributory factor in its death.

Leopard with dik-dik, not the sort of thing tourists would see every day

171

We, who were not there, were uncertain whether we really would have wanted to be. And one young American woman, her eyes bright with the retelling, paused and, to no one in particular, muttered, 'It was good, but it was a hell of a shame.'

That afternoon, as we set out again, there was a certain bloodlust in our bus; we wanted carnivores. On one of the main roads out across the plain our driver stopped another bus coming the opposite way. They chatted rapidly in Swahili, making much use of the magic words *simba* and *chui*. We were on the scent of a leopard ourselves now, and swung off towards a more densely wooded area, bounded on one side by a high rock outcrop. The leopard often rests here we learned, and so we threaded our way slowly over the rocks at the bottom of the wall, straining for a sight of spots. At the end of the rock, sunning itself at eye-level, was a rock hyrax, a delightful little animal that we surely would have stopped for that morning. We passed by without even slowing down, climbing above the outcrop onto a little plain. There the driver stopped beneath a larger than usual thorn tree. We saw the short vertical slashes on the trunk where the leopard had used its claws to climb up, and the remains of a Tommie wedged firmly in the canopy. But no leopard.

We drove on. Off in the distance were three stationary buses: a cheetah was posing magnificently on an old dead tree. He stood there, all lean muscle and potential energy, lording it over the grasslands. If we waited, perhaps we would see a kill. But there was nothing around to be killed. Eventually the cheetah stepped down, and we left it making its way through the grass. Time was growing late, a storm seemed to be developing behind us, and the driver and ranger both wanted to return to the lodge. On the way back the driver saw some tawny shapes off on the horizon and, despite his reluctance, could not ignore our enthusiasm for lions. After all, he had helped create it.

Four young females, their coats still faintly marked with the cub's spots, were around the carcass of a baby buffalo. One was eating; it looked as if she had just begun. The others lay resignedly by, two quite close and the other some way off. We had missed the kill, but so what? Off in the east were black storm clouds and rain, while to the west the sun was setting in a blaze of yellow; the lions and their victim were picked out in that sharp black light that some-times precedes a storm. Feasting our eyes, we were so close we could hear the calf's skin tear and instinctively we talked in whispers, which looking back seems foolish as nothing would have distracted the killers from their meal. Here was Nature red in tooth and claw, NRITAC as we had come jokingly to refer to it in our lusting, the red literally and liberally bespattered on the lioness's teeth, claws and muzzle. By now the driver was growing impatient. Just as we were on the point of leaving the fourth lioness stood up, stretched like an over-grown cat, and trotted determinedly towards the carcass. Cameras that had been put away were brought out again. She joined the one at the calf; there was

*Top* the mountain is Fuji, not Kilimanjaro, and this is Fuji Safari Park, not Africa.
In the real Africa (*above*), skyscrapers intrude on the view from Nairobi National Park

Spreading salt (*top*) attracts animals to Treetops. The baboons come for tea and put on a good show. Cape buffalo (*top right*) come in to drink. A fence and ditch stop them leaving the park. *Right* culling is a vital part of park management

Mzima Springs, a zoo facility in the wild, where you can watch hippos underwater

a furious fifteen seconds of snarling, and now two lionesses continued to work at the buffalo calf. Three vultures and a maribou stork waited nearby as we drove off, well satisfied. We had our own tale to tell.

It is a bit of a cliché these days to point out that the modern tourist on a game drive is like the white hunter of old, the camera substituting for the gun. A cliché, but true nevertheless. Of course there are far more tourists than there ever were hunters, and despite the self-imposed rigours of the holiday safari it is considerably more comfortable than hunting ever was, but the fact remains that, with the African game protected as it is by legislation, the game drive is the hunt of today. That, however, does not mean that there is no place for real hunting. A great deal of confusion exists on the question of hunting and its repercussions on conservation. Some people are against all hunting under any circumstances, saying that any killing of wild animals by man is bound to be detrimental. Others can see no circumstances in which hunting is not a good thing. The truth, as so often, lies somewhere between these two extremes, but exactly where depends on the particular species and the particular circumstances.

Hunters have conserved habitats for the very good reason that those habitats support the animals the hunters like to kill. Ducks Unlimited, an organisation of wildfowlers in the United States, is a good example of this kind of enterprise. It has bought up vast tracts of breeding marshes to ensure a continuing supply of huntable ducks. On the other hand, hunters are also accused of having put some species in jeopardy, although concrete examples of this are harder to come by. Sport hunting probably has done no such thing, although efforts to exterminate animals that compete with our agriculture have taken their toll, as has poaching.

The most important thing to realise about wildlife today is that in most places there are not enough predators. The reasons for this are complex, but come down in the end to one animal's way of life. Mankind, by his use of agriculture, has had more impact on wildlife than anything else. As land has been appropriated for crops or grazing domestic animals, so the wildlife that occupied it has been destroyed. The balance of nature has been upset.

I cannot stress too strongly that this balance is not a cosy confederacy of the animals for their mutual good. Rather it is the outcome of enlightened self-interest. The predator that reproduces very rapidly may do well in the short term, but if it over-exploits its prey it is doomed in the end. One that apparently shows restraint will succeed better in the final reckoning. The encroachment of agriculture, and to a lesser extent of poaching, was what put wildlife, particularly in Africa, in peril. The recognition that this was so led to laws protecting the wildlife, especially in specially designated parks and reserves. But these reserves, although they are better – much better – than nothing, are not natural. The primary problem is that they are too small.

177

That may sound absurd when one thinks of places like the Masai Mara and Serengeti reserves, which between them cover 10,138 square kilometres, but the truth is that protected areas represent a very small fraction of the land. In Zaïre about 2.5 per cent of the land is effectively protected. Tanzania does much better, with almost 30 per cent of its land in game reserves and controlled areas. Even so, game parks are like tiny islands of refuge in a sea of exploitation. That matters more to predators than prey because while it takes half a hectare of grassland to keep a wildebeest alive, a lion needs fifty wildebeest a year to sustain itself. Predators need far more space than their prey, and that is why, in the words of ecologist Paul Colinvaux, 'big fierce animals are rare'. They are rare everywhere, but when they are both rare and restricted to small islands the dangers are immense. Vagaries in the climate have always resulted in fluctuations in population, but if there were not enough food in one place the animals could move to another area where it was more plentiful. With island parks, however, it becomes much harder for an animal to shift localities. If all the lions in a park die during a drought, where are new lions going to come from when times improve? Animals on real islands have a fearful propensity to go extinct. The upshot of all this is that game reserves and parks must be managed by man if the animals in them are to survive, and that is why I regard them as zoos.

We have already seen how some of the parks are fenced. The intention is to keep the animals from wandering out to destroy neighbouring farms, but the fence insulates the park further. Elsewhere the problem is not keeping the animals in but keeping the people out. This applies not just to the local people but also, surprisingly, to the tourists. Microbuses and Land-Rovers are fine for travelling across the plains, but they destroy the grass. A single vehicle doesn't have too much effect, but the boom in visitors to Kenya's parks – Amboseli had nearly 100,000 visitors last year – has added car wheels to all the other threats. To combat this, in Amboseli, the World Bank agreed to give money for development only if tourists were restricted to the marked roads. Ditches were dug alongside the roads, and stones piled across certain of the smaller tracks to block them off. Rangers on patrol ensure that drivers found breaking the rules are punished. It is too early to say whether the range will recover, but the effect on the tourist is to make wild Africa more like the safari parks at home, and unfortunately little is done to explain why vehicles need to stay on the roads.

Tourism, and the money it brings in, is the major reason for the continued existence of Kenya's parks. But how are the local people, whose land has been appropriated to create the park, to benefit? Again, Amboseli is a prime example of the difficulties, and of the possibilities of overcoming them. Amboseli as an ecosystem depends on the long swamp that runs through its heart. In the dry season the game that is normally spread out over the Amboseli plain congregates in the area around the swamp. The swamp once also supplied the Masai and their cattle. Now the Masai have been told that they are not to bring their cattle into the park to water them, as they have done for hundreds of years. Worse, when there is water outside the park the game moves out and onto the Masai grazing lands, there to compete with the cattle for food. The Masai have shown their anger at this unfairness in many ways, most notably by spearing the game, especially the rhinos, that make Amboseli such an attraction. In the end agreements have been reached whereby the government provides boreholes and pipelines that supply water outside the park boundaries, and financially compensates the Masai for grazing damage by game. But the water supply is inadequate, and the Masai continue to bring upwards of 3000 cattle into the park during the dry seasons. The cattle graze on the way to and from water, further depriving the game.

Amboseli is in a precarious position. The presence of the Masai cattle detracts from its value as a park, and overcrowding by tourists interferes with the game. Cheetah are especially vulnerable. They hunt at dawn and dusk, but that is when the tourists are out on their game drives. The buses often crowd round the cheetahs, making it impossible for them to catch anything, so the cheetahs have been forced to hunt at midday, when the tourists are themselves eating, but they cannot afford to miss as many potential meals in the heat as they can at the cooler ends of the day, so much energy does a chase require. For all these reasons the better tour companies are beginning to avoid Amboseli, which could hasten its decline, and if it does go into a decline there will be no incentive for the Masai to respect the park. The problems are immense, and if Amboseli is to survive as a refuge for wildlife and a tourist attraction it will only be by virtue of a comprehensive management plan that takes into account the needs of all the parties.

Masai cattle need water. If they're not allowed in the park, it must be piped to them

Interference and management are everything, even in wild Africa. That is disturbing enough for people who imagine that all we need to do to save animals in the wild is enact laws to protect them. How much more disturbing is the simple fact that in the absence of sufficient natural predation we may have to go in and regulate numbers directly.

Culls are a regular feature of game management all over Africa, in Zambia, Malawi, Zimbabwe and Tanzania. It is exactly like the application of euthanasia to manage captive populations in zoos; because things are no longer wholly natural some wild individuals have to die that the species might live. When conditions dictate, the slaughter can be immense. Last year in Zimbabwe conservationists decided that they had to destroy 6000 of the country's 50,000 elephants. The cull was very efficient, aiming to wipe out whole herds so that there would be no traumatised survivors left, and in one park 2000 animals were killed in a month. One herd of sixty-five elephants was wiped out in just ninety seconds. Behind those gruesome figures lies another set of statistics that makes the cull necessary.

The elephant population in Zimbabwe had climbed from about 4000 at the beginning of this century to reach its present level. At the same time the human population had expanded even more – from about half a million to well over seven million – and the elephants were being squeezed into ever smaller areas. Two years of drought made matters worse; trees were destroyed faster than they could regenerate, and all the country's livestock was threatened. If the elephants had been allowed to live in such numbers, conservationists said, the damage to the habitat would take far longer to repair, and so some elephants had to die. There were immediate benefits, too. Meat was given to the local farmers, who lack protein, and the proceeds from the hides and ivory that were sold at auction went to further other conservation work.

This should not be taken as implying that culling is always the best, or even any, solution. The story of the elephants and trees in Amboseli makes that clear. In the early 1970s the acacia trees in Amboseli were dying off at an unprecedented rate. Elephant numbers had increased, and the animals were often seen ripping acacias apart for food. The conclusion seemed obvious; there were too many elephants. And the solution was equally obvious; get rid of the elephants, and the trees would recover. The obvious, however, turned out to be wrong.

David Western, an ecologist who has been instrumental in devising and implementing Kenya's wildlife policy, discovered that, paradoxically, it was rain that was killing the trees. During the previous few years there had been unusually heavy rains, particularly on the slopes of Kilimanjaro, south of Amboseli. The rain percolated down and raised the water table beneath the ground. The deep soil in Amboseli is very salty, and salt kills tree roots. Normally it is too deep in the ground to affect the acacias, but now the salt was lifted up to reach them, and the trees died. While the elephants would take advantage of the dying trees, they certainly were not the primary cause of their death. Getting rid of the imagined surplus of elephants would have done no good at all.

Nature is complex and culling is not always the answer. In other cases it can be demonstrated that it has become a valuable practice. The Tanzania Wildlife Corporation, Tawico, is a quasi-governmental organisation which oversees all sport hunting in that country. In 1982 Tawico earned $1 million in fees from hunters who killed about 1500 animals. In addition, Tawico conducts its own control hunts, killing animals for skins and meat, and capturing some alive for sale to zoos and other collections. Among the animals cropped are about 2000 zebra a year, each of which is worth $450 for its hide and $150 for meat. There is some opposition to Tanzania's use of hunting, or cropping as proponents prefer to call it, to bring in foreign revenue, but the fact is that it does produce much-needed cash, and is likely to continue for that reason.

Kenya banned all hunting in 1977 and has been reluctant to cull animals in the parks, but that is about to change. Some culling already goes on, mostly in response to specific complaints about particular beasts, but on a very small scale. The result is vast herds of herbivores, too vast to sustain. In Masai Mara herds of buffalo numbering 800 or more stretch to the horizon. At the moment they seem secure, but there is a danger that they are overgrazing the land, with the result that, when the slightest drought hits, the population will crash. Other parks suffer similar problems, and culling would be the best solution.

Rather than rush in, the government is trying to establish a system that will permit hunting, and bring in cash, but prevent the sort of abuses that might threaten the animals further without doing anything to improve the parks. I was very fortunate to be allowed to discuss this policy with the Honourable Maina Wanjigi, Minister for Tourism and Wildlife. He is aware that it was hunting that endangered the game in the first place. 'We will have to be very very careful that we don't overrun ourselves again,' Wanjigi told me.

The system will work through a network of registered professional hunters, under the supervision of the Director of Wildlife and Conservation. He will have to be satisfied that the hunters are men of integrity who will keep their clients under control; that, as Wanjigi put it, they will 'really play the game the way it should be done'. The government has already started to implement the system by permitting the resumption of bird hunting from March 1984. This, it is hoped, will ensure that the registration and control procedures work smoothly before hunting for big game is started. And when it does begin, not all species will be included. Quotas will be set on those that can be hunted, and the endangered species, notably rhino, cheetah and leopard, will not be touched. Unfortunately, regulating the registered hunters and their clients is perhaps the easiest part of keeping the killing of animals under control. By far the biggest threat to animals is illegal poaching, usually for trophies.

You have to have money, and a little courage, to hunt a wild animal. So trophies – stuffed heads and the like – have come to symbolise wealth and manliness. For far less money, and no expense of bravery at all, you can buy a trophy killed by someone else and imagine yourself to be a big game hunter. Poachers are only too willing to satisfy this kind of wish-fulfilment, and so controlling the sale of curios is probably even more important than controlling the hunters. Wanjigi is more than aware of this, and outlined the Kenyan plans to deal with the problem. 'We are not going to have any outlets locally for any of the trophies,' he told me. 'These will have to be paid for in foreign currency and will also not be available, even to the hunters, until they are ready to go.' The trophies 'will be handed back to them at the airport'. Any surplus trophies, not wanted by the hunters, perhaps, or resulting from the department's own culling operations, 'will be sold by us and through us, so that the old system whereby we had curio shops sprouting all over the place – that will not be allowed.' If the system works it should help to minimise the market for illicitly obtained trophies.

The Kenyan plans sound fine. If they can be implemented effectively the resumption of hunting will help to control the game and bring in revenue, a very important consideration. But the culling will have to be very carefully watched to ensure that it doesn't get out of hand. Ecosystems are not easy things to manage, and there is always a risk that in trying to manage game in parks we will actually make things worse, not better.

Killing selected animals is an important part of the management that all artificial collections of animals require. There are people who are willing to pay large sums of money to be allowed to kill animals. To discuss the ethical aspects of killing for trophies would lead me into a moral quagmire from which I doubt that I would emerge. My personal feeling is that it is regrettable that people find it necessary to kill animals for sport alone, but as long as they do, and are willing to pay, and as long as money is scarce and animals need to be killed to preserve the integrity of a park, then one would be foolish not to marry the two needs and get extra benefit from the animals that must die.

I have said that I find it regrettable that there are people who take enjoyment from killing another creature. This is not a view I can defend with any facts or figures – it's just my feeling. Because death has a definite place in wildlife management, however, I think that hunters can be very useful. But what is one to make of the burgeoning American phenomenon of hunting for species called exotics? In New Mexico you can shoot aoudad sheep, ibex and oryx. In Maryland there are Japanese sika deer and fallow deer from Europe. In Texas blackbuck from Pakistan strut across their territories, with sambar and barasingha introduced from India. And in Florida are the oldest of the exotics, wild pigs descended from the first Spanish colonists' domestic animals.

With the exception of the pigs, all the exotic species in the United States are descended from animals surplus to zoo stocks. On private ranches and on state-run reserves they have prospered and multiplied so that, for example, there are far more blackbuck in Texas than in their native Pakistan. And to go with the burgeoning herds there are increasing numbers of people wanting to hunt them.

I had the chance to join a hog hunt in Florida, but only as a spectator. My prowess with a gun is minimal, though according to our guide that is not something that deters a lot of American men. 'I always back them up,' he told me. We were bouncing along in a tractor trailer, looking for a meat hog, not a tough old trophy boar, nor a little weanling, but a young boar that would have some good eating on him. The sun was beginning to burn off the early morning mist that enwraps the palmetto scrub, and everyone scanned the horizon for game, just as we had on safari. A bunch of pigs trotting over to one side brought the convoy to a halt and the hunting party rushed out to investigate. The pigs vanished into a palmetto thicket, so we left them.

I wondered why we didn't just flush them out. Later Mike Acreman, our guide, explained to me that he is always after a fair chase, and that was why we abandoned those pigs. 'If I want to make it easy, we just go get a pack of dogs. Why, then we'd have five or ten hogs this morning, easy enough.' But he won't use dogs. 'Fair chase, no dogs. When it's man against the animal, that's when you come out with a fair chase hunt.' So we moved on, driving all over the ranch in search of the right kind of animal in the right kind of place.

After much bouncing over deeply rutted tracks, through scrub that scratched at us and open country where we could watch the progress of the dawn, Mike decided to try among the orange groves that provide the main crop of the farm. As soon as we entered the orchard Mike saw some hogs feeding down at the other end. He and his client stalked off between the rows of trees, accompanied by Mike's helpers and other members of the hunting party. I stayed behind in the trailer, reluctant to get involved and eager not to get in the way. The client, a fairly sprightly old man, followed Mike to where they had a good view of the pigs. He knelt, took aim, and fired. From my vantage point I could see what the client could not, that Mike was right behind him and fired at almost the same moment, ensuring that regardless of the client's aim the pig was felled. Backing him up, Mike had called it. Then the client walked over and administered the *coup de grâce* with his handgun. Mike and his helpers loaded the hogs, for two had been hit, onto the trailer and took them off to butcher.

It had been a good hunt. The client had had his fun, and had a heap of meat to show for it. Mike had earned another day's fees. The farmer would not have to worry about the hogs overrunning his crops. And I had gained a further insight into hunting and its importance, when properly conducted, in conservation. For, as long as they enjoy a good day's hunting, people like this

183

elderly hoghunter are as happy in pursuit of game near home as they would be in Tanzania. It costs less, too, and a rhino bred and dead on a Texas ranch might save one in Tanzania.

On balance, then, I think that hunting for exotics is a good thing, my only misgiving being that it preserves the mystique of the animal trophy. I look forward to the day when people hunt animals simply for meat and to manage populations. Even then, and knowing as I do that life depends on death, I suspect I will prefer the camera to the gun. Back on safari I had one last chance to get some very unusual views of the game.

At 6.20 in the morning the African night is still quite dark, although a red streak lights the eastern sky of the Masai Mara. Thirty minutes later the sun shoots over the horizon and, as the light rises, so does a huge billowing shape. Rex Rechs, balloonist, is preparing his craft to take us on a very unusual safari, floating above the plains of the Mara. The balloon is filled first with air, blown in by a little two-stroke propeller fan. With crew members hanging onto the fabric, Rex ignites the burners. Huge butane flames roar into the balloon, which begins to expand and rise, wobbling like a jelly. Soon the balloon, with its pattern of black, red, green and yellow crosses, an echo of Kenya's national flag, is towering 30 metres over the little wicker basket. We put on cycling helmets and climb in. After another couple of bursts from the burners we are lighter than air.

The climb is astonishingly smooth and rapid, and in no time we are drifting over the trees along the river-bank. We fly at dawn because the air then is relatively still, the sun not yet having had time to create the up-welling thermals that enable vultures to soar, but play havoc with balloons. A thermal will lift the balloon far above the plain in a matter of seconds, Rex explains, but worse, it can wring the hot air from the envelope and send the basket crashing down. But there are no thermals yet. It is quiet, and the note of the bellbird reaches us clearly, but not for long. It is the fact that hot air expands, and so is less dense than the surroundings, that enables us to float up here. But the air keeps cooling down, and Rex has to heat it up with deafening jets of flame. The butane burns with a loud roar that drowns out the bellbird, and the heat of the fire is almost uncomfortable as it cooks our upturned novice faces. Then all is cool and quiet again, save for the hiss of the pilot light and the occasional creak of the basket. At first, we all look up at the flaming jets. Later we will get used to them and enjoy the heat on our backs instead.

The wind, coming off the escarpment that surrounds the Mara, flows along the river valley, and we go with it. Below us three crested cranes flap out of a thorn tree and the top view of them is startling. Warthogs scurry along in Indian file, drawing attention to the tracks that cross the plain. Some are the parallel lines of vehicles, but the majority are single tracks that bend here and there without warning. There seems to be no good reason to prefer one route over another, and yet the animals wear and follow distinct paths. Perhaps that does less damage to the grazing.

Bleached white bones stand out below us on the dusty green, sometimes more or less complete skeletons, otherwise single bones, shoulder-blades, skulls, lower jaws, all lying where they were last dropped. There are lots of holes, too, of varying sizes; bat-eared foxes, hyenas, mongooses, jackals, all live underground. An African hare bounds away down a path, and as we skim just a few metres above the ground I can see little rodents jump for cover. Even when there is no game in sight there is plenty to look at; the escarpment, the sun, the other balloons, our shadow, the whole ecosystem spread out beneath us.

Off in the distance, near a grove of trees and directly downwind, are three dark shapes; elephants, not quite happy at our presence. As we approach we can see that there are two big ones and a baby, and then something extraordinary happens. They turn towards us and the biggest raises her trunk to taste our arrival. All three start to flap their ears, a sign that even the greenest tourist has learnt means danger. Then, to our amazement, they actually charge. Rex, who has flown over the Mara hundreds of times, has never seen anything like it, but there they are, trumpeting and running towards us. Even the baby joins in. And it works, because we pass over them and drift harmlessly away downwind over the trees.

Out on the plain the trees are sparse and spaced out, but where there is water, along the edge of the river, the forest is quite dense, the ground often invisible. Bird calls float up to us, and we can make out doves and pigeons flying in the canopy. Here and there the bleached ashen tracery of a dead tree marks the green. We pass over a pool, at the edge of which lies the almost clean skeleton of a hippo. The trees here are full of vultures, which flap away as we come close, alighting on the next tree downwind. Eventually they change tack and move upwind back to the carcass, desire for food overcoming apprehension.

We are over the open plains again, looking down on buffalo, topi, and a knot of giraffes. We have been up almost an hour, and we are running out of fuel. Rex dangles a 20-metre white rope over the edge, a signal to the ground crew that we are on our way down. Puffs of flame ensure our gentle descent, and soon the line is dragging on the ground. We drop lower and lower, and all too quickly the bottom of the basket is brushing the seed heads of the grasses. The support vehicle careers up, the crew races out, and after a slight lurch we are grounded. The traditional balloonists' toast – ersatz champagne – is followed by a delicious cooked breakfast out on the plains, with kites wheeling overhead hoping for some leavings. It has been a memorable experience, but nevertheless we retell the balloon safari straightaway to fix it in our memories. Elephants, the hippo bones, the vast mass of buffalo, all come alive again. By 9.30 we are back in camp.

A balloon safari, the best way to put the game parks in perspective

The balloon safari is a wonderful way to see the animals of Africa, a truly magical experience. All the interference – the park gates, the fences, the culling – is forgotten as you float over the savannah. The frailty of the parks and their game, and the precariousness of the control we exercise over them, remain in the background. The balloon trip provides, quite literally, a new perspective, offering a view of a whole integrated ecosystem. At the moment it is an experience that is by its nature restricted to a very few people, just a handful of the hundreds who visit the park each day, and that is a great shame. I wish everyone could enjoy this unique view of African life, because there is nothing like it to give an insight into your position on earth. Zoos can breed and preserve animals in captivity; floating over the Masai Mara, more than any argument or polemic, enabled me to appreciate why we ought to preserve them in the wild.

# Chapter Seven

# WATERY WORLD

Photographs taken underwater reveal an unknown world, where colours are brighter, shapes stranger, sizes odder than anything above. To check on the reality of those images can be very difficult, because people are not designed to spend any length of time underwater. But there is a very simple answer: an aquarium. If zoos contain animals that are out of place and managed for our benefit, then an aquarium, with its little pockets of another world, is perhaps the ultimate zoo. Most of the world's great aquariums are in cities by the sea, and often the aquarium itself is down at the harbour. But there is no need for this to be so. Just as land animals can be kept far from their natural home with the help of technology, so can fish in aquariums. Even so, the Sunshine International Aquarium in Tokyo is a bit of a surprise.

To get there you take the lift in Sunshine City, a tower block that contains shops, restaurants, offices and apartments. As you step out on the tenth floor you see ahead of you a tank containing two dolphins and a dugong. It is the first exhibit in the Sunshine Aquarium. If ever animals were out of place it is surely here, 30 metres or more above the endless traffic that clogs the streets of Tokyo. And yet the Sunshine International Aquarium, with dozens of exhibits containing hundreds of animals, is a great success. The Japanese crowd in to see not only the marine mammals but also the giant coral reef tanks, the spectacular collections of tropical fish, lungfish, axolotls, even a Baikal fur seal. Here you can check all those underwater pictures and discover that they do not lie, and you can do it comfortably and in the dry, without any special apparatus.

Fish in tanks are lovely, and it is not surprising that aquariums all over the world are very popular attractions. Part of the reason is that it is very easy to satisfy fishes' physical needs and that makes them easy to display well. A reliable supply of clean water is one essential – not usually a problem if the aquarium is by the water's edge. At Chicago's Shedd Aquarium they simply suck the water straight out of Lake Michigan. What does concern the fish is the temperature of the water, and its chemical composition. Keeping it cool or warm is not difficult; it just requires plant capable of doing the job. Chemicals, too, can be easily managed. Sea-water can be made artificially by adding the requisite salts in the right amounts. The home aquarist buys a packet of Instant Ocean, the Shedd Aquarium buys kilograms of the different chemicals and mixes up billion-litre batches of artificial sea-water. Filters keep the water clean by removing any suspended particles and biological treatment beds take out waste products, so that the water circulating through the tanks is far clearer than you would get in the wild. Measuring devices monitor the condition of the water continuously and any problems can be corrected more or less automatically by a computer.

So much for the physical needs of the fish. The visitors' needs are as easily fulfilled. Settings for the fish are made from fibreglass and resin, and because the scale is often so much smaller than in an exhibit for land animals, the work is that much more manageable. The water, despite being so clear, has a way of hiding imperfections, and because most people do not know what it really looks like under the surface there is less need for accurate detail. Water-weeds thrive under most conditions, and although I may have downplayed the human effort involved in setting up good aquarium tanks, the result is a series of beautiful and attractive cages housing all manner of strange aquatic animals.

If you have a taste for the macabre, the place to visit is the Danish Aquarium outside Copenhagen. The prize exhibit there is a shoal of large piranhas that occupies a tank overgrown with jungly plants. A waterfall plunges into the pool, and on the bottom are algae-encrusted skulls. I had expected piranhas to be evil, dark, drab fish, but in fact they are very lovely, with golden scales that catch the light. Hovering quietly in their lurex, they looked like a team of resting ballroom dancers, and like ballroom dancers they become supremely vicious when the occasion demands. It does so once a day when, as part of an educational display, the curator pours a small jar of meat extract into the waterfall. As the fish sense the blood they go into a frenzy and start flashing about in a whirling mêlée: a cod lowered into their midst is soon picked clean. Some of the piranhas suffer too, judging from the number with bite-shaped chunks missing from their fins.

Having demolished the cod they quieten down again, and their keeper calmly gets into the water with them. All that splashing has dirtied the glass and disturbed the visitors' view; it must be cleaned, and the only place that job can be done from is in the water. Those of us who have just seen the fish swing into action rather hope that they are sated. They aren't, as they demonstrate by tearing into another fish after the cleaner has got out unscathed, but – perhaps because he has been doing this since they were very small fry – they paid him no attention at all.

Little tanks of tropical fish are always pleasing to the eye, but since they are so easy to keep at home they are not the sort of thing one expects to find in an aquarium. At the Shedd, however, they show what the professionals can do. In a lovely room decorated in Chinese manner with carved red scrollwork and

Piranhas at Copenhagen, beautiful and educational

gilded bamboo is a collection of exquisite tropical tanks. Each has crystal-clear water, lush plants, lovely backdrops, and marvellous flashing jewels of fish. Shoals of gleaming neon tetras, swordtails, sharks, fancy guppies by the score, mollies, and all the old familiar tropical fish lifted out of the ordinary by the perfection of their presentation.

These small tanks are the bread and butter of the average aquarium, but there are new moves afoot to build bigger and bigger tanks, recreating a section of the ocean. One of the first was the Shedd's giant tank, which holds nearly 350,000 litres and houses a selection of warm-water reef fish. Corals are all but impossible to keep in captivity because they need very bright sunlight and a continuous swishing of water back and forth to keep them alive. But that hardly matters, because the living polyps of most corals vanish into their skeletons by day, and the dead skeletons are easy to collect and imitate, so the models look exactly as most people expect coral to look.

The Shedd's big tank is relatively small and obviously tank-like, but it was the forerunner of some startling new developments. Baltimore Aquarium boasts not one but two giant tanks, stacked one above the other. They are shaped like oval race-tracks, and a spiralling ramp guides visitors down the inside. The top tank contains $1\frac{1}{4}$ million litres of water, kept in place by acrylic windows that are 4 metres high and 7.5 centimetres thick. This tank is designed to be an Atlantic coral reef, stacked with artificial corals and stocked with the huge variety of fish normally seen in that kind of environment, and it works. I was particularly pleased to notice a triggerfish listing blissfully to one side while little cleaner fish buzzed about it removing bits of dead skin, parasites and the like, an example of natural behaviour successfully recreated in the tank.

The lower ring tank at Baltimore is slightly smaller but no less impressive. It mimics the open ocean, so there is no fancy scenery and the light is dimmer. Through the clear water, swimming against the current that circles the tank, the visitor sees the efficient shapes of sharks – lemon sharks, bull sharks, tiger sharks and nurse sharks – cruising by. Shoals of large snappers and groupers mingle with the sharks, and between them flap cownose rays and stingrays. The viewing ramp is often blocked by appreciative knots of people just watching.

Hong Kong's Ocean Park claims that its Atoll Reef is 'the nearest thing to a coral atoll ever created on dry land'. The reef is situated 30 metres above Hong Kong Harbour, with a view over Repulse Bay to Middle Island. The tank holds $1\frac{1}{2}$ million litres, an unimaginable quantity that is not made any more real by translating it into 2000 tonnes of water, and is designed to simulate a Pacific coral atoll in every detail. Walking into the building you confront the top of the tank, which has been cunningly decorated to look like the surface of a lagoon. Over on the far side a canoe lies tied up to a tree-trunk, and two plastic flamingos supposedly enhance the illusion. Moving around the outside of the tank you see a sandy bottom decorated with isolated coral heads, just as you would close inshore, but as you walk down the spiral ramp, as if you were moving deeper and further out, the light becomes dimmer, the coral more densely packed, and the fish more numerous. Down some steps you come to the region representing the outer slope of the atoll, where the corals and the fish are different from those in the shallows. More than a hundred species of fish live together in this section of the tank, choosing to remain at this depth because that is where they would be in the ocean. Lower still the light is very dim and here are the big fish of the open ocean.

Ramps and stairs are cleverly combined in the Atoll Reef to give you the feeling that you have travelled out a long way from the shores of the lagoon to the coral-free deeps, and as you stroll through the dimly-lit corridors it is quite easy to imagine that you are indeed walking freely on the bottom of the ocean. This is not as far-fetched as it sounds, for there are some places – Okinawa in Japan and Eilat in Israel – where you can walk along the ocean bottom. Under-water passages take you out onto the reef so that you can observe genuine coral populated by free fish. To be perfectly honest, though, while the technology of these undersea corridors is impressive, the fish are better seen in Ocean Park.

The culmination of this trend to bigger, more complete aquarium tanks, at least for the moment, is the dome tank at Seattle. It is not as big as Ocean Park, nor as heavily stocked as Baltimore, but it is special because it has turned the whole concept of an aquarium display inside out. Instead of being given a window onto the water the people are enclosed within a tank. Concrete spars hold thick panes in a dome, the better to withstand the pressure of the water, and the fish are not only in front of the people, they are also above and below them. Despite the bars, the experience is more like being underwater than is the case with any of the other giant tanks. Beyond the glass is a scene from Puget Sound, the harbour in which the Seattle Aquarium is located. In the water are ling cod and flashing salmon in numbers to make a fisherman drool. Shark prowl around the bottom among the forests of tall white sea anemones, and a giant Pacific octopus hides in the crevices. There are harbour pilings, old car tyres and all the rest of the debris that one would expect at the end of a busy pier; and they are all fake. Just outside the tank is the real end of the pier, with many of the same species swimming around real pilings, real tyres and real debris. In the tank, however, all is artificial, under control, and part of the illusion.

Because of our new-found ability to build monstrous tanks, capable of comfortably containing hundreds of fish of many different species, all living together in a remarkably lifelike environment, a good aquarium can be a sub-stitute for Nature in a way that no safari park can ever stand in for Africa. Giant tanks offer people an outstanding view of something most will never be able to see for themselves, and unlike the land-based attempts to do the same, they do not appear to compromise the animals or the visitors. Nevertheless, for the true enthusiast there is nothing to compare with being underwater above a coral reef, something which, if you are in the right place, can be remarkably easy to achieve.

There is always some nervousness and tension as you prepare to dive. The equipment, on which your life will depend, has to be checked thoroughly. Signals have to be agreed between you and your companion, so that you will understand one another underwater. Sitting around on deck is awkward and uncomfortable, the tanks heavy on your back, the wetsuit cloying and the fins ungainly. There is fear, too, mostly of unknown things that somehow always seem to lurk in the depths. But there is also a great sense of anticipation, because, clichéd though it may sound, being underwater really is like being in another world.

People were never intended to live in water. They cannot see without a face-mask, and must have a supply of air to breathe. With those two basic requirements met, however, an astonishing world is waiting below the waves, one that is invisible almost all the time. By just floating over a coral reef in tropical waters you will see more than you can ever imagine. Nothing can prepare you for the colours of the fish, the strange shapes of the corals, the tiny shrimps that hide among the crevices, the outlandish snails and sea-slugs, the all but invisible comb-jellies, shimmering with iridescent lights just in front of your face-mask. With a snorkel you need never take your eyes off the scene below, but if you are bitten by the underwater bug you will want to learn to use scuba and be free of the surface. And if you learn to dive in the cold waters around England, which are far from boring, you will nevertheless yearn for the excitement and colour of a tropical reef.

One of the easiest places in the world to enjoy the spectacle of coral reefs is the John Pennecamp Coral Reef State Park, off the coast of Key Largo in Florida. The park runs, in a band 13 kilometres wide, for 34 kilometres up the coast and it has been protected since about 1960. You don't even have to be a diver to enjoy the reef. Stationed at the park is a specially designed boat, the *Discovery*, which takes people on what is billed as the World's Only Undersea Tour. The *Discovery* has been modified to include an underwater observation room, a sort of fish tank in reverse, in which people can sit in comfort and gaze at the coral heads and fish outside the window, while an informative commentary identifies the organisms for the onlookers and also provides some history of the park. The trip is an excellent way for anyone, even a non-swimmer, to enjoy the beauty of a reef. Occasionally, though, those inside the observation room may catch sight of people outside, joining the fish in the water; and that is the way to experience the reef.

For snorkellers, nothing could be simpler. If you have all your own equipment you just sign up, pay up, and crowd on board one of the boats at the dock. If you have no equipment, you can soon be kitted up at reasonable cost. A swift ride takes you out to one of the well-known dive sites, where the boat ties up to a large buoy. Experienced hands are in the water in a flash, while those who have never snorkelled before get an instant lesson in the basics. For the next two hours the waters around the boat teem, not with fish but with people.

The reef fish are presumably used to this kind of disturbance, for they stay around even when surrounded by thrashing humans. Most of the snorkellers are beginners, content to float on the surface and avoid choking, marvelling at what they can see but not venturing down in search of further excitement. A few are more expert and explore some distance from the boat, where they are more likely to see some of the shyer species, but a small rescue boat circles round like a marine sheepdog and keeps them from straying too far. After two hours everyone gets back in the boat and they head back for land, novices and experts alike enthusiastically describing the sights they have seen.

For me, though, scuba is the way to experience the reef. The glass-bottomed boat lets you see well enough, and snorkelling can be great fun, particularly over shallower reefs, but the freedom that scuba offers is worth all the hassle above water. The dive shops hire equipment to anyone with evidence of scuba competence, and boats loaded with divers and their gear fan out from the dock every couple of hours. Speeding along the channel out into the park, past the fringing mangroves and lane markers, it is a matter of minutes before we are on a buoy above an area called French Reef. With no wetsuit to struggle into, getting kitted up is easy, and soon we have rolled back out of the boat and are heading under.

First of the big tanks, the coral reef exhibit in Chicago. Fish in the tank are fed by hand, accompanied by running commentary from the diver

*Top* (*both pages*) the sights that greet a scuba diver underwater off Heron Island are truly astounding. Giant anemones and clouds of fish compete for attention. *Facing* among the larger fish are imperial angelfish and banded angelfish, while a Fridman's dottyback hides in a crevice. A coral trout stops to be groomed by a cleanerfish. The branched fire coral is to be avoided, but most of the coral is completely harmless (*above*)

*Top* capture in the wild is still the only way to collect sharks for exhibit. *Above* Seattle's dome turns the tank inside out, putting visitors on the inside

Down on the bottom, about 14 metres according to the depth gauge, the main problem is deciding where to look first. Massive heads of brain coral sit on the bottom, interspersed with flat-branched elk-horns and the broad plates of table coral. Here and there are easily recognised colonies of fire coral, the stinging nettle of the sea (but worse) – to be avoided at all costs. Among the corals are their bigger relatives the sea anemones, some large with fat tentacles, others smaller and finer. All this, lovely though it is, is no more than a beautiful backdrop for the more lively members of the reef community.

The variety of fish is bewildering, and even with an underwater identification chart it is hard to be certain which is which. Most conspicuous are the large shoals of yellow-and-black striped sergeant-major fish, but I quickly cease to notice these. Parrotfish, with their hard jaws designed to nibble at coral and urchins, attract my attention, and soon I have spotted midnight and blue parrot-fish, and then the appallingly bright stoplight parrotfish. My attention turns now to the grunts, more adventurous than the parrotfish and often in small shoals; I tick a variety of these off on my list. I home in on a coral head and, eager not to miss anything, look for the tiny things that would otherwise go unnoticed; sea-slugs, shrimps, small egg cases of who knows what, tiny anemones, electric-blue yellow-eyed fish lurking in little holes, but it is hard to concentrate on them when there is still so much else to be seen. A queen butterflyfish saunters past, and as I watch it go I lift my eyes from the coral to confront the sleek silvery outlines of four or five barracuda. Although they are about 10 metres away I can see them quite clearly.

The best moment comes near the end of the dive, about five minutes before I am due to go up. A little black fish stationed above a branching coral head catches my attention and I go over to investigate. It is about 10 centimetres long, like a broad leaf with yellow markings on the fins, and my card identifies it as a French angel. I drift over and steady myself about 30 centimetres away, when the little thing darts over and starts attacking me. At first I'm not sure what's happening, and then I realise. It is defending its territory, not against me, a great hulking brute that could never be mistaken for a French angel, but against the fish that it sees reflected in the shiny chrome of my mouthpiece. To check, I take my mouthpiece out and move it slowly away from my face, and the fish obediently follows, rushing in and trying to bite its reflection. I back off and watch the fish for a while, but then it is time to get back up to the boat, and so reluctantly I leave this perfect little display of animal behaviour.

Other dives in John Pennecamp were just as entertaining. At Sand Reef, for example, there are long canyons between strips of reef, and I was able to glide down them, gazing from side to side while effortlessly pushed along by a gentle current. The sea life was much the same, except that instead of the barracudas we saw several big rays go flapping past. That is how it is at most of the marine parks of the world, especially those in warm waters. Plenty to see and easy,

197

well-organised diving. You need the initial expertise to enable you to get close to underwater animals, but with that accomplished, the variety of experiences to be had is almost limitless.

Scuba diving, of course, is available wherever there is water and enthusiasts to enter it, but there has been an enormous growth lately in places that cater specifically for divers. Not surprisingly, most of these are in tropical waters where the physical conditions are that much pleasanter and the profusion of easily observed animals is almost overwhelming. Few of the great diving locations are as easy to visit and enjoy as John Pennecamp, which is special because it is so accessible to complete beginners, but there are many other places where people can meet fish close up in the wild. A catalogue of dive sites would serve no great purpose, except to indicate the popularity of this sport which, I think, rests on the opportunity it offers to get close to wild animals, to become part of their world. But there is one place that divers talk about wherever they gather, which in England usually means in the comfort of a pub after a marrow-chilling dive.

Fifty kilometres off the Brisbane coast of Australia at the southern end of the Great Barrier Reef is a tiny speck of sand called Heron Island. There are many holiday resorts on the islands of the barrier reef, but Heron is one of the few that is actually out on the edge of the reef, rather than just offshore. It owes its fame to the efforts of Walt Deas and his wife Jean; while he was dive master on Heron they both devoted considerable time to hand-feeding the fish at many of the prime diving locations, with the result that Heron has gained its reputation as the place where the fish are friendly. For a diver, it is heaven.

My first dive at Heron was at a place called Hole in the Wall. As at Pennecamp, there are buoys for the boats to attach to so that they do not damage the coral, and we splashed over and went down the buoy's anchor line. I was diving with Cindy, one of the resort scuba staff, who had with her a plastic jar full of scraps from the kitchens. I had seen Walt's film of Heron, and talked to Cindy while we were getting ready, but I was not prepared for the reception we got at the bottom. Monstrous fish came crowding in and soon Cindy was all but invisible at the centre of a cloud of fish. She opened the jar and pulled out bits of sausage. These floated in the water, but only for a moment before they were snatched by eager hungry animals. It was quite alarming at times, not least because a water logged finger bears an uncanny resemblance to a sausage, as I discovered several times. The fish are not so much friendly as greedy, and while it may be something of a thrill to be able to say that I have been nibbled by a coral trout, it was also quite painful.

Once the jar was empty we swam away from the anchor rope in search of other sights. Some of the bolder grunts came after us, insisting that we must have more food for them, but eventually we left them behind and continued our exploring. What lay before us was very similar to what I had seen at Pennecamp, except that everything seemed bigger. The coral heads were more massive, even the fragile ones. There was an anemone that must have been a metre across, rippling in the current and sheltering three clownfishes in its tentacles. A brown-tipped reef shark swam past just within the limit of our vision and there were huge angel fish on almost every coral head.

Other sites around the island showed that this was a general feature; bigger fish and better coral. The human pressure on Heron is not nearly as intense as it is at John Pennecamp, which probably explains why the coral is so much more abundant, though the daily feeding must have something to do with the size of the fish. In any case, Heron underwater went well beyond my expectations. On one dive we came across a loggerhead turtle resting in a cave in the coral. As we approached she backed out and swam around us, even allowing us to ride on her. I was struck by how graceful turtles are underwater, compared to the lumbering single-mindedness of a female coming ashore to lay, and also by the fact that she could easily have swum away and left us behind if she had wanted to. Perhaps she did not want to abandon her sleeping hole, to which she retreated as soon as we left the area.

As at Pennecamp, you do not have to be a scuba diver to enjoy the reef life at Heron Island. When the tide is in you can snorkel in the lagoon, protected from the Pacific swell by the fringing reef. And when the tide is out visitors are encouraged to walk with a guide and explore the reef on foot. This is an activity fraught with contradictions, for while it introduces people to the reef and the animals and plants that live there, it also threatens the existence of the reef. Coral, despite being hard and seemingly indestructible, is actually very vulnerable. Some species are so sensitive that the mere touch of a hand will kill the polyps that build the heads. Even the tougher species cannot survive being trampled repeatedly, but despite requests not to do so, it is often easier to walk on the coral than round it. Lifting pieces to see what is under them does no good either, and as the coral dies the fish and other organisms that depend on it leave. The guides are aware of the problem, and candidly admit that interesting specimens are harder to find now than they were a few years ago, but the reef walks are one of the big attractions of Heron. Stopping them is apparently out of the question. One solution might be a catwalk floating on pontoons, so that people could reach the outermost parts of the lagoon without having to walk over the coral, but that would cost money and the management of Heron Island is possibly not as sensitive to the long-term problems of exploiting the environment as it might be.

A member of the Queensland National Parks and Wildlife Service, which has a research station on the island and administers the reef around Heron as part of a State Park, told me a story that indicated how shortsighted exploitation can be. The fringing reef has always made access to the island difficult, limiting

199

A walk on the Great Barrier Reef introduces people to the wildlife but slowly kills it

it to high tide. Some people arrive by helicopter, but all supplies and most of the visitors come by ship. To avoid having to time everything to the tides, the management decided to open a deep-water channel through the reef. They did not consult anybody, but simply went ahead and dynamited the narrowest part. After all, what harm would a short, thin path through the reef do to an island surrounded by more of the same?

Before this exercise in underwater landscaping, the tide used to ebb evenly over the whole lagoon. Now, twice a day, it sluices in a rush through the deep-water channel like bathwater through the plughole, and as it does so it scours the sand from the bottom and carries it away. The lovely beach that used to lie in front of the resort buildings is now almost gone, and the buildings themselves are still there only because an ugly retaining wall was built in time to save their foundations. So far Heron has not lost all its attractions, and the diving off the reef is a good as ever. People who go there will still have an excellent wildlife experience. But the lagoon is not as interesting as it once was, and the deep-water channel is a symptom of a more generalised lack of concern for the long-term health of the environment.

A more immediate problem underwater is the lack of communications. Talking is all but impossible, and getting across the simplest information, particularly if it involves anything out of the ordinary, like identifying a fish, leads to absurd pantomimes and misunderstandings. On one dive my friend asked me what fish had just swum past. It was a queen angel, which I duly mimed by putting on an imaginary crown and beating imaginary wings while wearing what I hoped was a beatific expression. He immediately grabbed me and headed for the surface, having understood that I had a splitting headache (a symptom of poisoning), was in severe pain, and needed help as I was too tired to swim. So providing information in an underwater park is extremely difficult. The guide can talk things over before and after the dive, but once down there it is very difficult to discuss anything. In that respect underwater exploration, quite apart from the equipment it requires, demands some expertise and enthusiasm if it is to be rewarding. Some underwater parks have solved the information problem by sinking underwater labels. If you dive at Buck Island Reef in the US Virgin Islands you can follow a self-guided tour round the reef, with trail markers to show you where to go and labels that identify the corals along the way. There are even signs identifying some of the fish, particularly the territorial species that are likely to stay around one coral head. The line between zoo and wild is thus further blurred, even underwater, where it is the people who are kept captive by their equipment.

One of the joys of underwater diving is the great freedom you enjoy. All the bulky equipment is weightless and you can come and go as you please, staying down as long as you have air. But the sight of a free diver surrounded by fish is

201

no longer a guarantee that the fish are in the wild. As aquariums master the skills of building enormous tanks, maintenance requires more than a long arm and a rolled-up sleeve. Divers have to go inside to clean the glass and repair any bits of broken scenery. Even more important, since the huge tank houses a mixture of species, it needs human intervention to ensure that every fish gets enough to eat. If food were simply dumped in the water the big fish would get most, and grow bigger, while the smaller and shyer specimens would starve.

The aquarium usually takes advantage of a diver having to enter the tank by featuring it as a special attraction. People are encouraged to stand by and watch as he swims through the tank handing titbits to the inmates. It is a grand spectacle wherever it is done, but one of the best organised of such shows is at the Shedd Aquarium in Chicago. The tank there is comparatively small, only 350,000 litres, and the diver is not completely free. He gets his air from a compressor that feeds him through an umbilical cord, called by divers a hookah rig. That has its drawbacks, chief among them being that the feed hose can get tangled up in the corals and bring them tumbling down, but it also has one great advantage: it allows the diver to be in two-way communication with the surface. Set into the mask is a microphone, through which the diver can talk to the crowd gathered outside and tell them exactly what he is doing. Alongside the wire carrying his messages up is another that brings sound down to an underwater earphone. A microphone in the crowd leads into the earpiece and allows onlookers to ask the diver questions, which he then answers immediately. He can point out specific fish, tell little boys that the sharks in this tank are not man-eaters, explain that the evil moray eel only wants to be cuddled, and so on. It is an excellent bridge between the people in the air and the fish underwater.

Being in the big tank at the Shedd gave me the chance to think about our relationship with fish. Perhaps it is because we normally see so little of them, despite the fact that water covers so much of the earth, that we find them so fascinating. Perhaps it is because they are so odd; it is very hard to empathise with a fish. Underwater, you come closer to imagining what it might be like, but you are still a long way from being a fish. I was floating weightlessly among the fish, but I could not control going up and down as easily as they could. I could feel currents of water as one of the bigger sharks cruised past, but fish are acutely sensitive to movements in the water. They can practically see things using this information, so sensitive are they. Most of all, I was constantly aware of my lifeline to the surface, while they of course were happily breathing water. So although I could get closer to them, I was still very much an alien, visiting their world.

The physical strangeness of life underwater is bad enough, but the mental life of a fish seems completely impenetrable. This is a disturbing thought, especially sitting in front of a lovely tank of jewelfish. If an animal moved

202

backwards and forwards incessantly round its cage I would say it was behaving abnormally. Fish keep circling all the time, but unlike the mammals they look good as they do so. We simply do not know enough about them to decide when they are psychologically healthy, and this worries me. People tell me that I am concerned for nothing, that fish do not have minds or psychologies, and that as long as they look good to us that is all that matters. Perhaps they are right as far as true fish are concerned, but trouble arises when they categorise as 'fish' everything that lives in the water.

Marine mammals certainly cannot be thought of as mindless. Indeed some people would have us believe that cetaceans – whales and dolphins – are more intelligent than we are. Yet we seem to treat them as we treat the fish in our aquariums, if not worse. Minnesota Zoo is very proud of its two beluga whales. Anookalik, the male, is 4 metres long and weighs 725 kilograms. His partner, Anana, is only 3.5 metres long and weighs 532 kilograms. The pair of them live in a bare green swimming pool of under 2 million litre capacity. If they are as intelligent as people claim, then surely they deserve better than that. The ocean may be as featureless as their pool, but whales are intensely social animals and I doubt that a single pair provides one another with all that much stimulation. But who knows? They seem to behave fairly normally and I hope they will confound me and breed (though a surplus of captive-bred beluga whales is a rather daunting prospect). The question remains of whether we really need to see animals such as these in captivity. I think not.

Dolphins caught in the wild, still unfortunately the main source of aquarium stocks

These arguments apply in even greater force to the other cetaceans commonly kept in captivity, dolphins and orcas. A recent survey in Britain discovered that the average lifespan of a dolphin in captivity is very short, just ten years compared to more than thirty-five in the wild, and that dolphins in captivity suffer all manner of diseases not found in their wild counterparts. Killer whales do even worse; in the wild they too can live thirty-five years, but in captivity they survive on average just two years and seven months. These animals are very popular, and hence profitable exhibits, as is borne out by the huge fees that are spent on vets to look after them. Clearly they are worth the investment. But I think it is up to the establishments that keep them either to improve their conditions or else to have the generosity to admit that they are not suited for life in a swimming pool.

In general, I think that even the most up-to-date aquariums are lagging far behind the best zoos in their approach to keeping animals in captivity. The prettiness of the exhibits is deceptive, quite unlike the bare barred cages of old, and in any case is not to the point. I have argued that much of the aesthetic appeal of zoo exhibits is for our benefit, not the animals', and the same is true of aquariums. What matters is the attitude of the people who are keeping the animals in captivity, and in that respect the aquariums of today are far too like the menageries of yesterday.

If we apply the old touchstone of reproduction, we find very little captive breeding occurring. There are exceptions, of course, like the four-eyed fish at Stuttgart, which are multiplying very well and can now be supplied to aquariums

Some breeding does go on, like these harlequin cichlids in Chicago and the four-eyed fish in Stuttgart

the world over from a captive-bred stock. At the Shedd Aquarium the cichlids breed well, though there is no concerted effort to breed them as a source of supply for other establishments. These African lake fish, incidentally, offer a spectacular display of types of territorial and parental behaviour. They suck up the sand and dig a nest for spawning, and many shelter the eggs and fry in their mouths. Visitors completely miss all this because they have no idea what to look out for, and the aquarium does not tell them. Some other places are trying to breed marine mammals. However, these examples are all exceptional. The vast majority of the animals on show in aquariums, including the marine mammals, were captured in the wild and will not breed during their stay in captivity. One survey revealed that of 217 fish species recognised as endangered by the International Union for the Conservation of Nature, only nine were breeding in captivity, and seven of those were being bred at only one establishment. The seas seem so limitless that the old approach holds; when something in an aquarium dies, go out and catch a replacement.

It was to get some new specimens that I was here now, steaming away from Miami on the Seaquarium's research vessel. As the gleaming skyscrapers of Miami Beach glided by our starboard side the captain explained what we were doing. Last night the boat had been out and laid down two lines, each 90 metres long. Every 5 metres along each line is a spur formed by a 2-metre rope that ends in a chain and a 15-centimetre steel hook. On each hook is a lump of bonito as bait. We were on a shark hunt, and the line with its spur is designed to allow the sharks, if any had taken the bait, to continue circling and thus continue breathing. For the Seaquarium we had to bring them back alive.

It took us about an hour to get to where the captain had set his lines. On the way I tried to talk to the two crew members, both workers at the Seaquarium. They were an odd pair. Dave was huge, blond and very well muscled, with a broken nose and tough face, and later on, watching him at work, I came to think of him as the sort of chap I would want on my side in a bar fight. Chuck was smaller, at least by comparison, darker and more intense. But they were both quiet with anticipation and reluctant to discuss the prospects of success. All Dave would say was that they usually got something. With forty baited hooks in these shark-rich waters, it would be hard not to; but what?

By now we were on the buoy marking the end of one of the lines, and the work began in earnest. Dave hauled the big orange float in and stationed himself at the gunwhale where the line came aboard. His mate was to the rear, and the captain had come down from the bridge to a small control panel amidships, where he had a clear view of the proceedings. Dave began to haul on the line. The first hook came up, bereft of its bait, and he and Chuck exchanged glances. Sharks do not nibble the bait without taking the hook, but smaller fish do: if a school had passed this way shortly after the lines had been laid they might have left forty unbaited hooks. Before these thoughts were complete, however, the second hook was on board, with a bonito head still firmly attached. We had worried for nothing. Chuck tore the bait from the hook and flung it into the sea.

They were a smooth team, Dave hauling in the line and Chuck removing the bait, if there was any, and slotting the hook into the rack along the transom. The rack was more than half full when Dave shouted 'I've got one'. Not much changed, except that the hauling became harder. Peering over the edge I could see nothing, but then I spotted a dark-brown shark, about 1 metre long. 'Bull shark. Dead,' said Dave. The rhythm was broken briefly as the two of them lifted the shark in and laid it on the deck. Then they resumed their work. After a further five or six empty hooks there was another cry as another shark came in view. 'Black tip. Dead', took its place alongside the bull shark.

We had almost finished the first line when Dave began to mutter that there was something really big on the end. He strained and pulled, the veins on his arms popping out, and got Chuck to join him. There was jocular but nervous talk of *Jaws III*, at that time not yet a finished film, which died down as the effort continued. The captain was making fine adjustments to the boat, trying to motor it back along the line rather than haul the line in. Whatever it was was very heavy. Suddenly the spell was broken. All we had hooked was a fisherman's lobster-pot. Without hesitating Dave put on a face mask, grabbed a knife, and jumped over to sever the other man's line. 'He'd've cut mine,' the captain said to nobody in particular.

With the lobster-pot no longer holding him up Dave soon hauled the remaining few hooks aboard, and after a short breather turned his attention to the line on the starboard side. Almost at once another dead black tip came in, and then there was a long wait, during which the captain reassured me that they don't normally get this many, or this many dead ones. About halfway down the line was something else, a hammerhead, cloudy eyes at the end of the grotesque fleshy stalks that give it its name. 'Hammerhead,' said Dave unnecessarily. 'They never survive.' That one they didn't bother to bring in, though I never learned why; they just retrieved the hook and let the big fish sink slowly out of sight.

Finally, about three-quarters of the way through the second line, we got what we were after. 'Bull shark. Big one, and alive.' Instead of lifting it in they unclipped its spur line and guided it back to the stern. The captain raised a gate there and, passing the line beneath it, they pulled the 2-metre shark through and into a flooded holding tank. Dave jumped in with it, sticking his hand into those fearful jaws to remove the hook, while Chuck brought in the few remaining hooks on the line. Carefully cradling the shark in his massive grip, Dave walked it round and round the tank, forcing water over its gills to keep it alive.

Satisfied with the shark's condition he helped Chuck tidy up the lines before the two of them set about dealing with the dead sharks on the deck. They measured them, and then deftly chopped their heads off. The bodies went overboard, the heads into garbage bags 'for a guy at Metro Zoo. He collects shark jaws for research.' A quick hosing got rid of the blood and we could all relax for the remainder of the trip back to the Seaquarium. The captain had radioed ahead, so we were greeted by a welcoming party, with all the equipment ready to transfer the shark to the aquarium.

The captain backed the boat into the quay and tied it off with a good gap behind the stern. A wooden crate, punctured with drainage holes, was slung from an overhead track behind the boat, and lowered into the water. The sliding door on the crate and the sliding gate on the transom were both lifted and Dave jumped in with the shark to steer it into the crate. When the two of them were safely in, the door was lowered and the crate lifted out of the water, pulled across on the rails, and lowered into the Seaquarium's shark pool. This is a large ring-shaped pool, about 6 metres across and 45 metres in diameter, filled with sharks of various kinds. Dave, brave though he was, did not guide the new inmate out, he simply shoved it through the now open door. The shark, to my horror, gave one or two strokes of its tail, bumped blindly into the wall, and sank inertly to the bottom.

As the captain explained, it had never before encountered an obstacle in his life, and would have to learn to avoid the walls. Every time he stopped, his supply of oxygen stopped too, so he had to be kept moving. We took turns with the long gaff pole, hooking him round a fin and pulling him through the water. Most of the time he remained a dead weight, but now and again he would stir himself and swim away off the hook. We would shout exultantly 'He's going,' only to have to grab the pole back and get him moving again after he had failed to negotiate a turn. After two hours or more the rescue bids were becoming less frequent, and he seemed to have everything sorted out, turning now rather than ploughing into the walls, and swimming quite strongly.

'One out of five's not a bad average,' the captain said. 'Let's hope we don't have to get another one too soon,' and off he went to see to his other duties Dave and Chuck had vanished for the day, and I was left watching the shark, my shark, adjust to his new surroundings. Bull sharks are not endangered. Being caught by aquariums is no threat to their continued existence. That four other sharks had died was unfortunate, but a lot less wasteful than taking, say, gorillas from the wild. Here in captivity the shark would give people something of a thrill, continuing the long tradition of the menagerie, perhaps helping to educate them. And when he did die, the captain and Dave and Chuck could always go out and get another one.

Sharks are awesome. There is something about them that inspires fear and wonder out of all proportion to their actual behaviour, and the sharks are the animals in aquariums that are most likely to be stared at in silent appreciation. I would like to think that this was because people recognise their superb adaptations, moulded by evolution and unchanged in aeons. More likely, though, it is the old fascination with the fearful. Sea World in Orlando, Florida, just along the road from Disney World, has recognised the deep hold that sharks have over us and turned it into one of the most awe-inspiring aquarium exhibits anywhere. Coral reef tanks may be lovely to look at and walk past, and giant open ocean tanks delight us with their massed schools of fish, but Sea World's Shark Encounter touches a very deep fear.

Visitors are prepared for their encounter in a special theatre in which they see very slick multi-media presentations that dwell on the ruthless feeding efficiency of the shark. Vast blown-up stills of sharks, many the prey's-eye view, magnify the horror, and the centrepiece of the show is a short film showing a feeding frenzy. 'Thus armed with a better understanding of the shark's role in the marine ecosystem,' as the PR manager put it to me, the visitors are ready for the Shark Encounter. The screens lift, and behind them is the giant shark tank. Some three dozen sharks patrol the waters, and there are Sea Maids on hand to point out the differences between the bulls and browns, nurses and tigers. Most visitors, however, are eager to move on to the next stage of the encounter.

A transparent tunnel leads beneath the aquarium, and along the 36-metre-long tunnel runs a moving walkway. Step onto it, and you are transported through and among the sharks. The mixture of fear and security is delicious. Acrylic, 10 centimetres thick, protects them from the menacing tiger sharks gliding by just above their heads. But didn't the mother shark in *Jaws III* bust through just such panels? Not only that, but the whole of that anti-biological fantasy took place at Sea World, in this very Shark Encounter. 'Could they escape?' seems to be the most frequent question, asked by children of all ages. Mouths drop open as the sharks, their own teeth exposed, swim overhead, but all too quickly the encounter is over.

At the end of the ride you are encouraged to hang around and watch the sharks through windows let into the sides of the tank, and perhaps the eeriest sensation of all is seeing more visitors still travelling down the tunnel, seemingly with nothing between them and the sharks. The Shark Encounter is a fine technological achievement, a tank holding $2\frac{1}{4}$ million litres of artificial sea water, 18 metres wide and 36 metres long with that terrifying tunnel through its heart. Just keeping it clean enough to sustain the thrill is a massive chore; two mornings a week the sharks are herded behind a net while two divers vacuum the floor and chamois the inside of the acrylic.

The sharks swim endlessly around the tank, up and over the tube often enough to scare the people within, completely at ease. The visitors cringe on the moving walkway, getting the safe fright that they came for. The exhibit is a success. But despite the newness of the technology on which the lives of the

sharks and the people depend, the Shark Encounter, like most aquariums, represents the oldest traditions of the menagerie; the exotic, the unfamiliar, the rare, the terrifying, firmly under our control. Animals in captivity to be gawped at.

All but one of the sharks in the Encounter were caught in the wild, and they will be replaced with more animals from the wild. That may not matter for the moment.

# Chapter Eight

# CLOSER AND CLOSER

Although the moon was full it was hidden behind thick clouds from which occasional huge drops fell. 'See those people up there?' Peering into the darkness I could just make out four slightly darker blobs seated up on the dunes. 'Yes,' I replied hesitantly. 'They're waiting for that log to start climbing out of the water,' my guide informed me, with ill-disguised superiority. We were on Mon Repos beach, in Queensland, Australia, one of the world's foremost turtle rookeries, and to tell the truth the log did look to me very like a turtle, waiting patiently as the surf washed over it.

'Come on,' said Duncan, 'they'll definitely be coming up further down the beach by peg eight.' Duncan is Duncan Limpus, and he knows Mon Repos beach and its turtles as well as you know your street and neighbours. As we walked down the strand, my eyes slowly becoming properly adjusted to the dark, I asked how many seasons he had been coming to Mon Repos. 'Thirteen.' 'And how old are you?' 'Thirteen.' Duncan is Colin Limpus's son, and Colin Limpus is a senior research scientist with the Queensland National Parks and Wildlife Service. He has been coming to Mon Repos since before Duncan was born, for fifteen years, and quite apart from the extremely valuable scientific research that he directs, he also makes it possible for tens of thousands of ordinary tourists to get close to animals; as close, if not closer, than they would be in a zoo but with the essential difference that these animals really are wild and free.

My attention had wandered to the unfamiliar sky, now clear, with the constellation of Orion upside down and high overhead. 'Three flashes,' Duncan whispered urgently. 'That's the signal. They've got one.' We hurried down the beach a further 100 metres and found Colin pointing out the track to an attentive group of people – families with young kids, teenaged couples, an elderly man. He showed us the marks made by the turtle's flippers and the bottom of her shell. The flipper marks alternated left and right up the beach like an open zipper. 'Turtles move in two ways,' Colin told us. 'Greens, hawksbills and flatbacks breaststroke up the beach using both flippers together. Loggerheads and ridleys alternate. We know this can't be a ridley because ridleys have never nested on Mon Repos, so it must be a loggerhead.' We all crouched to examine the tracks and verify what Colin had said, and then moved up to where the dunes rise up out of the beach itself. There, just as Colin had said, was a female loggerhead.

She had finished the so-called body pit, the broad depression that she scoops out of the sand, and was busy excavating the nest proper. But she had a problem. Colin quickly noticed that her left hind flipper was torn, probably the result of an encounter with a shark, and it was not terribly efficient at digging out the egg chamber. Until she had started laying she could be easily distracted so we were warned to sit quietly, no torches, no talking, and especially no photographs. It seemed a long wait, probably because the damaged flipper was holding her up. In the half-light I thought I saw Colin reaching down behind the black bulk of the turtle, and I fancy he was lending a helping hand with the egg chamber. In any case, he soon enough gave the all clear. 'OK, she's started to lay. You can put your torches on and take some pictures.'

Flashlights popped, children and adults alike gasped, and the loggerhead kept on laying. After a while Colin reached into the egg pit and brought forth a couple of white globes, glowing in the gas light. He handed them round for people to touch. Some were keen to do so, others reluctant. 'They feel like slimy ping-pong balls,' offered one boy of about six, and everyone agreed with him. Then, while the loggerhead obviously squeezed out eggs, Australia's leading turtle scientist answered the many questions we had to ask.

He told us first about this particular turtle. The monel tags on her front flippers indicated that she had last visited Mon Repos to lay five years ago; this was the fourth clutch she had laid this season. She was probably at least fifty, although it was impossible to tell how much older she might be. Her weight was around 135 kilograms, and a tape measure along the top of her high domed shell gave a reading of 174 centimetres. Between reproductive seasons she lives up around New Caledonia, some 2000 kilometres away, eating mostly squid, jellyfish, and other seafood. When she has enough reserves to make eggs she swims south to Queensland, where there are specific courtship areas. There she mates, probably with three or four males, and then continues her journey south to Mon Repos. She stores the semen from her matings and uses it to fertilise a batch of eggs. When they are ripe she makes her first trip up the beach, there to abandon 150 eggs to the care of the dunes. Back in the water she starts another batch of eggs, and two and a half weeks later she is up on the beach again laying a second clutch. A turtle may lay five, six, or even seven clutches. Then, her reserves exhausted, it is back to the feeding grounds off New Caledonia. Some will return for another laying season after two years, some after three. Ours had taken five, and Colin has records of turtles that have come back after a nine-year absence.

Why was she crying? How did she know where to dig? How did she find the beach? How do the hatchlings find their way to the sea? As she finished laying and started the clumsy business of disguising her nest we learned the answers to all this and more. Colin's own research has shown that turtles use the elevation of the horizon to orient. Coming up the beach the gravid turtle heads for the highest part of the horizon, the dunes. Emptied, she aims for the lowest horizon, the sea – the same technique that the hatchlings use in their mad scramble for the water. Colin wastes no opportunity to preach the dangers of mixing humans and turtle beaches unwisely. Humans use lights at night and they can dazzle the turtles and blank out their view of the horizon. The result is that the hatchlings mill about aimlessly and even more of them than usual are picked off by predators. Colin's account, straightforward and simple, is all the more poignant when you realise not only that he discovered much of this himself, but also that this very rookery is threatened by a proposed new housing development behind the dunes.

Perhaps the most amazing thing that anyone learned that night concerned the delicate question of turtle sex. Or rather gender. 'The turtle,' as Ogden Nash wrote, 'lives twixt plated decks, which practically conceal its sex.' There is no way, Colin told us, to tell from the outside whether a hatchling is male or female. But when you look inside you can tell, and you discover that it depends on the temperature in the nest. Warm nests produce only females, cool ones only males. Out on the reef the white sand and breezes keep the nests cool, and so the rookeries on the reef islands produce predominantly male loggerheads. The warmer brown beach at Mon Repos produces almost all females. Which is a shame, because it is far easier to protect a turtle rookery on an uninhabited island than one near a thriving town and port; but the beach at Mon Repos, because it produces many more females, is more important to conservation.

By now our turtle had truly finished. She turned around and started back to sea. Once again the lights were doused as we followed her slow progress down to the water's edge. The first wave sluiced over her and washed off some of the dry sand she had kicked onto her shell. I felt quite relieved that she had made it. She lunged forward with one last heave. Another wave picked her up and she was gone, to ripen a last load of eggs before the season ends, or perhaps to journey back north to the feeding grounds. With luck she will be back in another five years and Colin will be here to record her return. With luck the housing development will not materialise and she will be able to find her way into the dunes, where she will be available to educate another posse of tourists and to contribute to our understanding of turtle life.

As it happens I have been interested in sea turtles for some time and have written about their biology and conservation for the past five years or more, seen most of the species in captivity, and once even swam with a green turtle in the Mediterranean off Crete. Little that I heard that evening from Colin was new to me. But nothing had prepared me for witnessing the laying. The strength and determination of the female, her biological imperative to reproduce, had impressed me most powerfully. I strolled back along the beach with a renewed sense of wonder about natural selection. The other visitors, I am confident, were equally impressed, though perhaps in different ways.

The State of Queensland has recognised the unique importance of Mon Repos and exploited both its scientific worth and its appeal for visitors. As a result Colin Limpus, perhaps more than any zoo director, can honestly say that by offering people contact with animals he is truly furthering conservation and education. The whole spectacle is entertaining too, but in the best possible sense. Enthusiastic naturalists have always been able to satisfy their urge to be close to wildlife. The glorious thing about Mon Repos is that it is open to anyone, and most of the people who visit the turtles are ordinary holiday-makers. Mon Repos is not a zoo in the conventional sense of the word, but by judiciously managing the people and – to a lesser extent – the animals it fulfils many of the same purposes, and is just one example of a growing number of similar facilities. Australia boasts several such places where wild animals have been slightly stage managed to allow people to experience them more readily.

Sometimes it is a question of providing something the animal wants. The bird sanctuary at Currumbin, south of Brisbane on Queensland's Gold Coast, is an average sort of zoo with ample facilities for people to get among the native Australian animals and see them close to. Currumbin's fame, however, rests on a daily spectacle enacted at about 4 o'clock in the afternoon, and it depends on the co-operation of wild birds. The surrounding area is home to large flocks of gorgeously coloured rainbow lorikeets. These normally feed on the nectar of flowers, especially eucalyptus. But they have learned that a very acceptable substitute is to be had each afternoon at Currumbin and so especially when the rains have washed the nectar out of the flowers, in they come.

There is a small oval arena, grassed and containing two strange contraptions that look like some kind of complicated fairground ride. Each is made of a big wheel to which are attached several smaller ones. The wheels are fitted with perches and a plate-holder, and into the holder goes an aluminium pie plate filled with a sloppy mixture of water and honey with bits of soggy bread in it. The lorikeets cannot resist this hand-out. As they flock down in their thousands, the flapping of their wings makes the wheels turn, enhancing the fairground impression. But the crowds lining the arena have not come only to watch this spectacle. Everyone who wants it is given a plate of ersatz nectar, and the birds will flock to them too. The result is a curious sensation of being an especially attractive tree, with lorikeets all over you. They are on your head, up both arms, fluttering over the plate, everywhere. Now and again something alarms them, and the entire flock coalesces and whirrs off in a blur of colour, but they soon return to continue the feast, much to everyone's delight.

The lorikeets at Currumbin are wild, but come in close for a taste of honey water

Almost 1600 kilometres further south, off the coast near Melbourne, there is another wild zoo, and here no bribery takes place to bring you close to the animals; you just have to be in the right place at the right time. Phillip Island is confusing to a Briton because although all the town names have a familiar holiday ring – Cowes, Newhaven, Ventnor and Rhyl – they are in a completely unfamiliar geographic arrangement. That scarcely matters, though, since the island is not very big; and everywhere there are signs pointing to the Penguin Parade. Every night, after dark, the surfers and holiday-makers desert Summerland beach and it becomes the scene for a unique wildlife experience.

Fairy penguins are the only penguins that nest in Australia. Each day the birds abandon their burrows in the hills behind Summerland beach and go out to sea to feed. As night falls they return and waddle back up to the burrows. For the past fifty-four years people have been present nearly every night to watch the parade. What started with one man, who brought friends out in a horse and buggy to watch the penguins by the light of a kerosene lamp, is now a highly organised operation. There are concreted grandstand steps, a loud-speaker system and floodlighting, and it is visited by about 200,000 adults (and untold children) each year. The penguins have nonetheless gone from strength to strength, and fortunately continue to parade, regardless of their human audience.

As the sun sets the birds mass out beyond the breakers in large rafts but make no move towards the beach until after dark. Then they begin to swim to

215

shore until they are dumped unceremoniously on the sand by a wave. Pausing to gather their wits the elegant little birds, most of them less than a third of a metre tall, begin their march up the beach, leaning absurdly into the slope near the top. They head for two collection points where they are held back by human volunteers until enough of a group has gathered. Then they are released to make their way along a path through the crowds of people watching to the dunes behind the beach. White lines mark the penguin paths, and orderlies ensure that the people stay behind them. Once five or six groups have passed through, the crowds begin to disperse along the path up the hill. Along the way they stop to watch the penguins find their burrows, and in the breeding season they will be rewarded with the sight of adult and young greeting one another ecstatically before the parent regurgitates a load of fish for the chick.

The penguin parade on Phillip Island, like the turtles at Mon Repos and the lorikeets of Currumbin, gives people all that a zoo offers, and more. There is conservation, education, and above all entertainment and close contact with the animals. Similar set-ups, which aim to give ordinary people some of the experiences that have always been available to the keen naturalist, are springing up all around the world, an extension of the zoo to the wild and an expression of our growing concern for wildlife. The most impressive of these, an ocean away in California, combines the ancient pleasure of stalking one's prey with the newly acquired pleasure of touching it rather than killing it.

There isn't any easy way to tell you about it; the mystical is not my style and the factual will seem too prosaic. The sea is wet and a bit choppy. The whales are very big. Whale lice fill little dimples in the whale's skin, and barnacles encrust its head and tail. The whale feels exactly like a wet inner tube. When it comes up beside you and blows you can, if the light is right, see a spectrum surrounding its snout; a rainblow I call it. But all that doesn't even begin to convey what it is like to be on a whale-watching cruise.

Grey whales migrate each year from the plentiful icy waters of the Bering Sea down to the calm coastal lagoons of Baja California, the tongue of land that sticks down from California proper. The cows calve in the lagoons and the males follow them down to mate. Whalers in the last century, having discovered the lagoons, made short work of the grey whales, reducing the population as drastically as they reduced the whales' blubber for oil. Whaling for greys ended in 1873, when there were too few left to support the industry. A hundred years on, under stringent protection, the grey whales have recovered well, and now a different kind of whaler joins them each winter in the lagoons.

MV *Executive* is a 30-metre boat that spends nine months of the year taking sport fishermen out of San Diego. Between January and April, however, she runs ten-day cruises down the Baja pensinsula to visit the whales on their calving grounds. Different groups charter the *Executive*, and the one I was on had been organised by the Oceanic Society, an educational charity interested in all things maritime. Not all of us – there were thirty-two tourists on board – were members, but we all benefited from the two naturalists that the Society provided, in addition to the *Executive*'s own resident naturalist. There was information aplenty for those who wanted it, to complement the animals we were all expecting to see. And although we may have liked to think of ourselves as intrepid marine adventurers, the boat was new, very well-equipped, and served better food, and more of it, than many mainland restaurants.

Cruises in general attract many different kinds of people, and this one was no exception. Many were there escaping the winter, having a rest, getting some sun. Most were from California, but there was a good representative spread from the rest of the United States, and there was, as well as me, an English couple from Leeds. What united us all was a more than passing interest in natural history; and there was also a definite subgroup of whale freaks, people feeding a passion for cetaceans. One admitted that she was taking her eighth annual fix of whales. She hates camping, she told me, but has happily camped up on the New England coast where there are whales to be seen. Another explained that she was 'into dolphins', and spent most of her time the first few days absorbedly reading a mystical, and somewhat lurid, novel about a woman and a dolphin. There was a keen birder, a psychologist with an interest in astronomy, plenty of retired people enjoying themselves doing something different. We were all after whales, but we would accept any experience of wildlife that was offered.

Even before we had left the harbour there was considerable excitement. We stopped at the bait tanks to scoop up some anchovies; the *Executive* is a fishing boat, the crew are fishermen ready to go after any fish to be had. Meanwhile, we looked at the birds. All around us were gulls, big western gulls and small red-beaked Heermann's gulls. Lovely brown pelicans stood idly on the bait tanks. They may be awfully common around here, but still these birds, so close, gave us the feeling that we were off to a good start.

One day out of San Diego we reached the San Benito islands and anchored in a bay off the west island. Skiffs took us ashore, and we milled around on the beach poking among the smashed, but still lovely, abalone and top shells, looking for a specimen worth keeping. As we set off across the island the naturalists stopped us to point out some of the special plants of the place; there are six that are found nowhere else, but we were impatient to be moving on. The lecture the previous evening had told us what to expect, and we had all read the specially prepared guidebook: 'The northern elephant seal dominates the marine fauna of Islas San Benito.'

And it does. Coming up on the first sandy beach we saw the long brown streaks of elephant seal, 5 metres from trunk to toe and weighing up to 4 tonnes. At first they simply lay there, the three of them, apparently oblivious

At San Benito island you get as close to a bull elephant seal as you dare

to us. All around were bleating weanlings, lard sausages abandoned by their mothers, but we were oblivious to them. Most of the party was well content to admire and photograph the bull seals from afar, but a few of us were more intrepid and wanted to get up close. 'Go slow and keep low' we had been told, so that is what we did, one person per bull.

Creeping up through the beds of washed-up kelp and sea grass, alive with millions of hyperactive kelp flies, I felt thankful that the day wasn't any hotter; the smell was bad, but bearable. As I got closer to the big seal he turned his head a fraction to look at me, and I could see the scars on his chest, wounds that, like the kelp, were alive with flies. I could see his whiskers, thick and almost transparent, like the very strong monofilament used on the *Executive* to reel in marlin. I could smell him and, without knowing exactly how, was intensely aware of his enormous bulk. He shifted away, and ripples ran down his body, like a balloon full of water or a jelly set down on the table too suddenly.

The bull half-heartedly lifted his head up a couple of times to eye me. Then, just when I thought I had our meeting under control, he reared up and stared down his nose at me. His mouth was pink inside, his teeth yellow, and his trunk quivered with what I took to be rage, but it was the noise that was most startling. Not a roar, nor a bellow, but a series of staccato decrepitations, little explosions with a metallic ring to them, which you felt as well as heard. He stood his ground; I flinched back. Then he flopped down and rippled away. At first I thought I had won, but quickly realised that I had lost – the bull, and our encounter. Later, on reflection, it came to me that had he wanted to he could have flattened me with ease, and I felt even better about our meeting. Earlier in the season, when the beaches are crammed with cows and calves, and tempers among the bulls run high, I could not have got so close.

All around the island, every cove carries its quota of elephant seals. Each December the big bulls come ashore and begin to sort out their dominance hierarchy. The females arrive later in the month and give birth to the pups, who, on a diet of extraordinarily rich milk, quadruple their weight in a month. After giving birth the females are ready to be mated again, and this is when the bull's size and prowess pay off as he exercises his reproductive rights to the females in his group. This is when, without exaggeration, the beaches can run red. But by March, when we arrived, the fighting and mating were over. The beaches still held plenty of animals, mostly pups at this late stage of the season, but also bulls. Some were spent, the past breeding season having exhausted them utterly. The others were still relatively young. If they were lucky, and strong, their turn would come.

Navigation into the entrance of the Laguna San Ignacio is slightly tricky, so we were all banned from the area around the wheelhouse as the skipper brought us in. The lagoon is large, about 25 kilometres long and between 3 and 6 kilometres wide, but we dropped anchor near the mouth at a promontory called Rocky Point. The waters of the lagoon are a murky blue, and the peaks of the Santa Clara and San Francisco ranges crowd in, making Laguna San Ignacio seem like the gateway to a mountainous kingdom. For us, it was the gateway to an astonishing experience.

When the whalers discovered the lagoons of Baja California late in the 1850s, they had found a profitable sideline to their Arctic activities. In the summer they sailed up to the Bering Sea to hunt right whales – they were the right whales because they were slow, easy to catch, and floated conveniently when dead – but in the winter the fleets were idle. In the lagoons the whalers could catch grey whales and their calves, although it was by no means as easy as hunting right whales. Grey cows earned the name devilfish by turning on the harpoon skiffs and smashing them, and many men lost their lives in pursuit of them. A hundred years later, with the population recovered somewhat, the annual passage of the greys up and down the Pacific coast had become a tourist spectacle. People gathered on the cliffs to watch them go by. A few intrepid souls ventured out in boats to be among the whales, and some sailed down to the lagoons to see them on the calving grounds.

During the 1978–9 season the strangest thing happened. Certain cows allowed their calves to come right up to the little boats full of whale-watchers. It was almost as if the cows were indulging their calves' youthful curiosity. And the calves were so curious, and came so close, that the whale-watchers could reach out and touch them. The same thing has happened every season since, and some of the so-called friendlies are now big and on their own, probably friendly calves that have grown up into friendly adolescents. A new whaling trade had begun. Five years after the first contact the *Executive* was now in the Laguna

San Ignacio to see if we, too, could reach out to a friendly whale.

There isn't that much to it. You bundle up in waterproofs, put on a lifejacket, and get into a little skiff powered by an outboard motor. All around whale breaths fill the space above the waves, and the skiff operator, spray-drenched, takes you out to where the whales might be. The four skiffs go off in different directions and then they wait. If there are friendlies around, you don't find them, they find you, and when they do the thrill is unimaginable.

A huge head popped out of the water near the skiff, the paired nostrils tightly shut at first. They opened, and with a deep organ-pipe blow the whale breathed. Mother and calf circled the skiff, and as the mother passed directly under the boat I realised that her tail flukes were as broad as our skiff was long. Then, with no warning, the calf's head was up beside our gunwale. Eager hands stretched to touch it, to feel the wet rubber of a 10-tonne leviathan.

The mist of the blow smells sweet, unlike a humpback's foul breath, but it is lethal to cameras. One woman, the whale junkie, took a moment off from her tactile fix to tell me that on a previous trip whale breath had ruined her expensive equipment. 'But who cares,' she continued. 'I mean, I'd rather have a whale spoil it than have it stolen by some bum.'

Up close I could see the whale lice clustered in dimples on the whale's skin, and the barnacles that live nowhere in the world except on grey whales. The eye is set in a turret, like a chameleon's, and looks utterly inadequate for that huge head. At one point the whale rolled over, and I could see the white baleen curtains that it uses to strain its food from the sea. I recalled the ironical detail that the naturalists had pointed out to us the previous evening. Grey whales eat amphipods, small crustaceans that live on the bottom in the mud. The whale louse is not a true louse but an amphipod. Who is taking revenge on whom?

By now the other skiffs had joined us and our friendlies. They kept their distance, waiting for the whales to make the first move, and eager hands on board slapped the water urgently, hoping by some magic to attract the beast. They succeeded, for the calf went over to satisfy another curious skiff-ful. The mother and her calf played around us for half an hour or more and, incredibly, everybody in the boats was able to touch one or the other. Then, with as little warning as had heralded their arrival, they were gone, the choppy seas taut over their fluke prints.

On the way back to the *Executive*, soaking wet and wind chilled, idiot grins spread all over our faces, we tried to remember the experience, putting it into inadequate words in an attempt to give it permanence. It cannot really be done, not well. Somehow being able to talk has trapped people into using words when they are not really up to the job.

I think the thing that impressed me most was how utterly gentle and friendly the whales were. A sentimentalist might say that the devilfish had forgiven the

people who made it necessary to protect them, that they were trying to com-
municate with us. I don't know about that, in fact I doubt it very much, but I
do know that while we may control their destiny as a species, we humans have
no control over any particular grey whales. We can go where they are, and take
care not to alarm or disturb them, but we cannot make them do anything
except die. When a 35-tonne grey whale cow swims over to be touched, she is in
charge. She has chosen to come close to me, and that is something more rewarding than I can express.

Having touched a whale, what else can there be to do? Touch another one. On
our second day in the lagoon we went out in the skiffs again and repeated the
events of the previous day, which were no less exciting for being done a second
time. The weather blew up, however, and although we were supposed to spend
the afternoon as well with the greys, the skipper decided to leave early. We
steamed out of the lagoon, elated to have touched a whale, disappointed to
have to quit. Cutting through the heavy seas, pitching and rolling, most of us
were content to sit in the saloon and wait for something to happen. The weather
eased and something did. A whale was seen to blow out on the south-east horizon. As we changed course, the lookout spotted several more spouts. At this
stage we had no idea what we were after and there was a lot of excitement. If we
could get among them, this would be our first experience of whales in open
water, and we stood peering intently to sea. I'm slightly abashed to report that
the temptation to yell 'Thar she blows!' proved too much for most of us.

From a mile away the lookout was pretty certain that they were blue whales;
the colour, the placement of the little dorsal fin, the details of the high, columnar
blow, the sheer size of the beasts all indicated the largest animal on earth. Then
we were on top of them, and all of us could see the characteristic V-shaped
splashguard in front of the blowhole, like the windscreen on a powerboat.

There were at least ten animals, stretching out to the horizon, which led the
naturalists to speculate that we were perhaps on the edge of a larger group. A
mother and calf swam by, no more than 45 metres away, and another whale,
on its own, seemed noticeably smaller than the others. (Smaller, in this context,
being about 15 metres and perhaps 25 tonnes instead of 22 metres and 50 tonnes.)
Just ahead of our bows a blue whale defaecated, leaving a cloud of red sparkling
particles in its wake. The red comes from the carotene pigments that colour the
blue's food, mainly the shrimps called krill, but also perhaps pelagic swimming
crabs. Blue whales gulp their food, engulfing tonnes of water that distend the
grooves that run down the throat to behind the fins, ballooning the whale's
head before the excess water is strained out through the baleen plates.

Up at the wheelhouse the naturalists were timing the blows, part of the
valuable scientific information gathered on these cruises. The whales' behaviour
was carefully monitored to ensure that we were not disturbing them. If they

started responding oddly, diving deeper or longer, we would give up the chase. For the moment, though, everything was fine. The bows bristled with cameras, and every resonant blow was accompanied by the machine-gun sound of camera shutters. We were waiting to see the tail flukes lifted out of the water, the classic image of the disappearing leviathan. The blue's dorsal fin is tiny, and placed well back towards the tail, so every time we saw a fin we anticipated the flukes, shouting for them and willing them to appear. But none of the whales showed its tail. We had to content ourselves with blows, and sinuous yards of blue whale arching up out of the water, sometimes high and rounded, sometimes low and flat, always the tip of a living iceberg.

Two hours had flown by and the light was beginning to fail. We abandoned the whales and resumed our course. 'If it hadn't been for the wind in the lagoon,' the captain reminded a querulous passenger, peeved at having missed her second chance to touch a grey, 'we wouldn't have seen those blues. Does that make you feel better about the weather and your lost opportunity?'

By now we were in calm seas beneath a clear sky, and old sea hands were quietly expectant. The lower limb of the sun touched the horizon, and as the disc slipped into the sea all the binoculars were trained on it. An exultant shout went up. 'Wow,' said the woman who lost her cameras to whale breath, 'blue whales and a green flash in one day.' She had forgotten that that very morning she had touched a grey whale. It had been too full a day.

On the ninth day of the cruise, the last day but one, we headed south down the Sea of Cortez towards our final destination, La Paz. On the way we were going to stop at a place called Los Islotes, where we would have our last guaranteed close encounter with wild animals. Los Islotes are two tiny rocks a few hundred metres off the northern shore of Isla Partida Sur. They rise to just 14 metres above sea level, and are the final surface manifestation of a ridge that then plunges into the Sea of Cortez. On the flatter rocky platforms at the foot of Los Islotes lives a colony of California sealions, and those of us who wanted to would be allowed to swim over to them.

From where we stood on the deck we could hear them barking above the low rustle of the surf, and I for one was a bit worried. Like many pinnipeds, sealions operate a harem system. The bulls weigh about 270 kilograms, three times more than the cows, and while they are not as pugnacious as elephant seals they do fight one another for mastery of a patch of rookery. And, as it said in the guide, 'bulls not only patrol the land area of their harem, but also frequently take to adjacent waters.' What if one mistook me for a rival? Worse still, what if he mistook me for a mate? I mentioned my fears to the *Executive*'s naturalist, who drily pointed out that the breeding season is in June and July, still four months away. 'I don't think you'll have any trouble,' he said, adding, somewhat unnecessarily, 'we haven't lost anyone yet.'

222

Fears partially allayed I jumped into the sea, and a crowd of us began to fin over towards the sealions. As we got nearer we could see and hear them on the rocks, but there didn't seem to be any in the water. Then they were ahead of us, some bobbing upright and looking us over, others just swimming around lazily. I put my face beneath the water and could see their sleek shapes bulleting along, thrust forward by claps of their hind flippers. Mostly it was cows and smaller juveniles, but occasionally a big male would cruise straight by, sometimes pausing to look me over but decidedly less playful than the others. For some reason I did not feel in the least bit threatened. For a long time they seemed to keep away, always just out of reach, and as I floated panting on the surface I realised that there was no way I could ever catch them. I decided to stay still, finning slowly in towards the rookery, and was soon rewarded.

A young juvenile appeared from nowhere and hovered below my mask. Its deep liquid eyes looked slightly clouded, and trails of tiny quicksilver bubbles emerged from its fur. I took a deep breath and slipped under to join it, and to my delight it stayed where it was. We looked at one another, and then it turned and slowly swam away. I tried to follow it, but, coming up for air, appeared to have lost it. However, it had not lost me, and once again it appeared in front of me. We went through the whole business again, diving, looking at one another, and then swimming off together. The next time I came up for air it did not vanish, and off we went again. I got the distinctly romantic, and foolish, notion that it was taking me somewhere, but this thought barely disturbed me as I followed the young sealion, marvelling at how thoroughly it was at home underwater. Then, coming up for air again, I thought I had better take a look around to get my bearings, and it had indeed taken me somewhere.

Without realising it I had swum about 180 metres along the coast from the rookery, to a cleft between the two rocks that comprise Los Islotes. The sun was on the other side of the islets, and streamed through the underwater canyon, illuminating bright green shafts between the black shadows. It was truly beautiful, though I doubt that that was why my guide had come here. I floated there for a while, getting my breath back, and wondering what had become of the sealion, until I noticed several of them chasing each other way below me. I went down as deep as I could and they came up to meet me, hurtling around with astonishing speed. I had to surface, and they ascended with me to resume their game at less depth. They were twisting and turning all around me, showing off, it seemed, and wondering why this ungainly creature with the huge fins was so incompetent. I tried to show willing, diving and turning as quickly and as gracefully as I could, but my performance was pretty poor. I still don't know why I felt I had to try and be like them, but I did.

We frolicked in the water together for what seemed like only a few minutes, but was in fact an hour or more. I had become too cold to enjoy it any longer, and started slowly back to the *Executive*. At this point a new type of game started. A sealion would swim in front of me, then spurt ahead out of sight. I would dive down to see what had become of it, and as I looked around it would emerge from the shadows and swim towards me, fast and true. At the last minute it swerved aside, as I had expected it would, but still much to my relief. This happened several times on my way back to the boat, and on two occasions I felt a front flipper gently graze my side as its owner played undersea chicken with me. I fear I was not a very good playmate.

The sealions abandoned me about 90 metres from the *Executive* and porpoised off back to the rocks. I climbed on board and was surprised to discover how cold I had allowed myself to become. My lips were blue and even in the warm sunshine I shivered uncontrollably for about ten minutes and after two hot cups of coffee. But I can honestly say that I had never experienced anything like those sealions before. Confronting an elephant seal was exciting, and touching a grey whale rewarding in the extreme. I cherish the many sightings we had of whales out at sea. But swimming with sealions is far and away the most exhilarating thing I have ever done. I was close to wild animals, but more than that, I was aware of how superbly well-adapted they were to their environment, and how friendly to a visitor. The best had come last, and the next day I left the *Executive* far richer in experience.

Whales are powerful animals with enormous popular appeal. Very few people will ever see one in the wild, and an even smaller number get to touch one. I have dealt with the cruise at some length in an attempt to share the experience with as many people as possible. But what has a whale-watching cruise to do with the zoo of tomorrow? I could argue that it offers people the chance to appreciate wildlife, and redefine a zoo to include any such opportunity, but I think that would be misleading because the essence of even my new, extended definition of a zoo is that it involves some element of management, both of the people and of the animals. That applies, as I hope I have shown by now, in many circumstances that we do not at present think of as zoos, such as game parks, but I do not think it applies to whale-watching.

Paradoxically, it is because a whale-watch offers an experience of animals that no zoo could ever hope to duplicate that it is important. There is simply no substitute for seeing cetaceans at home on the open ocean, but I suspect that all the people who have ever seen a whale in the wild would be easily outnumbered by a good day's attendance at, say, San Diego Zoo. Zoos, however, while they cannot compete with a cruise like this, do offer an unparalleled opportunity to experience other animals. Indeed, for most people, most of the time, a zoo is the only way to get close to animals, and for this reason, good zoos are invaluable. But they are not the whole story; the wild is also important, and because we have preserved some animals in zoos, it does not mean we should abandon others in the wild.

# Chapter Nine

# TOWARDS ZOO 2000

**Z**oos are here to stay, because there is simply no substitute for what they offer. Critics argue that people are dissatisfied with zoos because they contrast ill with the spectacular wildlife films that can be seen all the time on television. I think the opposite is true; good wildlife films enhance the appreciation people have of good zoos. They know what an animal is capable of, and value it as much, if not more, in a zoo. It is also worth pointing out that some of the most startling 'natural' history footage seen on television has been filmed in good zoos. I have also even heard it argued that with the skills of model builders increasing so fast, there will soon be no need for zoos because people will see all the wild animals they want in the form of 'audio-animatronic robots' at places like Walt Disney World. This is so preposterous as to be unworthy of rebuttal. People go to the zoo because they like to be with animals and that is where they *can* be with animals. Until that desire vanishes, and I believe it never will, zoos will continue.

Audio-animatronic elephants at Disney World, supposedly an acceptable substitute

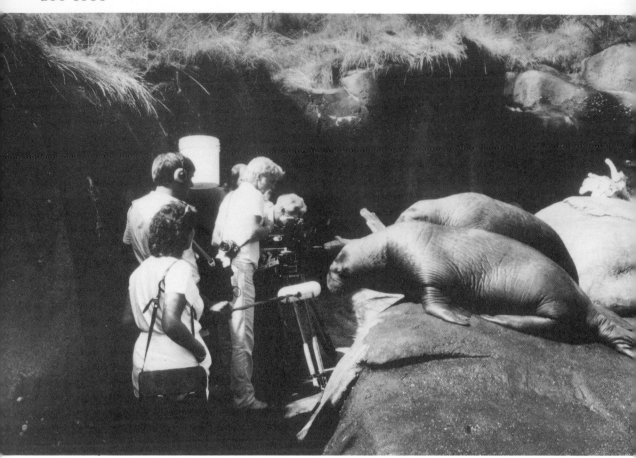

Much 'natural' history is filmed in good zoos

Zoos will survive, but they must also continue to evolve. There are still too many appalling zoos in existence today, ramshackle places with bare cages housing disconsolate and filthy animals. I have mostly chosen to ignore these in my account and to concentrate on the better zoos in the hope that things will change. Campaigns to abolish zoos entirely, and there has been a resurgence of such activity in the UK recently, take the opposite tack; they ignore the good and focus on the bad. To argue against them is futile because their passion stems from a moral conviction that all captivity is bad, and no amount of reason has any effect on such a belief. They would deprive the vast majority of people, who cannot go on safari or whale-watching, the chance ever to experience living animals, and I think that is bad.

I do, however, think that the objectors have a valuable role to play, if only they would be more discriminating. By all means let them campaign for the abolition of bad zoos, and I will join them, but let them also recognise that some zoos are very good. I have stressed this point throughout the previous chapters, and will not labour it now. I wish that there were no need to distinguish between good and bad zoos, that all zoos were automatically good, but they are not. Campaigners in the UK and elsewhere should emulate the Humane Society of the United States and acknowledge that there are grades of zoos. The truly awful should be shut down, but the mediocre can be made good, and even the best can improve.

Change can be imposed from outside, or it can come from within. People learned to dislike bars, so some zoos have given them animals in naturalistic cages. Those zoos have done well. Public taste will be a continuing force for change because, despite subsidies, zoos lose their will to live if people no longer visit them. An informed public should be able to select between good and bad zoos, and then, I hope, the bad zoos will wither away.

Just as some of the successful future zoo's adaptations will come from outside, others will have to start from inside the zoo movement, and will require a change of attitude from the public. Instead of simply talking about conservation and education, as too many of them do, more zoo directors will have to implement the ideals that they currently merely pay lip service to, becoming active contributors to zoos' welfare rather than scroungers on the backs of the better zoos.

So what will the good zoo be like in the year 2000? If they are to succeed, zoos will have to co-operate, managing each species according to the best principles of genetics and biology, and that will have all sorts of ramifications. For the public, the biggest change will be in display techniques. There will be more naturalistic displays and fewer postage stamp collections. Zoos will reduce the number of species they carry and increase the number of individuals in each species. There will be natural social groupings where appropriate, more interesting to watch and much more effective for captive breeding. The good zoos today already point with pride to changes in the composition of their collections; Bronx Zoo used to have 2900 specimens of 1100 species, but now has 3500 specimens of only 600 species. A multitude of single exotic specimens, far from being a badge of excellence, will become the mark of a bad zoo.

That means that each zoo will concentrate on the species best suited to it, although neighbouring zoos will probably have to get together to ensure that they do not duplicate one another's efforts. Forerunners in this area are the zoos of the Pacific north-west of America. Seattle has gorillas and its marvellous African savannah. Tacoma has the polar bears and other animals of the north. Portland specialises in Asian animals, and the Seattle Aquarium focuses on the inhabitants of the waters of the area. Zoo-goers decide what they would like to see that day and travel to the zoo of their choice. There will always be exceptions like penguins in the desert and gorillas in the snow, and some animals will always be tolerated as simple crowd pullers, but the public will have to modify its expectations too, coming to realise that they can no longer hope to see all the animals they want to on one trip to a single zoo; but I suspect that that particular change will come more easily when the animals are presented in a more interesting way.

Although some specimens will always be tolerated as a magnet for the public, the vast majority will have to earn their keep as an integral part of a managed breeding programme. Animals will have to be killed, and the biggest single challenge facing zoos today is to educate people about life and death. Basle is leading the way, but it has few followers. The public must be helped to accept that if we want to save species then we have to sacrifice individuals. The zoo of the future will take on this challenge, and although it will be hard work, the reward will be that zoos will in the end gain the trust and support of the public and will be able to manage their collections in the open and without subterfuge or fear.

A related problem is that of triage, discussed in Chapter Three. No single zoo can deal with this alone, but all should make an effort to explain their collective decisions. Shortages of resources mean that we will almost certainly be unable to save all the species of wildlife that we might like to. Some will have to go as we discover that five subspecies of tiger, for example, or two subspecies of orang-utan, are luxuries that we cannot afford. Indeed, when you consider the accelerating pace of ecological destruction, and the number of animals in zoos in relation to the untold millions of still unknown species that could be extinct by the year 2000, it is clear that we are not really saving anything.

With better display organised, and more co-operation, especially over breeding, the good zoo of the future will be involved in more scientific research. Some zoos are already famous for their scientific work, although to name San Diego, London, New York and Frankfurt would be invidious. Others do equally good research, although less of it, but far too many zoos today make no use of their collections to further our knowledge of wild animals. The information gathered can be of direct help to problems faced by zoos, or it may be indirectly beneficial. One of the biggest obstacles to successful captive breeding is perinatal mortality; far too many infants die just after birth, and a concerted scientific attack on the reasons would probably yield results very quickly. The promised benefits that wild animals hold for mankind are not likely to manifest themselves unbidden, and some basic research on the more exotic species could well turn up trumps. Zoo collections are a precious resource that should be used to the full, and that means conducting basic scientific research on as many representatives of the animal kingdom as possible.

Zoo 2000 will be many things. A very few will be wild places in which people are given the opportunity to be part of nature and its constituent animals and plants. The vast majority will be small, with naturalistic and informative exhibits of a few species. They will be sites of good scientific research and will co-operate extensively with their neighbours on matters of breeding and display. At the same time they will be entertaining and educate their visitors in the

A loggerhead turtle laying at Mon Repos, a super example of education, entertainment and conservation

*Above* Fairy penguins coming ashore provide a wildlife experience that is hard to equal
*Right* some things will never be done well in zoos, like swimming with sea lions, or watching
blue whales blow, but the zoo can help us preserve those things

Touching a grey whale is at once prosaic and dramatic, a singular experience. It reminds us that zoos cannot preserve all of nature. Saving species for eventual reintroduction to the wild is futile unless there is some wild left. Habitat destruction (*right*) proceeds apace, not just far away but close to home too, with the drainage of wetlands and burning of wastes

233

The subspecies of tiger:
*this page* Chinese, Javan,
and Siberian; *opposite*
Sumatran, Caspian and
Bali

Money to preserve works of art is much easier to raise than money to preserve the animals they depict. Why?

Basle is one of the few zoos to take its responsibility to animals seriously. When Giulia, a 25-year-old Indian elephant, had to be put down the reasons were clearly stated and it was done openly. *Below* the orang-utan exhibit at Zurich offers ample scope for animals and visitors

broadest possible sense. In effect, Zoo 2000 will use every means at its disposal to be part of a concerted effort to preserve selected species in captivity.

If it happens, it will be a wonderful achievement, but the question inevitably arises of why on earth we are bothering to save those few species we can in zoos. The usual answer is so that we can restock the wild from our arks when the flood of destruction has ebbed. I would like to think that this will be possible, but I doubt it because there is so little indication that there will be any wild to restock. By the time we realise what we are doing it may well be too late, and until we remove the threats there can be little point in releasing animals, but I suppose I should be optimistic and hope that we can save more of the wild habitats. Zoos, through education, may help achieve that aim, and will then be doubly useful if they have stocks for reintroduction.

Some people have argued that we should conserve wildlife because of as yet unknown benefits that it may provide for us. Who would have thought that armadillos would be useful in leprosy research, or that the rosy periwinkle would be the source of a potent anti-cancer drug? It is an excellent argument for conservation, but hardly one for zoos, except inasmuch as zoos can foster conservation. The tiny minority of species maintained in zoos might come up with beneficial surprises if we look, but that is not reason enough for them.

Quite honestly there can be no rational reason for saving wildlife in zoos. Life is a relentless struggle to survive and those that are ill-adapted to their surroundings perish. The different individuals of different species are just manifestations of different ways to approach that struggle. If one species, *Homo sapiens*, goes to the wall then that is neither here nor there, even if it drags countless others with it. We will simply have been an evolutionary failure, a rather brief-lived experiment. Life will go on, and there really is nothing sacred about extinction that we should try so valiantly to prevent it for its own sake. But that does not mean that we should abandon our efforts to improve our zoos and save as much of life as we can. Conservation may do us some good, directly and perhaps spiritually, but that is the only possible motivation for saving species from extinction. If we can save the whales and tigers we can save their habitats, and if we can save their habitats we may be able to save ourselves.

The best reason to conserve animals in zoos is simply that it gives us pleasure. There may be other benefits to come from a conservationist way of life, but those remain mostly conjectural. If we can preserve some natural habitat, and if we can offer people the chance to experience and wonder at the astounding diversity of life, that is reason enough to do it, and to do it properly. Those who come after us will not thank us if we impoverish their world.

I am honestly very annoyed that I will never see a living dodo, not even in a zoo, and I would hate to think that in the near future people might not be able to watch and take pleasure in the animals I now enjoy. It takes money to run a good zoo, and it is a dreadful irony that until very recently in Britain the government would pay for me to see paintings of animals, but not the living specimens. I can go to a museum to see a painted dodo and a stuffed quagga, and pay nothing for the pleasure, but London Zoo was on the brink of bankruptcy before it attracted a pitiful grant.

Good zoos, and I hope that in the future the word will include the whole panoply of interactions between animals and man, are a pleasure and a joy. They may act as reservoirs of genetic diversity, but so would a fridge full of embryos. They may be sources of information and knowledge, but so are books, films and photographs. What zoos offer, which nothing else can, is the simple pleasure of contact. For that alone, they are worth it.

One day on a visit to a zoo a little girl and her mother were watching the elephants. The mother was bored, and tried to persuade the little girl to move on, but the child was held fast by her fascination with them. Eventually, and somewhat exasperatedly, the mother pleaded. 'Do come on,' she said, 'you've seen elephants lots of times on TV.' Her daughter thought for a while and, without turning away from the animals, replied, 'Yes, but these are so big.'

Zoos are about real animals and real people, close together, and always will be

# FURTHER READING

Blunt, Wilfred, *The Ark in the Park: the Zoo in the Nineteenth Century* (Hamish Hamilton, London, 1976).

Durrell, Gerald, *The Stationary Ark* (Collins, London, 1976).

Fiedler, Walter, *Tiergarten Schönbrunn, Geschichte und Aufgaben* (VWGÖ, Vienna, 1976).

Fisher, James, *Zoos of the World* (Aldus, London, 1966).

Fitter, Richard and Sir Peter Scott, *The Penitent Butchers* (Fauna Preservation Society, London, 1978).

Hancocks, David, *Animals and Architecture* (Hugh Evelyn, London, 1971).

Klingender, Francis, *Animals in Art and Thought* (Routledge and Kegan Paul, London, 1971).

Markowitz, Hal, *Behavioral Enrichment in the Zoo* (Van Nostrand, New York, 1982).

Myers, Norman, *The Sinking Ark* (Pergamon, Oxford, 1979).

Zuckerman, Lord (ed.), *Great Zoos of the World: Their Origins and Significance* (Weidenfeld and Nicolson, London, undated).

I have also drawn on several scientific publications and the invaluable *International Zoo Yearbook*, published by the Zoological Society of London and currently edited by Peter Olney. Two zoo magazines, *Zoonooz* from San Diego and *Animal Kingdom* from New York, are well worth reading.

## PICTURE CREDITS

Arch. Phot. Paris/DACS 1984 page 8; Ardea pages 71 (Adrian Warren), 85 (top left, Pat Morris), 112 (M.D. England), 146–7 (Kenneth Fink) and 186 (Arthus-Bertrand); Arizona-Sonora Desert Museum page 65 (Al Morgan); Art Directors' Photo Library pages 52, 174 (bottom), 194 (centre left & right, bottom left & right), 195 (bottom left & right) and 226; Barnaby's Picture Library page 161 (Hubertus Kanus); Bildarchiv der Österreichischen Nationalbibliothek, Vienna pages 23 and 33; Howard Blakemore page 53; British Museum pages 9 and 20; Camerapix, Nairobi pages 160 and 166; Jeremy Cherfas pages 49, 151 and 156 (bottom); Gary K. Clarke page 154; Bruce Coleman pages 27 (top right, Jessica Anne Ehlers), 85 (bottom left, Jane Burton), 87 (William E. Townsend), 149 (whole page, Gunter Ziesler), 169 (Mark Boulton), 173 (bottom, R.I.M. Campbell), 174 (top, Jen & Des Bartlett), 175 (top right, Peter Davey), 176 (top, Timothy O'Keefe), 200 (Timothy O'Keefe), 203 (Timothy O'Keefe), 233 (top, Mark Boulton; bottom, Arne Schmitz), 234 and 235 (all, WWF/Helmut Diller); Currumbin Sanctuary page 215; Danmarks Akvarium page 189; Red Denner pages 150 (top) and 156 (top); Mary Evans Picture Library pages 16 and 35; Steve Foote page 218 (right); Jennifer Fry page 55; Fuji Safari Park, Japan page 173 (top); Carl Hagenbecks Tierpark, Hamburg page 38; David Hancocks pages 154 (bottom) and 155; Robert Harding page 179 (Brian Hawkes); Michael Holford page 25; Keystone Press Agency pages 18, 43, 73, 77 and 107; Kunsthistorisches Museum, Vienna pages 28–9; Moira Mann pages 92 (bottom), 145, 196 (top), 225 and 237 (bottom); Mansell Collection page 68 (top left); Richard Matthews pages 148 and 175 (top left); Metropolitan Toronto Zoo page 58; Miccosukee Tribe of Indians of Florida page 27 (top left); Harry Millen pages 76 and 152–3; C. Allan Morgan pages 218 (left), 231 and 232; New York Zoological Society pages 88, 89, 109 and 110; Liz Nicol page 229; A. Van Den Nieuwenhuizen page 204 (right); Oxford Scientific Films pages 86 (Survival/Jeff Foott), 92 (top, Ronald Templeton), 149 (inset, Survival/Alan Root), 171 (Survival/ Jen & Des Bartlett), 175 (bottom, Survival/Alan Root) and 176 (bottom, Survival/Alan Root); Photo Library of Australia pages 194 (top), 195 (top) and 230; Point Defiance Zoo & Aquarium page 239; Royal Zoological Society of Scotland (Chris Morris) page 130; Scala page 27 (bottom); Seattle Aquarium pages 132 (centre) and 196 (bottom); Sea World of Florida page 209; Shedd Aquarium pages 193 and 204 (left); Smithsonian Institution, National Zoological Park, Washington page 113; Times Newspapers page 82; UPI/Bettmann page 98; Washington Park Zoo page 127; Windsor Safari Park page 134; Zoo Anvers pages 78 and 132 (top left); Zoo Emmen pages 32, 51 and 61; Zoological Society of London pages 26, 30–1, 50, 68 (top right, bottom left & right), 85 (top & bottom right), 105, 116, 132 (top right) and 236; Zoological Society of San Diego pages 90, 91, 111, 136 and 150 (bottom); Zoologischer Garten Basel (Jörg Hess) pages 132 (bottom) and 237 (top). Drawing on page 6 by Jill Dow.

# INDEX

*Italic figures refer to illustrations*